THE

Lighthouse

HANDBOOK

New England

THE
Lighthouse
HANDBOOK
New England

2ND EDITION

{ THE ORIGINAL LIGHTHOUSE FIELD GUIDE }

By Jeremy D'Entremont

CIDER MILL
PRESS

BOOK
PUBLISHERS

Kennebunkport, Maine

13-Digit ISBN: 978-1-60433-262-9
10-Digit ISBN: 1-60433-262-X

This book may be ordered by mail from the publisher. Please include $2.99 for postage and handling.
Please support your local bookseller first!

Books published by Cider Mill Press Book Publishers are available at special discounts for bulk purchases in the United States by corporations, institutions, and other organizations. For more information, please contact the publisher.

Cider Mill Press Book Publishers
"Where good books are ready for press"
12 Port Farm Road
Kennebunkport, Maine 04046

Visit us on the Web!
www.cidermillpress.com

Design by Ponderosa Pine Design, Vicky Vaughn Shea
Typography: Baskerville MT, NumbersStyle Two, Post Antiqua, Salmiak, Swiss 721, Today SB
Photography and illustration credits on page 437

Printed in China

4 5 6 7 8 9 0
Second Edition

Contents

Foreword

Warning! Visiting lighthouses can be incredibly fun for the entire family—and addictive. Along the way you will also have the opportunity to make many new friends and experience breathtaking seascapes that offer some of the most serene and beautiful locations on earth.

So go ahead, stare deep into the light that beckons the admirer to come nearer, but know that its alluring powers can be both profound and permanent on one's heart and mind. For I can think of no other man-made structure that is capable of evoking our deepest emotions or inspiring the most moving of artistic achievements than a lighthouse.

Their mere presence exudes a powerful sense of protection and purpose. Even if a person is unaware of lighthouses and the reasons they were built, their unique and often beautiful construction conveys an undeniable sense of great importance, for these benevolent beacons of the sea are no ordinary structures.

At the foot of a lighthouse swirl the ancient secrets of the sea. The vastness of the deep and its crashing surf serve as a constant reminder that the serenity of these grand locations can be replaced in a moment's notice by the untamed power of the tempest, which historically wreaked havoc on many a ship, often causing tragic shipwrecks whose remains are strewn beneath the rocky ledges and shifting sands of our coastlines.

Before you can visit a lighthouse and experience its grand offerings of beauty and history, though, you have to first know how to get there, and let's face it: everyone needs a little help now and then when it comes to "finding our way."

Global Position Satellite (GPS) in one's care is great, but I'm of the belief that no technical instrument, regardless of capability, can ever fully replace that human "voice" when it comes to such topics as driving directions and intimate local knowledge.

If you are seeking out lighthouses, you do not just want to find them. Wouldn't it be nice to also be formally "introduced" to these guiding lights of the sea by someone in the know who has meticulously retraced the steps of the bygone lightkeepers before you?

No one is more qualified to serve as the companion "voice" on your personal lighthouse journey than Jeremy D'Entremont, New England's foremost lighthouse historian. Before you think that being "introduced" to a lighthouse is simply learning the driving directions, though, think again.

D'Entremont has traveled countless lonely roads to lighthouses, sought out and traversed their obscure walking paths, and in many instances, scaled the staircases of these stately beacons to obtain more than just travel information, which makes *The New England Lighthouse Handbook* a must-have for both the novice and tried-and-true lighthouse enthusiast.

Within the pages of this volume, D'Entremont demonstrates his prowess at being uniquely adept at presenting the entire realm of the lighthouse experience, from the important how-to-get-there information to the history and lore of each beacon, as well as fascinating tidbits of human interest that spark our imaginations and conjure up the golden age of lighthouses and their keepers.

Oh yes, there is something else you should know as you turn each page of *The New England Lighthouse Handbook*— the mere act of doing so can serve as the start of a new and exciting chapter in your own life. For on occasion, a visit to a lighthouse has been known to change the course of an individual's life, which is yet another fascinating possibility to ponder as you seek a temporary reprieve from the fast pace of society or perhaps the stress of your occupation.

With Jeremy D'Entremont's *New England Lighthouse Handbook* as your guide, plan your next trip to a lighthouse today, for time and the tides wait for no one. Along your journey from light to light, be prepared to experience unbridled fun and satisfaction, and remember to absorb every ounce of romance, mystery, strength, inspiration, and spiritual renewal that you can possibly derive from seeking out New England's beckoning beacons!

— Bob Trapani, Jr.
Executive Director
American Lighthouse Foundation

Introduction

I'm often asked, "What is it about lighthouses? Why do they mean so much to so many people?" I usually hem and haw before I attempt a reply because there is no simple, succinct answer to the question. Certainly, lighthouses are often pretty or ruggedly handsome, and they're usually in beautiful or dramatic locations. Some of them are marvels of engineering, the measure of the technology of their time. They're frequently among the oldest buildings in our coastal communities, and they serve as a link to centuries past. They remind us that our nation was built on maritime trade and that safe navigation was essential to the growth of that commerce. Beyond that, they speak to something deep inside us.

Lighthouses, perched defiantly on the turbulent line between land and sea, are symbols of steadfastness, hope, and strength. There's primal power in the image of a light in the darkness, guiding sailors safely home. It's no accident that churches, schools, and all types of businesses have utilized the positive symbolism of the lighthouse as a guiding light.

For me, it's the human history that grabs my attention above everything else. For centuries, keepers and families dedicated themselves, usually in obscurity and for little financial reward, to keeping the light lit at all costs. Connie Small, author of the classic book, *The Lighthouse Keeper's Wife*, once said that she and her husband, Elson Small, didn't see lighthouse keeping as a job; they saw it as a calling.

Time and again, keepers and their families saw past their own perils and discomforts. They did what had to be done to serve the good of all. They also lived their lives in rugged and extreme conditions that most of us would consider unbearable. For better or worse, with automation it's a way of life that's been relegated to the past in most of the world. With the passing of the age of the traditional keeper, a new form of keeper has evolved: the historic preservationist.

There's endless human drama (humor, also) to be found in the study of lighthouses. If you dig deep enough into the history of almost any lighthouse, you're likely to find stories of great heroism and heartbreaking tragedies. There's a good chance you'll find a ghost story or two and maybe something offbeat like a bell-ringing "fog dog." I hope this book will make you hungry for more of these stories.

The presentation of the lighthouses

in this book is roughly south to north and west to east. In addition to driving directions for mainland lighthouses, information is provided on cruises, flights, and tours that enable the aficionado to view lighthouses that are unreachable by car.

Information on cruises and tours is obviously subject to change over time. This new edition is up to date at the time of its publishing, but you should always check ahead with local chambers of commerce, tourism bureaus, and lighthouse organizations to learn about current cruise and tour offerings.

A brief glossary is included at the back of the book, defining some of the terms that appear in the text. I've tried to stay away from too much technical information in favor of human interest.

I hope this book will serve you well, and I hope it will make you want to learn more about these fascinating sites. I invite you to visit me online at www. lighthouse.cc "New England Lighthouses: A Virtual Guide."

Happy lighthousing!

—**Jeremy D'Entremont**
Portsmouth, New Hampshire
June 2011

KEY TO ICONS

For each lighthouse in the book, icons are used to help convey information on accessibility, as follows:

 indicates the lighthouse can be reached by car

 indicates the lighthouse may be viewed from one or more public cruises.

 means a boat ride to an island plus a car or other transportation are needed.

 indicates that a view (possibly distant) from shore is possible.

 means a significant walk is necessary to reach the lighthouse.

 means the site is closed to the public, even though it may be reachable by car.

 means that the lighthouse and/ or keeper's house are open to the public, at least on a limited basis.

 indicates there are overnight accommodations.

Connecticut

With a coastline that mostly borders Long Island Sound, Connecticut boasts twenty lighthouses from Greenwich to Stonington. Some were established as guides to local harbors, while others served primarily to help guide traffic through the sound to and from New York City.

There are several New York lighthouses that can be seen from the shores of Connecticut, especially in Fisher's Island Sound. Because the state of New York is not a part of New England, they're not included in this handbook. These include Latimer Reef Light, North Dumpling Light, Little Gull Light, Race Rock Light, and Orient Point Light, all of which can be viewed from the periodic lighthouse cruises offered by Captain John's Sport Fishing Fleet in Waterford, Connecticut; call 860-443-7259 or visit www.sunbeamfleet.com.

New London was one of the busiest ports in our young nation and thus is home to America's fourth oldest light station (1761). Nearby the stately New London Harbor Light (rebuilt in 1801) is New London Ledge Light, known widely for its striking architecture and its ghostly legends. I strongly recommend the tours of this structure offered by Project Oceanology in Groton.

Many travelers pass back and forth along bustling Interstate 95 without ever visiting some of the state's picturesque harbors and rivers. Aside from the lighthouses, coastal towns like Stonington, Old Saybrook, and Guilford are charming destinations in their own right. Connecticut also has New England's finest maritime museum, Mystic Seaport.

Only two of the state's lighthouses—Sheffield Island and Stonington—are open to the public on a regular basis. The grounds around a few others are easily accessible. Viewing most of Connecticut's lighthouses is a challenge, something that should never deter a true lighthouse buff.

Connecticut Lighthouses

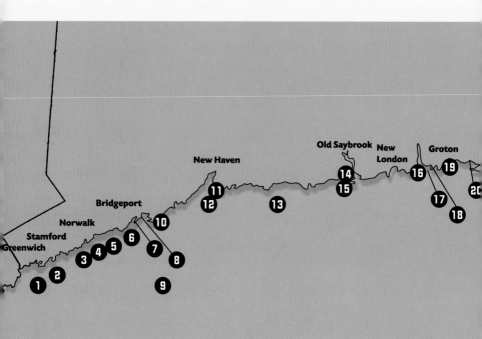

LIGHTHOUSE	PAGE

GREAT CAPTAIN ISLAND LIGHT

Accessibility: ⛵

Geographic coordinates: 40° 58' 54" N   73° 37' 24" W

Nearest town: Greenwich. Located on a 17-acre island a little more than a mile offshore.

Established: 1829. Present lighthouse built: 1868. Deactivated: 1970.

Height of tower: 51 feet. Height of focal plane: 74 feet.

Previous optic: Fourth-order Fresnel lens. Present optic: none.

Great Captain Island is named for Captain Daniel Patrick of the New Haven Colony, an early settler who was killed in 1643 in a dispute with a Dutch soldier. The island's location near the main shipping channel through Long Island Sound made it a perfect place for a lighthouse.

Keeper Adam Kohlman and his wife circa 1930s

The first lighthouse built on the site in 1829 was a 30-foot stone tower, described in an 1850 inspection report as "neglected and filthy." The station was rebuilt in 1868 as a handsome granite dwelling with a cast-iron tower mounted on its front end.

In 1904, a writer described the light station under Keeper Eugene Mulligan. Everything was "spic and span," but the keeper, whose wife had recently died, "bore the look of a constant sufferer." Mulligan had a series of knockdown battles with an assistant keeper. Once, when asked to clean the lighthouse stairs, the assistant blackened both of Mulligan's eyes.

In 1970, the lighthouse was darkened, and an automatic navigational light on a skeleton tower was installed nearby. Ownership of the lighthouse property went to the Town of Greenwich in 1973, and caretakers lived in the building for some years. The lighthouse gradually fell into poor condition, and the building was vacated for a few years; but it has

Fascinating Fact

The ownership of Great Captain Island was disputed between Connecticut and New York for more than a hundred years before a commission ruled in favor of Connecticut in 1880.

been restored recently.

During the summer months, there is a ferry service to the island from the Arch Street Dock in Greenwich. Call (203) 622-7814 or visit www.green wichct.org for information.

STAMFORD HARBOR LIGHT

Accessibility: 🚻 ⛵

Geographic coordinates:
41° 00' 48" N 73° 32' 31" W

Nearest city: Stamford.
Located less than a mile
offshore from the city's
Shippan Point section.

Established: 1882.
Present lighthouse built:
1882. Destaffed: 1953.

Height of tower:
60 feet. Height of focal
plane: 80 feet.

Previous optic: Fourth-
order Fresnel lens. Present
optic: 200 mm.

Characteristic: Flashing
white every 4 seconds.

For years, keepers lived with their families inside this typical cast-iron sparkplug-style lighthouse. Keeper John J. Cook, interviewed in 1908 about how he felt spending Christmas at the lighthouse, responded, "What more soul-stirring music could there be than that of wind and wave as they whistle and roar or moan and swish past our little home? And that light up aloft is a sermon in itself."

In August 1931, a Stamford woman called the police to tell them the light was out. Investigators soon found keeper Raymond Bliven's boat overturned about a mile from the lighthouse, and Bliven's body was later recovered. The medical examiner theorized that the keeper had fallen from the ladder, hit his head, and drowned. Others suspected foul play.

The tower was sold into private ownership in 1954. It changed hands several times and was owned by the city of Stamford for a time. In 1984 it was sold to New York banker Eryk Spektor, who spent hundreds of thousands of dollars restoring it. Spektor died in 1998, but the lighthouse is still owned by his family.

The lighthouse can be seen distantly from the Shippan Point section of Stamford. From Interstate 95, take exit 8 to Elm Street. Turn right at Jefferson Street. Turn left at Magee Street and follow through an intersection where it becomes Shippan Street. Turn right at Ocean Drive, then right at Fairview Avenue. Park on Fairview Avenue and walk to the small beach at its dead end.

In the past, cruises with Sound Navigation (203-219-3688, www.sound navigation.com) have provided views, but they may no longer be available. Some cruises offered by SoundWaters (203-323-1978, www.soundwaters.org) may pass by this lighthouse.

Stamford Harbor Light ca. early 1900s

Fascinating Fact

One of the early keepers at this offshore lighthouse built a dock and brought a chicken coop to the station, but a storm soon washed both away.

GREEN'S LEDGE LIGHT

Accessibility: 🏠⚓

Geographic coordinates:
41° 02' 30" N 73° 26' 38" W

Nearest city: Norwalk. Located on a shoal west of Sheffield Island, on the approach to Norwalk Harbor.

Established: 1902. Present lighthouse built: 1902. Automated: 1972.

Height of tower:
52 feet. Height of focal plane: 62 feet.

Previous optic: Fourth-order Fresnel lens. Present optic: VRB-25.

Characteristic: Alternating red and white flash every 12 seconds.

Fog signal: Two blasts every 20 seconds.

This lighthouse, a typical example of an offshore sparkplug-style cast-iron caisson tower, replaced the old Sheffield Island Lighthouse as a guide past dangerous ledges into Norwalk Harbor. Before its automation in 1972, this was a stag station, with male keepers.

Green's Ledge was the scene of a sequence of bizarre incidents. In March 1910, keeper John Kiarskon took the station's only boat ashore, leaving assistant keeper Leroy Loughborough alone. Kiarskon went AWOL, and Loughborough was discovered eleven days later after the light had gone dark. The assistant keeper had run out of food and was found barely conscious, with his dog at his side. Loughborough said he would have shared his last biscuit with the dog. His health never rebounded, and he died a year later at the age of twenty-seven.

Loughborough's brother, George, became the next assistant to principal keeper William Locke. In March 1912, George Loughborough was ashore when he learned of an aunt's illness, and he failed to return to the lighthouse. Locke was found sixteen days later, weak and exhausted. At this late date it's difficult to know whether George Loughborough was motivated by concern for a sick relative or revenge against the Lighthouse Service.

The lighthouse is still owned and operated by the Coast Guard and is not open to the public. A distant view is possible from South Beach in South Norwalk. You can get a much closer

Green's Ledge light, circa early 1900s

Fascinating Fact

Few keepers stayed more than a year or two at this isolated offshore lighthouse.

view from a charter cruise from Norwalk; visit www.chartermysearay.com or call 203-943-6946. You can also see Green's Ledge Light distantly from the ferry to Sheffield Island.

SHEFFIELD ISLAND LIGHT

Accessibility:

Geographic coordinates:
41° 03' 09" N   73° 24' 52" W

Nearest city: Norwalk.
Located on a 53-acre island
on the approach to Norwalk
Harbor.

Established: 1827.
Present lighthouse built:
1868. Deactivated: 1902.

Height of tower:
44 feet. Height of focal
plane: 51 feet.

Previous optic: Fourth-
order Fresnel. Present optic:
none.

Sheffield Island takes its name from an early owner, Captain Robert Sheffield. He sold the island to his son-in-law, Gershom Smith, and Smith became the first keeper when a lighthouse was established in 1827. The original lighthouse was a 34-foot stone tower, with a separate one-story dwelling, which still stands.

Keeper Gershom
Smith and his wife,
Temperance

Smith and his wife, Temperance, had twelve children between 1811 and 1836. Smith raised crops on Sheffield and other nearby islands, and his cows wandered across the sand bars from island to island at low tide. Smith lost his job in 1845 because of a change in the political winds, as often happened in that era.

The present granite dwelling-lighthouse combination was built in 1868. It's the same design as five other lighthouses built in southern New England and Long Island Sound around the same time. The two-story, ten-room dwelling had plenty of space for keepers' families.

After the turn of the twentieth century, it was decided that a light at Green's Ledge would be a more useful guide than the light at Sheffield Island. The old light was extinguished in 1902, and the property was sold into private hands in 1914.

In 1986, the Norwalk Seaport Association (NSA) purchased the property, and the island was opened for visitors on a limited basis the following year. In the ensuing years, the NSA was responsible for much restoration, and a caretaker was hired to live on the island in summer. Hurricanes and other storms have chewed away at the island's shores, but erosion control methods have largely kept the sea at bay.

Most of the island is now part of the Stewart B. McKinney National Wildlife Refuge, and there's a public walking trail and an observation platform. There's a wide variety of bird life on the island, and visitors might spot deer that have made the swim from the mainland.

To visit Sheffield Island, you can board a seasonal ferry at the Norwalk Seaport Association's dock, adjacent to the Stroffolino Bridge at the corner of Washington and North Water Streets in South Norwalk, near the Maritime Aquarium. Call 203-838-9444 or check online at www.seaport.org for the latest schedule. Visitors are given a tour that includes a climb to the top of the lighthouse—on a clear day you can see all the way to New York City. The Norwalk

Fascinating Fact

Captain Robert Sheffield, for whom the island is named, was the captain of a vessel captured in the American Revolution.

Seaport Association also offers sunset cruises and clambakes on the island by advance reservation; see www.seaport. org for details.

To reach the dock from I-95 South, take Exit 15. The exit ramp splits: stay to the right, following the signs for South Norwalk. Turn left at the light onto West Avenue. Bear left at the fifth light onto North Main Street. Turn left at the second light onto Marshall Street. From I-95 North, take Exit 14 in Connecticut. Go straight at the end of the ramp. Continue straight to the next stop sign. Continue straight down the hill to a traffic light. Turn right at the first light onto West Avenue. Bear left at the third light onto North Main Street. Turn left at the second light onto Marshall Street. Parking is available at the aquarium lot and garage. For directions from other major routes, see the aquarium's web site at www.mari timeaquarium.org.

SIDE TRIP: *Maritime Aquarium at Norwalk*

Here you can view more than 1,000 marine animals, enjoy a film in the IMAX movie theater, visit the gift shop, and dine in the Cascade Café. The Maritime Aquarium opened in 1988, and it has become an anchor for the revitalization of South Norwalk. The exhibits focus primarily on the marine life of Long Island Sound.

Maritime Aquarium at Norwalk
10 North Water Street
Norwalk, CT, 06854
Phone: 203-852-0700.
Web site: www.maritime
aquarium.org

PECK'S LEDGE LIGHT

This sparkplug-style offshore lighthouse had a short life as a staffed station— only twenty-seven years. There were three levels of living space for the male keepers inside the tower. The first keeper was George Bardwell, at a yearly salary of $600.

Accessibility: 🚶 ⛵

Geographic coordinates: 41° 04' 39" N 73° 22' 11" W

Nearest city: Norwalk. Located on a ledge at the northeast end of the Norwalk Islands.

Established: 1906. Present lighthouse built: 1906. Automated: 1933.

Height of tower: 54 feet. Height of focal plane: 61 feet.

Previous optic: Fourth-order Fresnel lens. Present optic: VLB-44 (LED).

Characteristic: Green flash every 2.5 seconds.

The structure narrowly avoided being destroyed by fire in 1913 when keeper Conrad Hawk left some tar near the kitchen stove. Flames were spreading fast when Hawk discovered the fire, but he quickly extinguished it with buckets of seawater.

On December 5, 1921, the steamer *J. C. Austin* of Brooklyn, New York, developed a leak, and the four crewmen on board escaped to a lifeboat. The keeper at Peck's Ledge, Charles Kenney, set out in the small lighthouse boat in rough seas with two assistants and rescued the drifting crewmen. The men were so exhausted that the keepers had to carry them up the ladder into the safety of the lighthouse.

A distant view (about two miles) is possible from Calf Pasture Beach Park in South Norwalk. Directions: From I-95, north or south, take exit 16 to East Avenue. Drive south on East Avenue past two traffic lights and under a railroad bridge. Bear left after the third traffic light to Cemetery Street, then bear right onto Gregory Boulevard and continue south to a traffic circle. Bear left and follow Calf Pasture Beach Road to the beach parking area; the lighthouse can be seen from here. There is a parking fee during the summer. For more information, call Norwalk Recreation and Parks at 203-854-7806.

You can get a much closer view from a charter cruise from Norwalk; visit www.chartermysearay.com or call 203-943-6946.

Peck's Ledge Light ca. early 1900s

Fascinating Fact

This is a tricky location for the Coast Guard personnel who service the light. They have to step off their boat onto a 15-foot ladder, often with heavy equipment—no easy feat when seas are high.

PENFIELD REEF LIGHT

This handsome building, with its mansard roof and Second Empire details, is very similar to several other lighthouses built around the same time, including one fairly close by in Bridgeport Harbor. It's perhaps best known as one of New England's most haunted lighthouses.

Accessibility:

Geographic coordinates: 41° 07' 00" N   73° 13' 18" W

Nearest town: Fairfield. Located on a dangerous reef in Long Island Sound, near the border between Fairfield and Bridgeport.

Established: 1874. Present lighthouse built: 1874. Automated: 1971.

Height of tower: 35 feet tall. Height of focal plane: 51 feet.

Previous optic: Fourth-order Fresnel lens. Present optic: VRB-25.

Characteristic: Red flash every 6 seconds. Fog signal: One blast every 15 seconds.

Drawing from the original plans for Penfield Reef Light

Three days before Christmas in 1916, keeper Fred Jordan set out for the mainland in one of the station's small boats so that he could bring his hand-made Christmas presents to his family. The seas were growing increasingly rough, and assistant keeper Rudolph Iten watched helplessly from the lighthouse as Jordan struggled against the gale. The keeper's boat capsized, and his lifeless body was later recovered.

Keeper Rudolph Iten

Iten later told a reporter that a few days after Jordan's drowning, he observed a "gray, phosphorescent figure" emerge from the room formerly occupied by Jordan. The figure passed silently to the stairs and disappeared in the darkness below. Iten claimed that other keepers also saw the ghost and that they were all prepared to sign an affidavit to that effect.

Ghostly sightings at Penfield Reef have been reported periodically. Clark Ellison, one of the light's last Coast Guard keepers, says he heard disembodied footsteps coming slowly up the creaky stairs on more than one occasion. The first time, he and another crewman hunted in vain for the source of the sound, but after that, they "did not get up to seek the ghost in person."

Nineteenth-century engraving of Penfield Reef Light

In 1969, the Coast Guard announced plans to replace the lighthouse with a light on a simple pipe tower. Local residents and politicians objected, and the plan was scrapped. After its automation and destaffing in 1971, the building developed some structural problems. The Coast Guard installed a new stainless steel lantern roof in 2003 along with other renovations.

In 2008, under the provisions of the National Lighthouse Preservation Act, the National Park Service announced that ownership of Penfield Reef Lighthouse would be conveyed to Beacon Preservation, Inc., (www.beacon preservation.org). At this writing, a dispute over the submerged lands under the lighthouse has thrown the ownership situation into confusion, and it appears the lighthouse will revert to the federal government for an auction to the general public.

Penfield Reef Light can be seen distantly from Fayerweather Island, at the end of Seaside Park in Bridgeport. Better views are available from regular harbor cruises aboard the 40-foot former Navy launch *Chief,* leaving Captain's Cove Seaport in Bridgeport. See www. captainscoveseaport.com/cruises.htm or call 203-335-1433 for information.

SIDE TRIP: *Captain's Cove Seaport*

Since opening in 1982, Captain's Cove Seaport, located on historic Black Rock Harbor in Bridgeport, has grown into a very popular maritime and amusement center. There are charming shops built to look like a New England seaport village, a 400-seat restaurant, and Club Titanic. There are music events and festivals, and you can take a harbor cruise from here that includes views of the Penfield Reef and Fayerweather Island lighthouses.

Captain's Cove Seaport
1 Bostwick Avenue
Bridgeport, CT 06605
Phone: 203-335-1433
Web site: www.captainscove seaport.com.

Fascinating Fact

Penfield Reef was once a peninsula that supported the grazing of cows. The land wore away until only a jagged reef was left.

FAYERWEATHER ISLAND LIGHT
(Black Rock Harbor Light)

Accessibility: 🚗 🚶 ⛵

Geographic coordinates:
41° 08' 33" N   73° 13' 00" W

Nearest city: Bridgeport. Located on a seven-acre island at the entrance to Black Rock Harbor, Long Island Sound.

Established: 1808. Present lighthouse built: 1823. Deactivated: 1933.

Height of tower: 47 feet.

Previous optic: Fifth-order Fresnel lens. Present optic: none.

Bridgeport's Black Rock Harbor was once an important center for trade and shipbuilding. All that's left of this light station is the 1823 rubblestone tower, which replaced the original lighthouse after it was destroyed in a hurricane. The keeper's house was destroyed by fire in 1977.

The most fascinating character in Fayerweather Island's history was Kate Moore, daughter of keeper Stephen Tomlinson Moore. When her father became disabled, young Kate took over most of the lightkeeping duties. Kate maintained a garden, cared for a flock of sheep, carved and sold duck decoys, and had a thriving oyster business. When her father died in 1871, Kate finally was appointed as the official keeper; she resigned eight years later. After retirement, Kate was asked if she missed her old home. "Never," she answered. "The sea is a treacherous friend."

Keeper Kate Moore

After the light was discontinued, the tower fell into disrepair. The island later became part of Bridgeport's Seaside Park, a 370-acre recreation area established largely through the efforts of favorite son P. T. Barnum. The Black Rock Seaport Foundation, affiliated with the Black Rock Community Council, oversaw a 1998 restoration of the lighthouse. Solar-powered lights illuminate the tower at night, but the lighthouse is not an aid to navigation.

The lighthouse itself is not open to the public, but you can reach the grounds via a mildly strenuous walk from the western end of Seaside Park. From I-95 South, take exit 27 (Lafayette Boulevard). Take the University of Bridgeport/Transportation Center ramp. Continue straight on South Avenue for 0.2 miles. Turn left onto Park Avenue and follow to the park. From I-95 North, take exit 27 (Lafayette Boulevard). After a short distance, turn left onto Myrtle Avenue, and then turn right onto Railroad Avenue. After 0.4 miles, turn right onto Park Avenue and continue to the park.

From Park Avenue, follow Waldemere Avenue to the west. Waldemere leads onto Barnum Drive, then Barnum Boulevard. Park at the far western end of Barnum Boulevard and walk across the breakwater to the lighthouse. From

Fascinating Fact

Kate Moore lived here for sixty-two years as the keeper's daughter and later as keeper herself. She was credited with at least twenty-one lives saved.

the island, you can see Penfield Reef Lighthouse offshore about 1.5 miles to the south.

Call 203-576-7233 for more information on Seaside Park. There is an admission fee to the park in summer. You can also view this lighthouse from harbor cruises leaving Captain's Cove Seaport in Bridgeport. Visit www.captains coveseaport.com/cruises.htm or call 203-335-1433 for more information.

Nineteenth-century view of Fayerweather Island Light

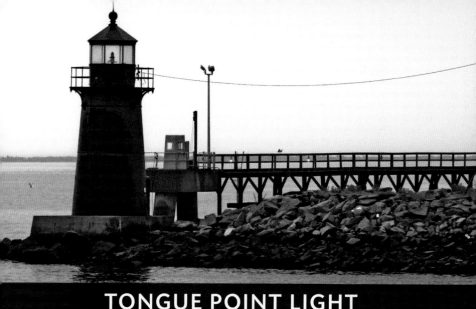

TONGUE POINT LIGHT
(Bug Light, Bridgeport Breakwater Light)

Diminutive "Bug Light," as it's known locally, was originally about 500 feet offshore at the end of a breakwater at the entrance to Bridgeport's inner harbor. The first keeper was S. Adolphus McNeil, long-time keeper of the old Bridgeport Harbor Lighthouse, which burned down in 1953. There was never a dwelling built here, so McNeil constructed a little shanty on the breakwater where he'd sometimes spend the night.

Accessibility:

Geographic coordinates:
41° 10' 00" N 73° 10' 39" W

Nearest city: Bridgeport. Located on the grounds of the Bridgeport Harbor Generating Station at the west side of the entrance to Bridgeport Harbor.

Established: 1895. Present lighthouse built: 1895. Automated: 1954.

Height of tower: 31 feet. Height of focal plane: 31 feet.

Previous optic: Sixth-order Fresnel lens. Present optic: 155 mm.

Characteristic: Green flash every 4 seconds.

When McNeil died in late 1904, his widow, Flora Evans McNeil, replaced him. Flora was a sea captain's daughter and expert boater. In stormy weather, she could be seen dashing out on the breakwater in a rubber coat and boots. "I suppose some people would think it an impossible thing to do," she told a reporter, "but I am almost as much at home on or in the water as I am on land, and I have no real fear of the water even when it is angry."

The breakwater was shortened in 1919, and the lighthouse was moved to its present location, 275 feet closer to shore. The light was automated in 1954. It stands today on the property of the Bridgeport Harbor Generating Station, and the grounds are off limits to the public.

An excellent view is possible from the Bridgeport-to-Port Jefferson (NY) ferry, which passes the lighthouse soon after it departs from Bridgeport. See www.portjeffferry.com or call 631-473-0286 (NY) or 203-335-2040 (CT) for details. Sailing time is 75 minutes, and you also get a distant view of Stratford Shoal Light on the trip.

Fascinating Fact

Flora Evans McNeil, one of this light's keepers, also ran a manicure business in Bridgeport.

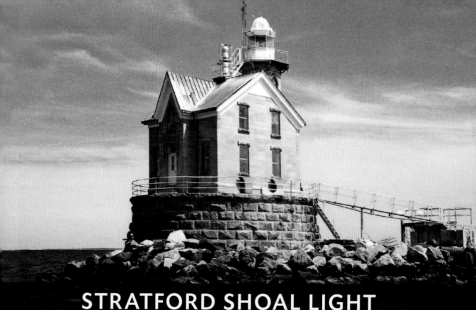

STRATFORD SHOAL LIGHT
(Middleground Shoal Light)

This granite lighthouse—also known as Middleground Light because of its location in the middle of Long Island Sound—looks a bit like a ghostly castle from the ferries that pass it. The building took three years to erect, with storms causing numerous delays.

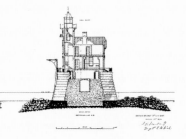

Drawing from the original plans for Stratford Shoal Light

Accessibility: ⛵

Geographic coordinates: 41° 03' 35" N   73° 06' 05" W

Nearest town: Stratford. Located at Stratford Shoal, also known as Middleground Shoal, about midway between the New York and Connecticut coasts in Long Island Sound.

Established: 1877. Present lighthouse built: 1877. Automated: 1970.

Height of tower: 35 feet. Height of focal plane: 60 feet.

Previous optic: Fourth-order Fresnel lens. Present optic: VRB-25.

Characteristic: White flash every 5 seconds. Fog signal: One blast every 15 seconds.

This was a stag station, with male keepers only. Life was lonely and stressful at the isolated location. In 1905, an assistant keeper named Julius Koster went into a rage and locked himself in the lantern room. He threatened to destroy the light and managed to stop its rotation for a while. First assistant keeper Morrell Hulse valiantly defended the light from Koster, going five days without sleep. It's been claimed that Koster's ghost later haunted the lighthouse, slamming doors and hurling chairs against the walls.

Stratford Shoal Light, circa late 1800s

The shoal itself has a ghostly legend. In the early 1800s, it's said that a ship called the *Trustful* left Bridgeport in stormy seas with a cargo of church bells. It seems some of the crew decided to stay behind because of the rough conditions, and the captain told them that if the ship sank, the bells would peal a dirge for the "white-livered folk" who stayed behind. The ship met its doom at the shoal, and the crew was lost. To this day, so they say, if you listen closely at Middleground Shoal, you'll hear the sound of muffled church bells clanging beneath the sea.

The light was automated and destaffed in 1970, and the building is not accessible to the public. It can be seen distantly from the Bridgeport-to-Port Jefferson ferry (www.bpjferry.com). These Web sites provide information on charter boats in the area that might be able to provide a closer look: www.ctsportfishing.com and www.ct-fishing-charters.com.

Fascinating Fact

One of the most unusual rescues here was in June 1955, when two Coast Guard keepers picked up a test pilot who had parachuted into the sound when the engine failed in his F-84 Thunderstreak fighter plane..

STRATFORD POINT LIGHT

The first lighthouse built here in 1822 was a 28-foot octagonal wooden tower. It was replaced by the extant 35-foot conical cast-iron tower in 1881, and the tower's central red band was added in 1899.

Accessibility: 📷 ⛵

Geographic coordinates: 41° 09' 07" N 73° 06' 12" W

Nearest city: Stratford. Located at the west side of the mouth of the Housatonic River.

Established: 1822. Present lighthouse built: 1881. Automated: 1970.

Height of tower: 35 feet. Height of focal plane: 52 feet.

Previous optic: Fourth-order Fresnel lens. Present optic: VRB-25.

Characteristic: Two white flashes every 20 seconds.

Undated aerial view

Benedict Lillingston became keeper in 1868. His young granddaughter, Lottie, lived at the station. Lottie tended a flock of Spanish hens and helped with the gardening. During a bad storm in October 1871, Keeper Lillingston and his son, Frederick, left to aid a vessel in distress. Lottie was left alone with her invalid grandmother.

Lottie decided to check the light at about 10:30 p.m., knowing that a ferry was due to pass by. She found that the light had gone out. Acting quickly, Lottie stopped the rotating mechanism, lit a small brass lantern and hung it inside the lens. The ferry captain reported that the light was dim for a half hour. But without that dim light, the steamer might not have made it safely past Stratford Point.

Local native Theodore "Theed" Judson was keeper from 1880 to 1921. He earned the nickname "Crazy" Judson because of incidents like his 1886 sea serpent sighting. The monster was "easily 200 feet in length," with whis-

kers that were "the rich deep green color of bog hay," he told a reporter. In a 1915 article, Judson claimed he had seen mermaids off Stratford Point on a number of occasions. He almost caught one, he said, but she got away after making a hissing sound that "matched well to her temper." His friends never got him to retract his fishy tale.

The station serves as housing for a Coast Guard family and is off limits to the public. You can get a partial view of the station from the gate at the end of Prospect Drive in Stratford. For good photo opportunities, you need a private boat or charter. These Web sites provide information on charter boats in the area: www.ctsportfishing.com and www.ct-fishing-charters.com.

Fascinating Fact

Agnes Judson, a 17-year-old daughter of the keeper, swam out and rescued two fishermen in heavy seas in July 1897.

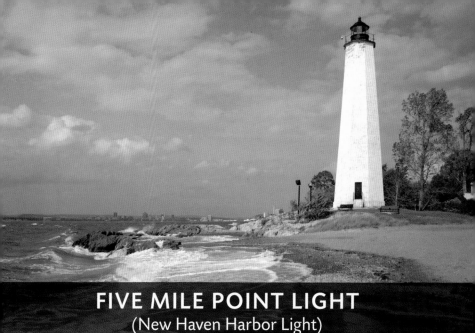

FIVE MILE POINT LIGHT
(New Haven Harbor Light)

This stately brownstone tower stands at Five Mile Point, so-called because of its distance from downtown New Haven. The first lighthouse, built in 1830, was a 30-foot octagonal wooden tower. The light was too low to be of much help to navigation, so a new taller tower was constructed in 1847. The stone for the tower was quarried in East Haven and brought to Five Mile Point in horse-drawn drays.

Accessibility: 🚗

Geographic coordinates: 41° 14' 58" N 72° 54' 13" W

Nearest city: New Haven. Located at the east side of the entrance to New Haven Harbor, at Lighthouse Point Park, 2 Lighthouse Point Road.

Established: 1805. Present lighthouse built: 1847. Deactivated: 1877.

Height of tower: 80 feet. Height of focal plane: 97 feet.

Previous optic: Fourth-order Fresnel lens. Present optic: none.

The 1877 Southwest Ledge Light, in a more advantageous position offshore, replaced this light as a guide into New Haven Harbor. East Haven native Elizur Thompson was keeper at Five Mile Point from 1860 to 1877, minus a two-year gap in the middle. He served as the first keeper at Southwest Ledge. After his 1882 retirement, he returned to Five Mile Point to fly storm signal flags for the U.S. Weather Bureau.

The lighthouse property was transferred to the War Department in 1896, and it passed to the City of New Haven in the 1920s. The city's parks commission created Lighthouse Point Park. The grounds around the lighthouse are open all year. A carousel established at the park in 1916 has been restored and operates in a pavilion close to the lighthouse.

To reach Lighthouse Point Park, take I-95 South to exit 51. At the first traffic light, turn left into Townsend Avenue. Turn right onto Lighthouse Road and follow to the park. From the south, take I-95 North to exit 50 (Woodward Avenue). At the second traffic light, turn right onto Townsend Avenue. Turn right at Lighthouse Road and follow to the park. (Watch for the green signs along Townsend Avenue directing you to the park.)

For more on Lighthouse Point Park, call 203-946-8790 or visit www.cityofnewhaven.com/Parks/Parks Information/lighthousepoint.asp. There is a $20 parking fee for non-residents. From the park, you can see Southwest Ledge Light about a mile offshore to the southwest.

Tourists at Lighthouse Point in the early 1900s

Fascinating Fact

Babe Ruth and Ty Cobb were among the players who competed in baseball games at Lighthouse Point Park.

SOUTHWEST LEDGE LIGHT

This cast-iron, wood-lined lighthouse was established to mark a dangerous ledge near the main channel into New Haven's harbor. It replaced the old Five Mile Point Lighthouse on the mainland. Work on the tower began in 1873 but was delayed by storms, and the light didn't go into service until January 1, 1877. The tower's architecture is unusual and striking, with Second Empire detailing and a mansard roof.

Accessibility: 🚶

Geographic coordinates: 41° 14' 04" N 72° 54' 44" W

Nearest city: New Haven. Located at the southwest end of the east breakwater at the entrance to New Haven Harbor.

Established: 1877. Present lighthouse built 1877. Automated: 1953.

Height of tower: 45 feet. Height of focal plane: 57 feet.

Previous optic: Fourth-order Fresnel lens. Present optic: VRB-25.

Characteristic: Red flash every 5 seconds.

Fog signal: One blast every 15 seconds.

Elizur Thompson, formerly keeper at Five Mile Point, was the first keeper. A newspaper story reported that a piano was brought to the lighthouse for Thompson and his wife. The piano took on some water during the trip from shore, but it "was found to serve well enough to cheer up the evening after the lights had been lit within."

Assistant keeper Nils Nilson

Like many offshore stations, this was a tough assignment for keepers. It appears that the poor conditions and isolation contributed to the 1908 suicide of assistant keeper Nils Nilson. He had been the recipient of a gold lifesaving medal a few years earlier.

The lighthouse was destaffed in 1953. For some years, a civilian "lamplighter" onshore kept an eye on the station and did maintenance as needed.

Southwest Ledge Light can be seen in the distance, about a mile to the southwest, from the area near Five Mile Point Lighthouse at Lighthouse Point Park in New Haven. There are currently no public cruises passing nearby, so the only way to get a close view is by private boat or charter.

Southwest Ledge Light in the early 1900s

Fascinating Fact

Assistant Keeper Edward Grime resigned in 1916 because of damp conditions and rampant cockroaches.

FAULKNER'S ISLAND LIGHT

Abisha Woodward, who also built the 1801 lighthouse at New London, constructed this handsome octagonal brownstone tower. The first keeper was Guilford sea captain Joseph Griffing.

Early 1900s aerial view of Faulkner's Island

Accessibility: 🔭 ⛵

Geographic coordinates:
41° 12' 43" N 72° 39' 13" W

Nearest town: Guilford. Located on a three-acre island about four miles offshore from Guilford Harbor, Long Island Sound.

Established: 1802. Present lighthouse built: 1802. Automated: 1978.

Height of tower: 46 feet. Height of focal plane: 94 feet.

Previous optic: Fourth-order Fresnel lens. Present optic: VRB-25.

Characteristic: White flash every 10 seconds.

Eli Kimberly, keeper from 1818 to 1851, was a local man who had been a crewman on a revenue cutter. Ten of the Kimberlys' twelve children were

Fascinating Fact

British soldiers from a warship visited the light station during the War of 1812, when Solomon Stone was keeper. The keeper's three daughters were entertained as guests of the officers on the ship.

born during the family's long stay on the island. The Kimberlys gained a reputation as excellent hosts to the summer people who gathered on the island; they even built a bowling alley for visitors.

Oliver N. Brooks followed Kimberly as keeper. In November 1858, he was praised for a daring rescue of five people aboard a disabled schooner in heavy seas. The keeper and his two daughters played a variety of instruments and often gathered for lively musical sessions. They were sometimes joined by the family's Newfoundland dog, Old Tige, whose "singing" was described by

Faulkner's Island Light circa early 1900s

a writer as not howls or barks, but a "wonderful something in between."

Coast Guard personnel staffed the station beginning in 1941. An accidental fire in March 1976 destroyed the keeper's house, and the Coast Guard crewmen were reassigned. The light was soon automated.

A preservation effort began in the late 1980s and eventually developed

into the all-volunteer Faulkner's Light Brigade, a commission of the Guilford Preservation Alliance. Government funds were combined with local donations, and the lighthouse tower was restored in 1999. Federal funding has paid for extensive erosion control on the island in recent years.

Faulkner's Island is owned by the U.S. Fish and Wildlife Service and is part of the Stewart B. McKinney National Wildlife Refuge. Faulkner's Island is an important nesting site for

common terns and endangered roseate terns.

You can see the lighthouse very distantly from Guilford Harbor. Faulkner's Light Brigade usually holds a public open house in September. For information on the open houses and other events, visit www.lighthouse.cc/FLB/ or call 203-453-8400. You can see the lighthouse very distantly (bring your binoculars) from Guilford Harbor, but for a closer look you'll have to be in a private boat or charter cruise.

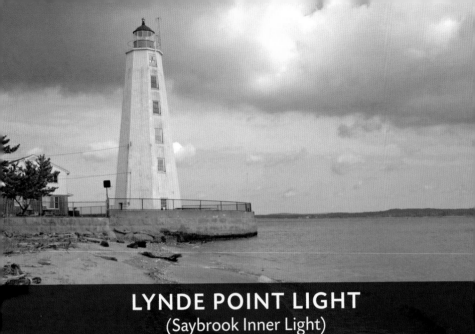

LYNDE POINT LIGHT
(Saybrook Inner Light)

Accessibility: 🏛 ⛵

Geographic coordinates:
41° 16' 17" N   72° 20' 35" W

Nearest town: Old Saybrook. Located on the west side of the mouth of the Connecticut River.

Established: 1802. Present lighthouse built: 1838. Automated: 1978.

Height of tower:
65 feet. Height of focal plane: 71 feet.

Optic: Fifth-order Fresnel lens.

Characteristic:
Fixed white.

The first lighthouse built at this point in 1802—a 35-foot wooden tower—was deemed too short, leading to the construction of the still-standing brownstone tower in 1838. The tower is similar to the octagonal masonry towers at New London (1801), Faulkner's Island (1802), and Five Mile Point (1847).

John Ninde Buckridge, a native of New York City, was keeper from 1883 to 1902. Buckridge had lost a leg in the Civil War. He and his wife, Margaret, had six children. Their daughter Minnie was married at the lighthouse in 1890, "amid the hoarse screech of congratulatory steamer whistles," according to a newspaper account.

Keeper John Ninde Buckridge

Elmer Gildersleeve, the next keeper, raised eight children with his wife in 34 years at light stations in New York and Connecticut. The keeper's son, Lawrence Gildersleeve, caddied for golfers at a course near the lighthouse—five cents for 18 holes, with an additional 25-cent tip when he was lucky.

The 1858 keeper's house was demolished and replaced by a modern duplex in 1966. The light was automated in 1978, but the Coast Guard retained the duplex dwelling for housing for two families.

The light station and the road leading to it are not open to the public. Distant views are possible from some points along the shore, including the South Cove Causeway. To get there, take exit 67 off I-95 South and follow Elm Street south, then turn right onto Route 154 (Main Street). Continue on Route 154 as it makes a right turn onto Bridge Street and follow to the causeway. You'll have to park on a nearby street and walk out on the causeway.

The best photo opportunities are from the occasional lighthouse cruises offered by Captain John's Sport Fishing Fleet (860-443-7259, www.sunbeamfleet.com) in Waterford. Connecticut River Expeditions (860-662-0577, www.ctriverexpeditions.org) of Essex passes the lighthouse on their South Sunset Cruise.

Fascinating Fact

When Keeper Daniel Whittlesey died in 1841, his wife, Catherine, became keeper. An 1850 inspection report praised her, stating that everything was in first-rate clean order."

SAYBROOK BREAKWATER LIGHT
(Saybrook Outer Light)

Accessibility:

Geographic coordinates:
41° 15' 48" N   72° 20' 34" W

Nearest town: Old Saybrook. Located at the end of a stone breakwater on the west side of the mouth of the Connecticut River.

Established: 1886. Present lighthouse built: 1886. Automated: 1959.

Height of tower: 49 feet. Height of focal plane: 58 feet.

Previous optic: Fourth-order Fresnel lens. Present optic: 300 mm.

Characteristic: Green flash every 6 seconds.

Fog signal: One blast every 30 seconds.

Two stone breakwaters were built at the mouth of the Connecticut River in the 1870s, and a channel was dredged between them. It was decided that a lighthouse was needed at the end of the west breakwater, so Congress appropriated $38,000 for that purpose. The cast-iron sparkplug-type lighthouse was completed in 1886.

Living quarters were inside the tower. The walk to shore across the breakwater was often dangerous, especially in winter, so the keepers generally traveled by boat. The first keeper, Frank Parmele, lasted only four years, and turnover was frequent.

In May 1896, the *New York Times* reported that Keeper John D. Skipworth had sighted a "monstrous sea serpent sporting on the surface of the Sound." Skipworth said the monster was 300 feet in length and that it spouted water from its head like a whale. He may have been trying to top the 1886 sea serpent sighting by Keeper Theed "Crazy" Judson down the coast at Stratford Point.

Sidney Gross was principal keeper at the time of the great hurricane of September 21, 1938. Gross and an assistant keeper were trapped in the lighthouse as the tide rose. Oil and gasoline tanks and a walkway to the breakwater were carried away, as were the station's boat and the platform that encircled the tower.

By 6:00 p.m., the seas crashed through a second story window, flooding the tower. "I certainly did not expect to see another sunrise," Gross wrote in his log. When daylight came and the seas subsided, the keepers sur-

Fascinating Fact

Actress Katherine Hepburn lived for many years in a house neighboring this lighthouse.

veyed the wreckage and realized how lucky they were. About 700 people died in the storm along the New England coast, including seven at light stations.

The lighthouse is in a private community, and the best views are from the water. Captain John's Sport Fishing Fleet (860-443-7259, www.sunbeam fleet.com) in Waterford includes it in their periodic lighthouse cruises. Connecticut River Expeditions (860-662-0577, www.ctriverexpeditions.org), with cruises leaving from Essex, also provides a viewing opportunity on their South Sunset Cruise.

Saybrook Breakwater Light in the early 1900s

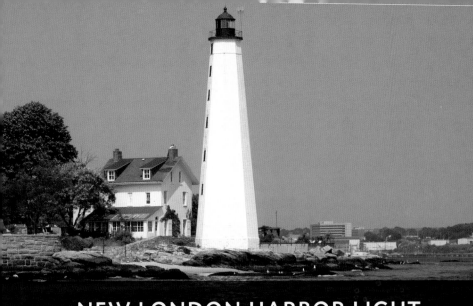

NEW LONDON HARBOR LIGHT

Accessibility: 🏛️ ⛵

Geographic coordinates:
41° 19' 00" N 72° 05' 24" W

Nearest city: New London. Located at the west side of the entrance to the Thames River.

Established: 1761. Present lighthouse built: 1801. Automated: 1912.

Height of tower:
89 feet. Height of focal plane: 90 feet.

Optic: Fourth-order Fresnel lens, (1857), still in use.

Characteristic: 3 seconds white, alternating with 3 seconds darkness.

This elegant tower stands as a reminder of the days when New London trailed only New Bedford and Nantucket as a whaling port. The first lighthouse at this location was a 64-foot stone tower with a wooden lantern, erected in 1761. The lighthouse was financed by a local lottery. In 1790, ownership was ceded to the federal government.

New London Harbor Light in the early 1900s.

Fascinating Fact

This is Connecticut's oldest and tallest lighthouse.

The extant octagonal brownstone lighthouse was built in 1801 after its predecessor developed a major crack. The builder was New London resident Abisha Woodward, a veteran of the American Revolution.

Writer Arthur Hewitt interviewed Keeper Charles Field in 1904. Field told Hewitt about a particular night when "the fog was so thick yer could have cut it with a knife and it fairly stuck in yer throat." Field heard a strange sound in the fog and realized it was a vessel's sails in the wind. He shouted to the vessel, and they managed to divert course just before running up on the rocks.

In 1912, the light was converted to automatic operation, and the keeper's house was sold into private ownership. Under the National Historic Lighthouse Preservation Act, ownership of the lighthouse tower was transferred in 2009 to the New London Maritime Society, which operates the city's Custom House Maritime Museum. See

SIDE TRIP: *U.S. Coast Guard Museum*

This museum is located in Waesche Hall on the grounds of the Coast Guard Academy in New London, Connecticut. The museum contains a first-order Fresnel lens from Thacher Island, Cape Ann, Massachusetts. There are also ship models, figureheads and other carvings, uniforms, medals, and more. The museum is open Monday–Friday, 9:00 a.m. to 4:30 p.m. and occasional weekend days; it's closed on all federal holidays. Admission is free, but you will need a government-issued photo ID to enter the campus. At this writing, the museum will be closed for a construction project at least until May 2012.

Coast Guard Museum, U.S. Coast Guard Academy

15 Mohegan Avenue

New London, CT 06320-4195

Phone: (860) 444-8511

Web site: www.uscg.mil/hq/g-cp/ museum/museumindex.asp

www.nlmaritimesociety.org or call 860-447-2501 for more information.

For now, it's nearly impossible to photograph the lighthouse in its Pequot Avenue location. Visitors are warned by no trespassing signs to stay off the property, and the presence of trees make photos from the sidewalk difficult. The best views for photography are from the water. The lighthouse is included in the periodic lighthouse cruises offered by Captain John's Sport Fishing Fleet (860-443-7259, www.sunbeamfleet. com) in Waterford. DownEast Lighthouse Cruises (860-460-1802, www. downeastlighthousecruises.com) in Groton can also provide a good view.

Public ferries leaving New London provide views, although they may not pass as close as the lighthouse cruises. For the ferry from New London to Ori-

ent Point, NY, call Cross Sound Ferry Services at 860-443-5281 or visit www. longislandferry.com. For the ferry from New London to Fishers Island, NY, call 860-442-0165 or see www.fiferry.com. A seasonal ferry goes from New London to Montauk (Long Island), NY; call 631-668-5700.

SIDE TRIP: *Custom House Maritime Museum*

This museum is the home of the New London Maritime Society, founded in 1983 to save New London's Custom House from commercial use after the government declared it surplus property. New London's only downtown museum is housed in a handsome federal-style granite building designed by Robert Mills in 1833. The exhibits preserve and promote the city's maritime history, while the building continues to house an active office for the U.S. Customs Service. Of primary interest to lighthouse buffs is the beautifully preserved fourth-order Fresnel lens from New London Ledge Light.

Custom House Maritime Museum
150 Bank Street
New London, CT 06320
Phone: 860-447-2501
Web site: www.nlmaritimesociety. org

New London Harbor Light in the early 1900s

NEW LONDON LEDGE LIGHT

As New London transitioned from whaling port to industrial city, the old New London Harbor Lighthouse wasn't sufficient to guide large, modern ships past dangerous ledges at the mouth of the Thames River. The Lighthouse Board determined that a lighthouse was needed in a more advantageous position at the river's mouth. A giant crib made of southern yellow pine was sunk into position, and then filled with concrete, gravel, and stone, and then topped with a three-foot layer of concrete.

Accessibility:

Geographic coordinates: 41° 18' 18" N   72° 04' 42" W

Nearest town: Groton. Located near the center of the mouth of the Thames River, on the approach to New London Harbor.

Established: 1909. Present lighthouse built: 1909. Automated: 1987.

Height of focal plane: 58 feet.

Previous optic: Fourth-order Fresnel lens. Present optic: VRB-25.

Characteristic: Three white flashes and one red flash every 30 seconds.

Fog signal: Two blasts every 20 seconds.

A three-story combined dwelling and lighthouse was built on this foundation. The style of the building is usually classified as French Second Empire, but it also shows the influence of Colonial Revival architecture.

Keeper Howard Beebe

Howard B. Beebe, a native of New London, was the principal keeper during the memorable hurricane of September 21, 1938. Beebe later recalled that waves were pouring through the second floor of the dwelling during the storm. Eleven tons of coal stored in the basement was washed away by the angry seas.

Early photo of New London Ledge Light

Under the Coast Guard, two or three crewmen lived at the lighthouse. Stories of ghostly visitations were common during the Coast Guard era. The men told of doors that opened and closed by themselves. The TV turned itself on and off, and a deck swabbed itself. Visitors said they felt a mysterious presence watching them at night. Actual ghost sightings were rare; supposedly only women have seen the spirit who became known as "Ernie."

The usual story that's told is that a keeper named Ernie, circa 1930s, jumped from the roof of the building to his death after learning that his wife ran away with the captain of the Block Island ferry and that Ernie took up permanent residence as the lighthouse ghost. This story doesn't jibe with the known facts; there is no record of a keeper named Ernie and no evidence that a keeper ever died at the station. The stories persist, however.

In August 2006, members of a paranormal investigation team called the New England Ghost Project spent a night at the lighthouse. No ghost appeared, but the team's psychic medium, Maureen Wood, apparently

made contact with an angry male spirit. The entity claimed that he was a worker performing maintenance on the roof of the dwelling and that his coworkers locked him out as a prank. As he attempted to get inside, he slipped and fell to his death. The accident, said the spirit, was covered up by those involved. There's no hard evidence to support this story, but it offers an intriguing alternative to the usual tale about Ernie.

The New London Ledge Lighthouse Foundation, a chapter of the American Lighthouse Foundation, now cares for the building; see www.ledge lighthouse.org. Only distant views are possible from shore. Project Oceanology, located in Groton at the Avery Point Campus of the University of Connecticut, has offered public tours to the lighthouse. See www.oceanology.org or call 860-445-9007 for more information and the current schedule.

The periodic lighthouse cruises offered by Captain John's Sport Fishing Fleet (860-443-7259, www.sun beamfleet.com) in Waterford afford a

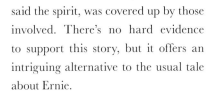

Fascinating Fact

It's been said that the elegant style of this lighthouse is the result of requests of wealthy local residents who wanted a structure that would not look out of place compared to their own homes.

great view of this lighthouse. DownEast Lighthouse Cruises (860-460-1802, www.downeastlighthousecruises.com) in Groton can also provide photo opportunities. Ferries leaving New London also pass close to the lighthouse; see the end of the section on New London Harbor Lighthouse for details.

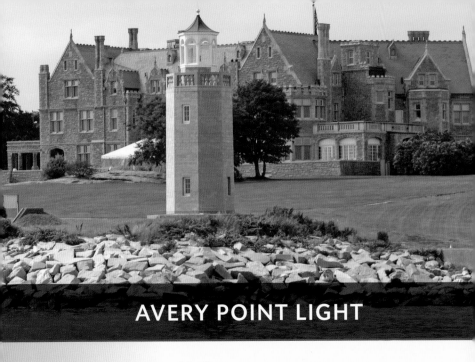

AVERY POINT LIGHT

Accessibility: 🚗

Geographic coordinates: 41° 18' 54" N 72° 03' 36" W

Nearest town: Groton. Located on the east side of the Thames River.

Established: 1944. Deactivated: 1967. Relighted: 2006.

Height of tower: 41 feet. Height of focal plane: 55 feet.

Optic: Solar powered LED.

Characteristic: Green flash every 4 seconds.

The University of Connecticut's Avery Point campus in Groton was once the 70-acre estate of wealthy industrialist Morton F. Plant. The estate was sold to the State of Connecticut in 1942. It was eventually sold to the federal government, and a Coast Guard training facility was established on the site.

Avery Point Light circa 1996, before restoration

The octagonal lighthouse was constructed of brown concrete blocks, topped by a wooden lantern surrounded by a railing that incorporated Italian marble balusters salvaged from the Plant estate. The light aided mariners headed for a cove east of Avery Point and those traveling in Fisher's Island Sound and Pine Island Bay. After the Coast Guard left the site in 1967 and the light was deactivated, the property was converted into a campus of the University of Connecticut.

After years of abandonment, the lighthouse was falling to ruin by the 1990s. Help came in the form of concerned local citizens who founded the Avery Point Lighthouse Society (P.O. Box 1552, Groton, CT 06340, www.averypointlight.com), a chapter of the American Lighthouse Foundation.

With state, federal, and private funding, restoration of the tower began. The wooden lantern was removed from the tower in 2001, and a replica lantern was created by the West Mystic Wooden Boat Building Company. The outer faces of the concrete blocks were replaced, and the old blocks were strengthened with cement and steel reinforcement. The restoration was completed in late 2005, and the tower was relighted at a gala ceremony in October 2006. With a solar-powered LED (light-emitting diode) installed, the lighthouse is now an official private aid to navigation.

To visit the lighthouse, take I-95 north or south to exit 87 onto CT Route 349 (Clarence B. Sharp Highway). Turn right at the second traffic light (still Route 349). At the next traffic light, turn left onto Benham Road (still Route 349). Continue for about 1.5 miles. The road curves sharply left at the end of Route 349, and the road becomes Shennecossett Road. The entrance to the University of Connecticut's Avery Point campus is here. Enter the property and head straight back toward the water. Follow the circular drive and park in one of the visitor parking areas. Walk to the east and you'll see the lighthouse near the edge of the water.

Fascinating Fact

This was the last lighthouse built in Connecticut. It's been said that it was intended to serve as a memorial to all lighthouse keepers.

MORGAN POINT LIGHT

Accessibility: 🛥

Geographic coordinates:
41° 19' 00" N 71° 59' 22" W

Nearest town: Noank (a village of Groton). Located on the west side of the mouth of the Mystic River.

Established: 1831. Present lighthouse built: 1868. Deactivated: 1919.

Height of tower:
52 feet. Height of focal plane: 61 feet.

Previous optic: Sixth-order Fresnel lens. Present optic: none.

This light station was established in 1831 to help mariners entering the Mystic River and the harbor of Noank, a thriving center for shipbuilding and fishing at the time. The first keeper was Ezra Daboll, a veteran of the War of 1812. When Daboll died in 1838, his wife, Eliza, succeeded him as keeper.

Morgan Point Light circa early 1900s

The original 25-foot granite tower and six-room dwelling were replaced by a new combined lighthouse/dwelling in 1868. The handsome granite building is similar to the lighthouses constructed around the same time at Connecticut's Great Captain Island and Sheffield Island and several other locations. A cast-iron light tower was attached to the front end of the dwelling.

In 1921, the lighthouse was discontinued and replaced by an automatic light to the east on Crooks Ledge. The lighthouse was sold to a private party for $8,625.

In 1991, Jason Pilalas of San Marino, California, purchased the property. Pilalas, a partner in an investment management firm, grew up in Greenwich, Connecticut, near the Great Captain Island Lighthouse that is almost identical to the one at Morgan Point. The building's interior was

Morgan Point Light during its "headless" period

in disrepair, but Pilalas had it adapted into a comfortable living space. A major addition at the rear of the building

SIDE TRIP: *Mystic Seaport Museum*

This is one of America's best maritime museums, with 300,000 visitors annually and a volunteer corps of more than 1,400 people. You can get an intimate view of American maritime history here as you explore historic tall ships (most notably the whale ship *Charles W. Morgan*) and stroll through a recreated nineteenth-century New England seaport, including a replica of Brant Point Lighthouse (with an actual Fresnel lens).

The exhibits alone are more than enough to keep you occupied for many hours, but you can also get out on the water aboard the vintage steamer *Sabino*, the classic power launch *Resolute*, or the catboat *Breck Marshall*. There's an extensive museum store and art gallery and multiple choices for dining. You'll want to spend at least a few hours here.

Mystic Seaport
75 Greenmanville Avenue
P.O. Box 6000
Mystic, CT 06355-0990
Phone: 860-572-5315
Web site: www.mysticseaport.org

includes additional living space and an office. The rebirth was capped with the addition of a new replica lantern; the original had been removed years earlier. The new lantern is slightly oversized so it can serve as a comfortable sitting room with a spectacular view.

The lighthouse is not accessible to the public, but it can be viewed from the periodic lighthouse cruises offered by Captain John's Sport Fishing Fleet in Waterford; call 860-443-7259 or visit www.sunbeamfleet.com. DownEast Lighthouse Cruises in Groton can also provide a close view; see www.downeast lighthousecruises.com or call 860-460-1802. And the 1908 steamboat *Sabino* (a national historic landmark) travels from the Mystic Seaport Museum to the mouth of the Mystic River, fairly close to the lighthouse. See www.mystic seaport.org or call 860-572-5315.

Fascinating Fact

Civil War veteran Thaddeus Pecor was keeper here for a remarkable forty-eight years (1871–1919). Some have claimed that his spirit haunts the lighthouse.

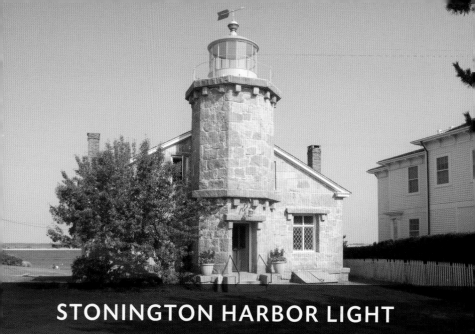

STONINGTON HARBOR LIGHT

The harbor of Stonington was busy with whaling and sealing vessels in the early 1800s. The first lighthouse, built in 1823, was a 30-foot stone tower with a separate stone dwelling. The first keeper, William Potter, was paid $300 yearly. When Potter died in 1842, his wife, Patty, became keeper. Patty Porter retired in 1854 at the age of 71.

Accessibility:

Geographic coordinates:
41° 19' 43" N   71° 54' 20" W

Nearest town: Stonington. Located on the east side of Stonington Harbor.

Established: 1823. Present lighthouse built: 1840. Deactivated: 1889.

Height of tower: 35 feet. Height of focal plane: 62 feet.

Previous optic: Sixth-order Fresnel lens. Present optic: none.

Inside Stonington's Old Lighthouse Museum

Coastal erosion led to the rebuilding of the station farther from the water. The handsome new building, with a 35-foot octagonal tower at the front of a one-and-one-half-story dwelling, went into service in 1840.

A breakwater was built at the entrance to the harbor in the 1880s. The Lighthouse Board established a 25-foot cast-iron lighthouse on the breakwater in 1889, and the old lighthouse was rendered superfluous. The building eventually became the home of the Stonington Historical Society's Old Lighthouse Museum, housing an eclectic collection that includes China trade items, pre-1935 Stonington pottery, items relating to military history, a fourth-order Fresnel lens, and a display on Long Island Sound lighthouses.

Visitors to the museum are invited to climb the stairs to the lantern, where they can enjoy a view that encompasses parts of three states. For the hours and more information on the Old Lighthouse Museum, call 860-535-1440 or visit www.stoningtonhistory.org. In the 2011 season, the museum was open daily (10 a.m. to 5 p.m.) in summer, with a later closing (8:00 p.m.) on Thursdays.

To reach the museum, take exit 91 off I-95. Turn south on Route 234 (Pequot Trail), and continue 0.4 miles to North Main Street. Turn left on North Main and continue 1.5 miles to the stoplight at the intersection with US Route 1. Cross Route 1 and continue straight to a stop sign. Turn left and then take the next right over a viaduct (railroad bridge) onto Water Street. Follow Water Street through Stonington Village to the end. Park at the end of the point and walk up to the lighthouse.

Fascinating Fact

This lighthouse was constructed from stones and other materials from the original (1823) tower and dwelling, which had to be relocated due to coastal erosion.

Stonington Breakwater Light circa early 1900s. This lighthouse was dismantled in 1926.

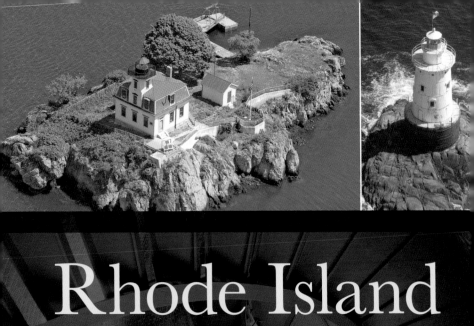

Rhode Island

Tiny as it is, the Ocean State has more than 400 miles of scenic coastline. It's said that if you're driving in Little Rhody, you're never more than thirty minutes from the water's edge. It should come as no surprise that thirty lighthouses were built in the state, twenty-one of which still stand. Most of them are within the confines of Narragansett Bay, a sheltered area of some 147 square miles.

Beavertail is America's third oldest light station, a testament to the importance of Newport as an early center of maritime commerce. The city—now best known as a yachting capital—was also the home of America's most celebrated lighthouse keeper, Ida Lewis of Lime Rock.

The development of Providence as a manufacturing center north of Narragansett Bay on the Providence River had a great deal to do with the establishment of many light stations. In addition to several lights built to guide traffic through the east and west passages of the bay, five lights were established on the river itself. Only one of the river lights, the pretty station at Pomham Rocks, survives today.

No tour of Rhode Island is complete without a ferry trip to Block Island, the "Bermuda of the North." Block Island Southeast Light can lay claim to iconic status. Architecture, scenic beauty, and history combine to make this an essential destination.

Rhode Islanders are justifiably proud of their maritime heritage. The state has had a lighthouse renaissance in recent years, with impressive restorations completed at several locations. For most Rhode Island lighthouses, you'll have to be content with views from the water. Luckily, some excellent cruises are available. Beavertail, Rose Island, and the two Block Island lights rank as the state's must-sees; all of them have exhibits that are open to the public in season.

Rhode Island Lighthouses

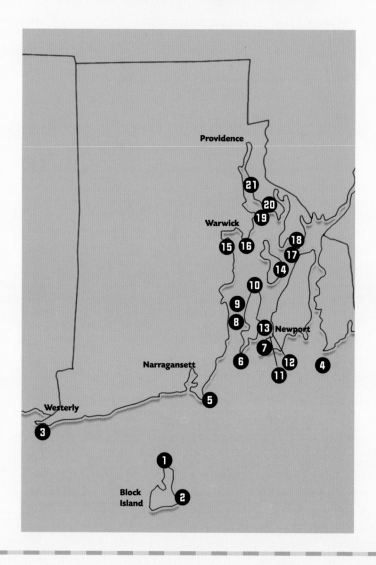

Providence

21

20

19

Warwick

18

15   16   17

14

10

9

8   13   Newport

7

Narragansett   6   12

11   4

5

Westerly

3

1

Block   2
Island

LIGHTHOUSE   PAGE

BLOCK ISLAND NORTH LIGHT

Accessibility: ⛵ + 🚗 🚶 🏠

Geographic coordinates:
41° 13' 40" N   71° 34' 33" W

Nearest town: New Shoreham. Located at Sandy Point, the northern tip of Block Island, about 12 miles south of the Rhode Island coast.

Established: 1829. Present lighthouse built: 1868. Automated: 1956. Deactivated: 1972. Relighted 1989.

Height of tower: 55 feet. Height of focal plane: 61 feet.

Present optic: Fourth-order Fresnel lens.

Characteristic (skeleton tower): Flashing white every 5 seconds.

Block Island is a popular vacation spot today, but the ten-square-mile island was long known by mariners for its treacherous shoals. Countless vessels ran up on the long sandbar that extends from Sandy Point at the island's north end, which led Congress to appropriate $5,500 for a lighthouse at the point in 1829. The station initially consisted of a small, one-story dwelling with two lights, about 30 feet apart from each other, mounted on the roof.

The station was rebuilt farther from the sea in 1837. It was again a dwelling with two lights on the roof. From the sea, the two lights blended into one. A new single lighthouse tower was constructed along with a new dwelling closer to the end of the point in 1857. The encroaching sea soon threatened the buildings. In 1868, a sturdy new combined lighthouse/dwelling was constructed, similar to the contemporary lighthouses at Sheffield Island and Great Captain Island in Connecticut.

Block Island North Light circa early 1900s

Hiram Ball served as keeper from 1861 until his death in 1891. Ball first went to sea at age thirteen as the cook on a West Indies–bound schooner, and he eventually captained a variety of vessels. His brother, Nicholas Ball, was largely responsible for the development of Block Island as a resort. Ball was followed by Elam Littlefield, who served thirty-two years (1891–1923) as keeper.

In February 1907, the passenger steamer *Larchmont* sank in stormy seas off Watch Hill. Some of the passengers escaped in lifeboats and made it to

Fascinating Fact

The huge granite blocks for this lighthouse were delivered to Block Island by a schooner, then hauled by oxen to Sandy Point.

Block Island, where keeper Littlefield and his family cared for them. More than one hundred people perished in the disaster.

In late 1972, the Coast Guard extinguished the light and replaced it with a nearby light on a utilitarian steel tower. The abandoned lighthouse fell into severe disrepair. Ownership eventually passed to the Town of New Shoreham (Block Island's sole town). The North

Light Commission manages the lighthouse; the nonprofit North Light Association was later established to raise funds for the lighthouse.

After much work on the building, the lighthouse was opened to the public as a museum in 1993. The lighthouse has undergone extensive renovation during the last few years under the tireless stewardship of North Light Commission Chair Rob Gilpin. In June 2008, the lantern was removed for an overhaul. After work on the building and the lantern was completed, the lighthouse was relighted on October 23, 2010.

Block Island is accessible via ferry from Point Judith and Newport, RI (www.blockislandferry. com, 401-783-7996) and from New London, CT (www.goblockisland. com, 860-444-4624). The lighthouse is a very long walk from the ferry terminal; if you don't bring your own car, a bicycle is recommended, or you can hire a taxi.

Reaching the lighthouse from the parking area requires a walk of about 20 minutes on a sandy beach. At this writing, following the recent restoration, the interpretive center in the building is expected to reopen seasonally. For more information, contact the North Light Commission, P.O. Box 220, Block Island, RI 02807, 401-466-3213.

BLOCK ISLAND SOUTHEAST LIGHT

In 1872, local merchant Nicholas Ball circulated a petition for a lighthouse at the southeastern corner of Block Island, claiming that vessels passing through the area were "exposed to as much danger as at almost any other place on the entire coast of the United States." Congress appropriated $75,000 for a lighthouse, and a 10-acre plot of land on Mohegan Bluffs was purchased. The building was designed to be an architectural showcase, and the melding of Italianate and Gothic Revival styles makes it unique.

Accessibility:

Geographic coordinates: 41° 09' 10" N   71° 33' 04" W

Nearest town: New Shoreham. Located at the southeast corner of Block Island.

Established: 1875. Present lighthouse built: 1875. Deactivated: 1990. Relighted: 1994.

Height of tower: 52 feet. Height of focal plane: 261 feet.

Earlier optic: First-order Fresnel lens. Present optic: First-order Fresnel lens (installed 1994).

Characteristic: Flashing green every 5 seconds.

Fog signal: One blast every 30 seconds.

{ 59 }

The keeper's house, attached to the tower, was a two-and-one-half-story duplex residence with twin kitchen wings in the rear. The building is brick with a granite foundation and trim. The octagonal tower is capped by a 16-sided cast-iron lantern.

The first keeper was Henry W. Clark, who married the daughter of Keeper Joseph Whaley of Point Judith Light. Their son, Willet Clark, served as an assistant and later as principal keeper, spanning a total of forty-four years (1886–1930). His granddaughter, Jean Napier, later summed up the lives of the keepers: "They had a great pride of service." She recalled that her grandfather claimed he could smell fog before anyone could see it, and he'd always have the boilers going for the fog signal before it was needed.

Nineteenth-century view of Mohegan Bluffs and the lighthouse

The hurricane of September 21, 1938, New England's worst ever, did tremendous damage to the station. The radio beacon was knocked over, the oil house was demolished, windows were blown out, and all power was lost. The keepers had to turn the lens by hand for several days.

The Coast Guard deactivated the light in 1990 and replaced it with a steel tower. By the early 1990s, 115 years of erosion had put the lighthouse on the endangered list. The building, once over 300 feet from the edge of the bluff, was then only 55 feet from the brink. A dedicated group of volunteers, the Block Island Southeast Lighthouse Foundation, raised about $2 million in federal and private funds to pay for moving the lighthouse.

In August 1993, International Chimney Company of Buffalo, New York, and Expert House Movers, Inc. of Virginia moved the historic structure to its present location about 300 feet from the bluff. The first-order lens had to be removed because it rested on a potentially dangerous mercury bed. It was replaced by a first-order lens originally from Cape Lookout Light in North Carolina. The restored light was relit on August 27, 1994. The res-

toration of the building is proceeding, with the ultimate goal of a museum and overnight accommodations inside.

The Block Island Southeast Lighthouse Foundation operates a small museum and a gift shop in the lighthouse, and tours of the tower are offered in the summer. For more information or to help with the ongoing restoration, contact the Block Island Southeast Lighthouse Foundation, Box 949, Block Island, RI 02807; phone 401-466-5009.

The Southeast Light is a mildly strenuous walk of around twenty to thirty minutes from the ferry dock, reached by following Water Street, then Spring Street, to the south. There are bike rentals near the dock and taxis for hire. (See the ferry information for Block Island under the entry for Block Island North Light.)

Fascinating Fact

This is the highest lighthouse above water in the New England states.

WATCH HILL LIGHT

Accessibility: 🚗 🚶 🏠

Geographic coordinates:
41° 18' 12" N 71° 51' 30" W

Nearest town: Westerly. Located at the juncture of Block Island Sound and Fisher's Island Sound, at the southwestern corner of Rhode Island.

Established: 1808. Present lighthouse built: 1856. Automated: 1986.

Height of tower: 45 feet. Height of focal plane: 61 feet.

Optic: Fourth-order Fresnel lens. Present optic: VRB-25.

Characteristic: Alternating red and white flash every 2.5 seconds.

Fog signal: One blast every 30 seconds.

To aid mariners passing through Watch Hill Passage between Block Island Sound and Fisher's Island Sound, the first lighthouse was established here in 1808. The original 35-foot wooden tower and small dwelling were threatened with erosion by the 1850s. The extant square granite tower was erected in 1856 along with a two-story brick dwelling.

Jared S. Crandall was keeper in August 1872, when the steamer *Metis* collided in heavy seas with the schooner *Nettie Cushing*. Crandall took part in the rescue of a number of passengers from the sinking steamer, and he and several other local men received gold lifesaving medals for their efforts. When Crandall died at the age of 56 in 1879, his wife, Sally Ann Crandall, was appointed keeper. An 1886 article reported that "Aunt Sally," as she was known, kept the station "neat as wax."

During the hurricane of September 21, 1938, keeper Lawrence Congdon and assistant keeper Richard Fricke took refuge in the keeper's house, as winds up to 125 miles per hour battered the station. The seas crashed over the lighthouse, breaking the lantern glass and damaging the lens.

The station was again punished by Hurricane Carol on August 31, 1954. As the storm intensified, Coast Guard assistant keeper Bill Mack tried to get the foghorn going. The waves were throwing rocks the size of baseballs against the fog signal building, smashing the windows. Mack had to retreat to the keeper's house. The storm eroded much of the land near the fog signal building.

The foghorns after Hurricane Carol in 1954

Fascinating Fact

The first keeper here, Jonathan Nash, took in seasonal boarders. After he lost the keeper position with a change in the political winds, Nash opened the Watch Hill House, which was the first waterfront hotel in the area.

After automation, the Watch Hill Improvement Society signed a thirty-year lease for the maintenance of the station. A subgroup of the society, the Watch Hill Lighthouse Keepers Association, was formed. The group has been responsible for many improvements to the keepers' house. The house is currently rented to individuals who also serve as caretakers. To learn more about the Watch Hill Lighthouse Keepers Association, visit www.watchhill lighthousekeepers.org online.

You can reach Watch Hill by following Route 1A from Westerly. The lighthouse is at the end of Lighthouse Road, which originates at Larkin Road near the corner of Bluff Avenue. There is no street sign, but there is a sign marking the road as private. The elderly and those with handicapped plates are permitted to drive to parking areas near the lighthouse; a gate is open from 8:00 a.m. to 8:00 p.m. Other visitors must park in the Watch Hill village and walk to the station (about 15 to 20 minutes). Parking in Watch Hill can be hard to find in summer.

There's a small museum in one of the station's buildings, featuring the lighthouse's old fourth-order Fresnel lens and its clockwork mechanism. The museum is open to the public on Tuesday and Thursday afternoons in July and August, from 1:00 to 3:00 p.m. There's a fence immediately around the light station, and the gate to the property is open only when the museum is open.

Watch Hill Light circa early 1900s

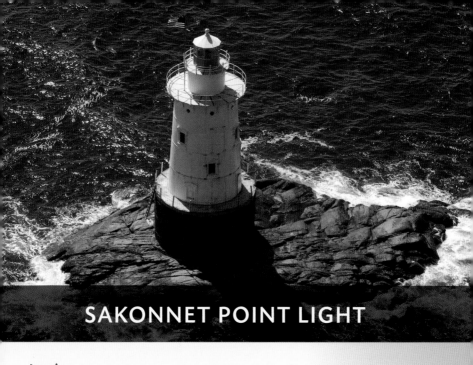

SAKONNET POINT LIGHT

The Sakonnet River, actually an inlet of the Atlantic Ocean, separates the easternmost part of Rhode Island from the busier Aquidneck Island to the west. The lower part of the river was an important harbor refuge, leading Congress to appropriate $20,000 for a lighthouse to help mariners entering the river. A rocky ledge known as Little Cormorant Rock was chosen as the location. Construction was difficult and slow at the rugged, exposed location. Work began in early 1883 and was completed late in 1884.

Accessibility:

Geographic coordinates:
41° 27' 12" N   71° 12' 12" W

Nearest town: Little Compton. Located on a ledge a little more than a half-mile offshore, at the southeastern corner of Rhode Island.

Established: 1886. Present lighthouse built: 1886. Deactivated: 1955. Relighted: 1997.

Height of tower: 66 feet. Height of focal plane: 70 feet.

Previous optic: Fourth-order Fresnel lens. Present optic: 300 mm.

Characteristic: White flash every 6 seconds, with red sector.

The keepers lived inside the tower, with the first floor serving as a kitchen and living area. The second and third floors were bedrooms, and the fourth level was a combined bedroom and storage area. More than 50 men served as keepers or assistants at the isolated station before the Coast Guard took over in the early 1940s.

The hurricane that struck without warning on September 21, 1938, was especially hard on Sakonnet Point. Keeper William Durfee later wrote his account of the storm: "By three o'clock the wind blew a gale and the sea began to go higher and higher. . . . At five o'clock all outside doors had been carried away and all windows from the first floor to the third floor were stove in, so

that we were practically flooded out of our home. At five-thirty I went into the tower to light up. While there, we took what was called a tidal wave. . . . That sea, when it hit the tower, sounded like a cannon. And it hit with such a force as to knock me off my feet."

When day broke, Durfee and the assistant keeper were amazed to see the damage to the lighthouse and onshore, where much of Sakonnet Point's fishing community was wiped out. A major crack in the caisson was soon repaired, and the lighthouse remained in operation.

Hurricane Carol in 1954 caused additional damage, and the Coast Guard elected to decommission the light. Carl Haffenreffer, president of Narragansett Brewing, bought the lighthouse for $1,111.11 at auction in 1961. In 1985, the structure was donated to the Friends of Sakonnet Lighthouse (P.O. Box 154, Little Compton, RI 02837; www.sakonnetlighthouse.org). Workers and volunteers dug out pigeon guano two feet deep, sandblasted the tower, and repainted it, among other repairs.

With the help of the Coast Guard, a new optic was installed, and the light went back into service on March 22, 1997. Major restoration work was

Fascinating Fact

Nearby West Island was considered as the site for this lighthouse, but the members of a fishing club on the island convinced the government to look elsewhere. Presidents Chester A. Arthur and Grover Cleveland were among those who fished in the vicinity.

carried out in 2010–11, funded by a grant from the federal Transportation Enhancement Program.

The lighthouse can be seen from a beach at Sakonnet Point, but you'll need a long camera lens for decent photos. To get there, head south on Route 77 in Tiverton. Take Route 77 to its terminus near the beach in Little Compton. On the left, just before the beach parking area (free), walk down a narrow paved lane to a walled beach overlook. In summer, the beach is open to residents only, but you can see the lighthouse from the overlook, a little more than a half-mile offshore.

It can also be seen from the Sachuest Point National Wildlife Refuge in Middletown, RI, but the view from here is even more distant—about two miles. The best views are from the water or from the air; unfortunately, no regularly scheduled public cruises pass close to here. (See the information on Bird's Eye View helicopter tours from the Newport Airport in the appendix.)

POINT JUDITH LIGHT

Accessibility:

Geographic coordinates: 41° 21' 42" N 71° 28' 54" W

Nearest town: Nearest town: Narragansett. Located on the west side of the entrance to Narragansett Bay.

Established: 1810. Present lighthouse built: 1857. Automated: 1954.

Height of tower: 51 feet. Height of focal plane: 65 feet.

Optic: Fourth-order Fresnel lens.

Characteristic: White light; 5 seconds on, 2 seconds off, 2 seconds on, 2 seconds off, 2 seconds on, 2 seconds off.

Fog signal: One blast every 15 seconds.

Point Judith extends more than a mile from the Rhode Island coast, marking the entrance to Narragansett Bay to the north and Block Island Sound to the south. The first lighthouse was built here in 1810 for $5,000. The octagonal wooden tower was destroyed in a hurricane in September 1815; the keeper's house was damaged, but keeper John P. Whitford and his family escaped injury. A 35-foot octagonal stone lighthouse tower was erected the following year.

In November 1850, keeper Edgar Ravenswood Eaton received a warning from the local lighthouse superintendent, who had received a complaint that the light was out for more than two hours in the pre-dawn hours one day. The superintendent called the occurrence "altogether inadmissable." Eaton explained that he had been tending a sick child, but that was not considered a valid excuse. The light had to be on, no matter what.

Keeper Joseph Whaley

The present octagonal brownstone tower was erected in 1857. A family dynasty of keepers began in 1862, when local native Joseph Whaley took charge. Whaley was keeper for twenty-seven years and was succeeded by his son, Henry, who stayed until 1910. At the time of his retirement, Joe Whaley voiced some resentment about complaints: "Why, every sailor man in the world has his eyes open to catch the lighthouse keepers and complain of them, and they do it every time they get a chance."

The keeper's house was demolished after automation in 1954. The lighthouse underwent a major restoration in 2000, with some of the original brownstone blocks being replaced. The new blocks were quarried in the same area in Connecticut where the original stone was quarried.

The lighthouse stands on the grounds of Coast Guard Station Point Judith; the station's prominent main building was constructed in 1937. The grounds of the station are open to visitors during the

Fascinating Fact

Some say Point Judith is named for the wife or mother-in-law of an early landowner, and others say it's after the book of Judith in the Apocrypha of the Bible. There's also a legend about a sea captain who was traveling by the point with his daughter, Judith, in thick fog. The daughter announced that she sighted land. The father, not seeing anything, exhorted his daughter: "Point, Judith, point!"

day, but the lighthouse itself is not open. To reach the station, take Route 108 to the south from Route 1 in Wakefield. Follow Route 108 to the end, and then turn right onto Ocean Road. Follow Ocean Road to the parking lot at the end, near the Coast Guard station.

You can also view the lighthouse from the water aboard the light-

Point Judith Light's fourth-order Fresnel lens

house cruises offered by Snappa Charters, leaving from the Galilee section of Narragansett. Several cruises are offered for small groups. Call 401-782-4040 or visit www. snappacharters.com to learn more. For information on other charter boat opportunities in the area, visit www.ufish. com/regions/ri.htm.

BEAVERTAIL LIGHT

Beavertail Point, at the southern end of 6,000-acre Conanicut Island, marks the dividing line between the east and west passages of Narragansett Bay. The early settlers erected a watch house at the point by 1705 and then a lighted beacon, tended by local Indians, in 1712. The first true lighthouse built here in 1749 was a wooden tower 69 feet tall. The original tower burned down in 1753, but a new tower was quickly erected on the same spot.

Accessibility: 🚐 🏠 ⛵

Geographic coordinates: 41° 26' 58" N 71° 23' 59" W

Nearest town: Jamestown. Located at the southern tip of Conanicut Island.

Established: 1749. Present lighthouse built: 1856. Automated: 1972.

Height of tower: 45 feet. Height of focal plane: 64 feet.

Previous optic: Third-order Fresnel lens. Present optic: DCB 24.

Characteristic: Flashing white every 6 seconds.

Fog signal: One blast every 30 seconds.

When the British evacuated Newport during the American Revolution in October 1779, they set fire to the tower and took the lighting equipment. Repairs were soon completed, and the equipment was recovered.

Early 1900s view of Beavertail Light

One of the most colorful keepers here was George T. Manders, who was in charge from 1913 to 1937. One of his hobbies was carving miniature baskets from peach stones to be used as watch charms, but Manders was best known as a raconteur. He once claimed to have seen a white whale from Beavertail, but locals pointed out that on that particular day the fog was so thick you couldn't see your hand in front of your face.

Carl Chellis succeeded Manders as keeper. Chellis was in charge during the terrible hurricane of September 21, 1938. Chellis and assistant keeper Edward Donahue escaped injury, but Chellis's daughter perished when the school bus she was riding in was swept off a causeway. The hurricane had one positive effect: it uncovered the foundation of the original lighthouse, which still can be seen at the edge of the bluff.

The Coast Guard automated the light in 1972. In the 1980s, 170 acres around the lighthouse were developed as Beavertail State Park. A museum in the former assistant keeper's house is maintained by the volunteers of the Beavertail Lighthouse Museum Association (BLMA). There are exhibits on Rhode Island lighthouses and keepers, and a

Fascinating Fact

In 1817, this lighthouse was the scene of experiments conducted by David Melville, a pioneer in the field of gas lighting. The use of coal gas had some advantages, but the whale oil industry was too powerful for Melville's innovative ideas to catch on.

fourth-order lens is on display. There's also a small gift shop. The fog signal building has saltwater tanks displaying specimens of local marine life. The museum is open seasonally, seven days a week from mid-June to mid-September. Check www.beavertaillight.org or call 401-423-3270 to confirm the schedule.

After being awarded grants from the Champlin Foundations and the Rhode Island Historical Preservation and Heritage Commission, the BLMA hired the Abcore Restoration Company, Inc. of Narragansett to carry out the restoration of the tower. The project was completed in October 2009. The exterior stonework was repointed, and the lantern and interior were fully restored. At the same time, significant repairs were carried out on the two dwellings.

This is the third oldest light station in the nation and an essential destination for New England lighthouse seekers. Many people consider the view from Beavertail Point the most beautiful in Rhode Island, and on a pleasant summer day you're likely to see many people simply sitting along the rocky shore, soaking it all in. Beavertail State Park and the lighthouse are easily reached from Route 138 from the east or west. (From I-95 South, follow Route 4 South to Route 1 South to Route 138 East.) After crossing the Jamestown Bridge from North Kingstown on Route 138 East or the Newport Bridge from Newport on Route 138 West, follow the signs to Jamestown Center. Continue to the south past Mackerel Cove Town Beach to Beavertail State Park at the tip of the island.

The lighthouse cruises offered by Snappa Charters, leaving from the Galilee section of Narragansett, also can provide a great view. Several options are offered for small groups. Call 401-782-4040 or visit www.snappacharters. com. Some of the harbor cruises from Newport may also provide views. Contact the Newport County Convention and Visitor's Bureau (www.gonewport. com, 1-800-976-5122) for the latest offerings.

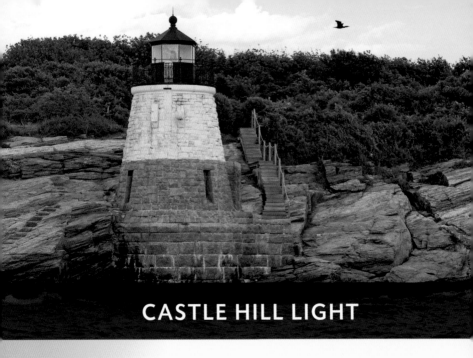

CASTLE HILL LIGHT

Accessibility:

Geographic coordinates:
41° 27' 44" N 71° 21' 47" W

Nearest city: Newport. Located on the east side of the entrance to Narragansett Bay, at the westernmost point of Newport.

Established: 1890. Present lighthouse built: 1890. Automated: 1957.

Height of tower: 34 feet. Height of focal plane: 40 feet.

Previous optic: Fifth-order Fresnel lens. Present optic: 300 mm.

Characteristic: 3 seconds red alternating with 3 seconds darkness.

Congress first appropriated $10,000 for a fog signal here in 1875. The Lighthouse Board wanted to establish the signal on land owned by famed biologist and industrialist Alexander Emanuel Agassiz. Agassiz at first refused to sell, but he later gave a suitable portion of his property to the government. The Agassiz cottage was sold to J. T. Connell, who eventually transformed the property into an inn. The property is now known as the Castle Hill Inn and Resort.

The 34-foot-tall granite lighthouse was first lighted in May 1890. The first keeper was Frank W. Parmele, formerly at the Saybrook Breakwater Light in Connecticut. The keeper's house was about 300 yards east of the lighthouse, at Castle Hill Cove. It still stands and is a private residence.

On February 10, 2005, a near disaster occurred when a 350-foot freighter was caught on the rocks near the lighthouse. Luckily, there were no fuel leaks, and none of the crew was injured.

The granite tower blends nicely with its rocky surroundings, and this is a favorite place to sit and watch the sailboats on the east side of the entrance to Narragansett Bay. A short walk through the woods from the parking area at the marina near the Castle Hill Inn and Resort will get you to the lighthouse. In Newport, take America's Cup Avenue and Thames Street to Wellington

Avenue and turn right. Turn left at Halidon Avenue, then right onto Harrison Avenue. Turn right onto Castle Hill Road, then left onto Ocean

Early view of light with fog bell

Drive. Turn right at a paved road with a small Inn at Castle Hill sign. Turn right to the Castle Hill Cove Marina and park there. The quarter-mile trail to the lighthouse begins opposite the marina entrance.

This lighthouse can be viewed from lighthouse cruises offered by Rhode Island Bay Cruises, leaving from Quonset Point in North Kingstown; see www.rhodeislandbaycruises.com or call 401-295-4040. It can also be seen from some sightseeing cruises leaving Newport. Contact the Newport County Convention and Visitor's Bureau (www.gonewport.com, 1-800-976-5122) for the latest offerings. Charter cruises offered by Snappa Charters in Narragansett can also provide a great view. Call 401-782-4040 or visit www.snappacharters.com. For more information on the Castle Hill Inn and Resort, visit www.castlehillinn.com or call 888-466-1355.

Fascinating Fact

The lighthouse was partly based on a design by the famed architect H. H. Richardson, designer of Boston's Trinity Church.

DUTCH ISLAND LIGHT

Accessibility: 🏛 ⛵

Geographic coordinates:
41° 29' 48" N 71° 24' 16" W

Nearest city: Jamestown. Located at the southern tip of an 81-acre island in the West Passage of Narragansett Bay.

Established: 1827. Present lighthouse built: 1857. Automated: 1947. Deactivated: 1979. Relighted: 2007.

Height of tower: 42 feet. Height of focal plane: 56 feet.

Characteristic: Red light; two seconds on, four seconds off.

Previous optic: Fourth-order Fresnel lens.

Present optic: LED.

Dutch Island is in the middle of Narragansett Bay's West Passage between Jamestown to the east and Saunderstown (a village of North Kingstown) to the west. The West Passage became a major route for vessels traveling north to Providence, and Congress appropriated $5,000 for a lighthouse at the island's southern end in 1825–26.

The first lighthouse tower, 30 feet tall, went into service in 1827. The first keeper was William Dennis, a twice-captured privateering captain during the American Revolution and former sheriff of Newport County. Dennis remained keeper until the age of 93.

The first tower and dwelling were damp and poorly constructed. A new 42-foot-high square brick tower and attached two-story dwelling were built in 1857.

Ernest Homer Stacey arrived as keeper in 1937 and stayed for a decade, leaving when the light was automated in 1947. Stacey's son, Robert, had to row ashore for school every day. Because the trip was often hazardous, Robert eventually boarded with his grandmother on the mainland during the school year.

Keeper Ernest Stacey

The keeper's house was demolished in 1960. In 1979, the Coast Guard replaced the lighthouse with a lighted buoy offshore. The abandoned tower soon fell victim to neglect and vandalism. In 2000, concerned local citizens formed the Dutch Island Lighthouse Society (DILS). (P.O. Box 435, Saun-

Fascinating Fact

Dutch Island got its name from a Dutch trading post established on the island in the 1630s.

derstown, RI 02874, www.dutchisland lighthouse.org)

DILS received a grant of $120,000 in Transportation Enhancement funding, and Abcore Restoration was awarded a contract for the restoration of the lighthouse. The work was completed in November 2007, and the lighthouse was relighted as an aid to navigation. Restoration included interior and exterior repairs to the brick lighthouse tower, replacement of floors and metalwork, and the repair of interior stairs. The tower now has a white stucco finish.

Dutch Island is closed to the public because of safety concerns related to the ruins of old military structures on the island. The lighthouse can be viewed distantly (recommended only if you have a good long lens for your camera) from the Fort Getty Recreation Area. There is a fee to enter the area, but if you explain that you just want to photograph the lighthouse, you might be allowed in for free for a short visit.

To reach Fort Getty from the west, follow Route 138 East to Jamestown via the Jamestown Bridge. Take the Helm Street exit onto an access road and go straight at the stop sign. Continue to a stop sign and take a right onto North Road. Go straight at a four-way intersection and continue past Mackerel Cove Beach. After the beach, take the first right onto Fort Getty Road and continue to the recreation area. From the east, follow Route 138 West over the Newport Bridge. Take the Jamestown exit. Bear right at a yield sign and continue to a stop sign. Turn left onto Conanicus Avenue and go straight at the intersection. Follow approximately a half mile and turn right onto Hamilton Avenue. Go straight at a stop sign and continue past Mackerel Cove Beach. Take the first right onto Fort Getty Road and continue to the recreation area.

This lighthouse can be viewed from lighthouse cruises offered by Rhode Island Bay Cruises, leaving from Quonset Point in North Kingstown; see www.rhodeislandbaycruises.com or call 401-295-4040 for the schedule.

PLUM BEACH LIGHT

This lighthouse was established to help mariners through the busy and dangerous West Passage of Narragansett Bay. During the construction process, a schooner lost anchorage and was swept down the passage; it was saved by a cable near Beavertail. The contractor complained that the bay was "the stormiest place we have ever worked."

Accessibility:

Geographic coordinates: 41° 31' 49" N 71° 24' 19" W

Nearest town: North Kingstown. Located in the West Passage of Narragansett Bay, just north of the Jamestown-Verrazano Bridge.

Established: 1899. Present lighthouse built: 1899. Deactivated: 1941. Relighted: 2003.

Height of tower: 53 feet. Height of focal plane: 54 feet.

Previous optic: Fourth-order Fresnel lens. Present optic: LED.

Characteristic: White flash every 5 seconds.

A basement in the light-house provided storage for oil, coal, food, and water. The first level was a kitchen and living area, and the second and third levels contained bedrooms for the principal keeper and an assistant keeper. Many visitors in the 1915–25 period were treated to tours given by keeper Charlie Ormsby. The guests were impressed by the immaculate condition of the lighthouse and by the breathtaking view of the bay from the lantern.

Keeper George Troy circa 1912

During the hurricane of September 21, 1938, Edwin S. Babcock, a substitute keeper, and assistant keeper John O. Ganze took refuge in the fourth level of the lighthouse. Thirty-foot waves broke open a door in the tower, washing away furniture and the station's boats. The two men lashed themselves back-to-back to the pipe that contained the weights for the clockwork mechanism that rotated the lens. They felt a gigantic wave, possibly a tidal wave, strike the lighthouse. Finally, by early in the evening, the storm subsided. The hurricane reopened old cracks in the lighthouse and did great damage to the entire structure.

The completion of the first bridge between North Kingstown and Jamestown in 1941 made the light obsolete. Birds took possession of the abandoned tower, and it became an eyesore. The nonprofit Friends of Plum Beach Lighthouse gained ownership in 1999.

Restoration work by the Abcore Restoration Company of Narragansett began in late June 2003. An astonishing 52 tons of pigeon guano was removed from inside the tower with the help of

Fascinating Fact

This was one of a small number of American lighthouses built by the pneumatic caisson method. A massive wooden caisson, topped with the first few courses of a cast-iron cylinder 33 feet in diameter, was lowered to the floor of the bay. The water was pumped out of the caisson, and workers entered it to dig into the bottom, allowing the structure to sink 30 feet into the floor of Narragansett Bay.

Clean Harbors Environmental Services. The Abcore crew under Keith Lescarbeau removed a half-inch layer of rust from the outside of the caisson and added reinforcing steel bands to the caisson to prevent further damage. The stone riprap around the caisson was also reinforced. The upper gallery and its railing were repaired, new doors and windows installed, and eight new glass panels were installed in the lantern.

The Coast Guard approved the return of a light to the lighthouse, once again making it an active aid to navigation.

The lighthouse can be seen distantly from shore and as you're driving over the Jamestown-Verrazzano Bridge. It can be viewed from lighthouse cruises offered by Rhode Island Bay Cruises, leaving from Quonset Point in North Kingstown; see www.rhodeislandbay cruises.com or call 401-295-4040.

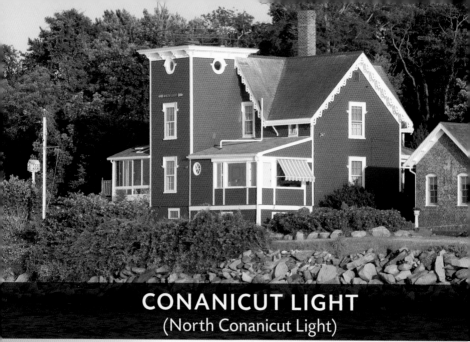

CONANICUT LIGHT
(North Conanicut Light)

Accessibility: 📷 ⛵

Geographic coordinates:
41° 34' 25" N 71° 22' 18" W

Nearest town: Jamestown. Located at the northern point of Conanicut Island in Narragansett Bay.

Established: 1886. Present lighthouse built: 1886. Deactivated: 1933.

Height of focal plane: 47 feet.

Previous optic: Fifth-order Fresnel lens. Present optic: none.

For some years, the Newport and Wickford Railroad maintained a simple light and foghorn at the northern tip of Conanicut Island. The Lighthouse Board decided a proper lighthouse was needed at the location, as a guide for vessels heading south on their way to Newport or the Atlantic Ocean. The lighthouse took the form of a Gothic Revival house with six rooms and a square tower attached to the northeast corner. The first keeper was Rhode Island native and Civil War veteran Horace Arnold.

Late 1800s view of Conanicut Light

It was decided in the early 1930s that money could be saved by transferring the navigational light to an unattended 50-foot steel skeleton tower about 55 feet east of the lighthouse. The property was sold at auction to a private party for $2,785.

In its location on North Bay View Drive, it's difficult to get a good view of the entire lighthouse from the road due to the surrounding trees. If you do visit the location, be sure to be respectful of the privacy of the owners. Better photographic opportunities are possible from the water. A good view is achievable from the lighthouse cruises offered by Rhode Island Bay Cruises, leaving from Quonset Point in North Kingstown; see www.rhodeislandbaycruises.com or call 401-295-4040 for the schedule.

Fascinating Fact

Keeper Horace Arnold once made a risky walk out onto the ice to assist the passengers of a stranded vessel. The boat's skipper presented the keeper with a captain's chair for his considerable efforts.

LIME ROCK LIGHT
(Ida Lewis Yacht Club)

Accessibility:

Geographic coordinates:
41° 28' 39" N   71° 19' 34" W

Nearest city: Newport. Located on the south side of Newport Harbor. (The street address is 0 Wellington Avenue.)

Established: 1854. Present lighthouse built: 1854. Deactivated: 1927.

Height of tower: 13 feet. Height of focal plane: 30 feet.

Previous optic: Sixth-order Fresnel lens.

With increasing maritime traffic in Newport Harbor, Congress appropriated the modest amount of $1,000 for a light on March 3, 1853. During the following year, a small stone tower was erected on the largest of the Lime Rocks, a cluster of limestone ledges about 900 feet from shore. Hosea Lewis, a native of Hingham, Massachusetts, was appointed keeper.

Keeper Ida Lewis

In 1857, a keeper's house was built at the station. A narrow, square column of brick built into the building's northwest corner was surmounted by a small lantern, which held a sixth-order Fresnel lens showing a fixed white light.

Soon after moving to the offshore home, Hosea Lewis suffered a paralyzing stroke. His wife took over much of the lighthouse work, but from the time of her father's stroke, their young daughter Idawalley Zoradia Lewis— better known as Ida—played a substantial role in the management of the light and household. Ida's rowing skills and courage were to come into play many times during her years at Lime Rock. Her first rescue was in the fall of 1858, when she was only sixteen. Ida rushed to a capsized sailboat and saved four young men who were desperately struggling to stay afloat.

Another of Ida's best-known rescues occurred in 1867, when she saved three men and a valuable sheep they had been transporting for wealthy banker August Belmont. Interviewed years later about one of her rescues, Ida said. "I don't know if I was ever afraid. I just went, and that was all there was to it."

As Newport grew into a prime resort for the rich, Ida Lewis became one of

SIDE TRIP: *Museum of Yachting*

This museum explores the ways in which yachting demonstrates human achievement in the arts, technology, and design. Exhibits include the America's Cup Gallery and the Single-Handed Sailors' Hall of Fame. The museum is home port to the *Courageous*, the legendary two-time America's Cup winner and Rhode Island's state yacht. Of special interest to lighthouse fans is the *Rescue*, a beautiful rowboat presented to Ida Lewis by Newport citizens in 1869. The museum is located at Fort Adams State Park on Harrison Avenue in Newport. For more information on Fort Adams, visit www.riparks.com/fort adams.htm or www.fortadams.org.
Museum of Yachting
P.O. Box 129
Newport, RI 02840
Phone: 401-847-1018
Web site: www.moy.org.

Fascinating Fact

Longtime keeper Ida Lewis was credited with eighteen lives saved, and it's believed the actual number may have been as high as thirty-five.

Nineteenth-century engraving of Lime Rock Light

SIDE TRIP: *Museum of Newport History*

This museum, operated by the Newport Historical Society, is a must for first-time visitors to Newport. The museum offers decorative arts, artifacts of everyday life, colonial silver, ship models, historic photographs, paintings, and audio-visual programs to tell Newport's story. There's also a museum store with books and gifts.

Museum of Newport History
127 Thames Street
Newport, RI 02840
Phone: 401-846-0813
Web site: www.newporthistorical.org

the nation's most famous women. It was estimated that 10,000 people visited Lime Rock in 1869. Ida and her parents were paid a visit by President Ulysses S. Grant in 1869. Hosea Lewis died in 1872, and Ida finally received the official appointment as keeper in 1879.

In a 1907 interview, she said, "There's a peace on this rock that you don't get on shore. There are hundreds of boats going in and out of this harbor in summer, and it's part of my happiness to know that they are depending on me to guide them safely." Ida Lewis died on October 25, 1911, at the age of 69. The bells of all the vessels in Newport Harbor tolled for Ida that night, and flags flew at half-staff throughout Newport.

In 1924, the state legislature voted to change the name of Lime Rock to Ida Lewis Rock. An automatic optic on a skeleton tower was installed near the old dwelling in 1927. The buildings at Lime Rock were sold in 1928 and became the Ida Lewis Yacht Club. Club personnel keep the building's lantern illuminated in summer as a tribute to Ida Lewis.

The yacht club is not open to the public. You can photograph the light from Wellington Avenue. To reach the site, take Thames Street in Newport

Lime Rock Light House, Ida Lewis under Light, Newport, R.I.

Lime Rock Light and keeper Ida Lewis circa early 1900s

(one way) south to Wellington Avenue and turn right. The yacht club can be seen at the end of a long boardwalk. A good view is available from adjacent King Park with its statue of Rochambeau, who brought the French army to Newport to help win the American Revolution.

Harbor cruises in Newport offer views of the yacht club. Contact the Newport County Convention and Visitor's Bureau (www.gonewport. com; 1-800-976-5122) for current information.

The yacht club can also be viewed from lighthouse cruises offered by Rhode Island Bay Cruises, leaving from Quonset Point in North Kingstown; see www.rhodeislandbaycruises.com or call 401-295-4040 for the schedule.

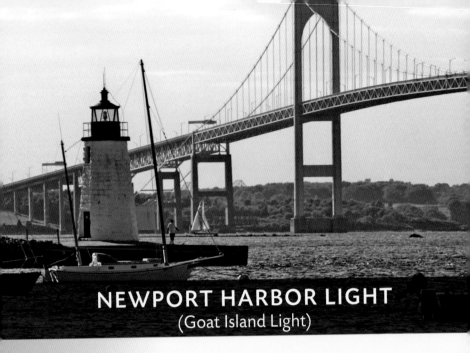

NEWPORT HARBOR LIGHT
(Goat Island Light)

Accessibility: 🚗

Geographic coordinates:
41° 29' 36" N   71° 19' 37" W

Nearest city: Newport. Located at the northern tip of Goat Island, on the grounds of the Hyatt Regency Newport Hotel, on the north side of Newport Harbor. (The street address of the hotel is 1 Goat Island.)

Established: 1824. Present lighthouse built: 1842. Automated: 1963.

Height of tower: 35 feet. Height of focal plane: 33 feet.

Previous optic: Fourth-order Fresnel lens. Present optic: 250 mm

Characteristic: Fixed green.

Goat Island, about six-tenths of a mile long in a north–south direction, has been home to a fort, a torpedo station, and condominiums. The first lighthouse here, a 20-foot stone tower built by contractor David Melville, went into service on New Year's Day in 1824. In the late 1830s, a breakwater was constructed over a reef at the north end of the island, and it was decided that a new lighthouse would be erected at the end of the breakwater. The extant 35-foot stone tower went into service in 1842.

A new keeper's house was constructed next to the tower in 1865. This was a family light station, and several families came and went before Charles Schoeneman's arrival in 1883. Schoeneman was in charge until 1922, becoming such a fixture that the lighthouse was popularly known as Schoeneman's Light.

In November 1921, a 155-foot-long submarine accidentally rammed the breakwater and caused damage to the foundation of the keeper's house. The house was soon demolished, and personnel from the island's torpedo station looked after the light for some years. It was automated in 1963. The area between the shore and the lighthouse was filled in when a hotel was constructed.

The Coast Guard licensed the lighthouse to the American Lighthouse Foundation (ALF) in 2000. In late 2006, a new picket fence was built around the perimeter of the foundation for safety reasons. To learn more about the ongoing preservation of this lighthouse, contact the American Lighthouse Foundation, P.O. Box 565, Rockland, ME 04841; www.lighthousefoundation.org; 207-594-4174.

The grounds around the lighthouse,

Newport Harbor Light circa late 1800s

adjacent to the Hyatt Regency Newport Hotel, are open. From Route 114 South in Newport, take the first right after a police station onto Marlborough Street. Continue straight to a traffic light and make a right turn onto America's Cup Avenue. At the next light, turn left at the Goat Island Connector Road. This road becomes the causeway. At the stop sign, proceed over the causeway to the Hyatt Regency Newport. From the west, drive over the Jamestown Bridge, then over the Newport Bridge. Take the first exit after the bridge for Route 238. Turn right at the stop sign at the end of the exit ramp and proceed to the second traffic light. Turn right onto Route 238/America's Cup Avenue. Turn right onto the Goat Island Connector Road. This road becomes the causeway. Proceed over the causeway to the Hyatt Regency Newport.

Park at the Hyatt Regency Newport

Hotel or the nearby marina. The grounds of the lighthouse are accessible by passing through the lobby of the hotel or by walking all the way around the hotel. You can also get a good view from the lighthouse cruises offered by Rhode Island Bay Cruises, leaving from Quonset Point in North Kingstown; see www.rhodeislandbaycruises.com or call 401-295-4040 for the schedule. Some of the harbor cruises in Newport may also provide views. Contact the Newport County Convention and Visitor's Bureau (www.gonewport.com, 1-800-976-5122) for current information.

Schoeneman was responsible for saving the lives of several sailors from the destroyer Myrant in 1912. The men were fishing from a sailboat that was overturned by a squall. The keeper was in his seventieth year at the time.

Fascinating Fact

At the age of 70, keeper Charles Schoeneman rescued several sailors from the destroyer *Myrant*. The men were fishing from a sailboat that capsized in a squall.

Early 1900s view of Newport Harbor Light

ROSE ISLAND LIGHT

Congress appropriated funds in 1868 for a lighthouse on Rose Island to serve as a guide through the bay's East Passage and to warn of dangerous shoals north of Newport Harbor. The handsome wooden dwelling was topped with an octagonal lighthouse tower on the west-facing side of its mansard roof.

Accessibility:

Geographic coordinates: 41° 29' 44" N 71° 20' 34" W

Nearest city: Newport. Located on an 18-acre island north of Newport Harbor, about a mile offshore in the East Passage of Narragansett Bay.

Established: 1870. Present lighthouse built: 1871. Deactivated: 1970. Relighted: 1993.

Height of tower: 35 feet. Height of focal plane: 48 feet.

Previous optic: Sixth-order Fresnel lens.

Characteristic: White flash every 6 seconds.

The first keeper, John Bailey Cozzens, was succeeded in 1872 by George C. Williams, a twice-wounded Civil War veteran. The keeper who stayed the longest was Charles Slocum Curtis, whose thirty-one-year stay began in 1887. Many stories about Curtis's years at the station have been preserved through the keeper's grandson, Wanton Chase. "My grandfather was fastidious in everything. He whitewashed everything that didn't move," Chase remembers. Besides his lighthouse work, the keeper was busy all day with his chickens and a large garden.

Keeper Charles Curtis

Keeper George S. Bell was at the lighthouse with his daughter Charlotte during the hurricane of September 21, 1938. The two bailed buckets of water out of the dwelling at the height of the storm, managing to escape injury.

With the completion of the Newport Bridge close by, the lighthouse was deemed obsolete in 1970. The light station property was transferred to the City of Newport in 1985, and the Rose Island Lighthouse Foundation was formed to work for the restoration of the abandoned lighthouse. By the early 1990s, much restoration had been completed, thanks to several grants and many in-kind donations. The building's second floor was converted into an apartment for caretakers, and the first floor became a living museum of lighthouse life circa 1912. Restoration climaxed with the relighting of the lighthouse as a private aid to navigation on August 7, 1989.

The upstairs apartment is now available for week-long stays for those who want to enjoy the beauty of the island and to learn about lighthouse life. Guests bring their own food and perform daily chores. The downstairs bedrooms are also available for overnight stays. Guests are responsible for cleaning up after themselves, changing the linens, and having the rooms back in order before the museum opens at 10:00 a.m. the next day.

Public tours of the lighthouse and parts of the island's Fort Hamilton are available from early July until Labor Day. (From April 1 to August 15, access to the rest of the island is limited for the protection of nesting birds on the island.)

The Newport and Jamestown ferry (401-423-9900, www.conanicutmarina. com/ferry.html) makes daily loops in summer between Jamestown and Newport and will stop at Rose Island on request. Visitors are encouraged to use the ferry, as there is no dockage for private boats. (Kayaks and small boats are welcomed; they must be pulled up on the beaches on either side of the lighthouse landing.) The ferry also stops at Perrotti Park, Bowen's Wharf, and Fort Adams in Newport.

To reach the ferry from I-95 North, take exit 3 (Route 138 East) and follow the signs to Jamestown. Continue on 138 East and take the last exit on the right to Jamestown, before the Newport Bridge. (Signs read "Last exit before toll bridge" and "Welcome to Historic Jamestown"). Follow Conanicus Avenue until you get to a stop sign at Narragansett Boulevard (about 1.5 miles). The water will be on your left. At the stop sign, you'll see the Town Dock/Ferry Wharf and shops ahead on the left. Go straight through the stop sign and turn left to the Ferry Wharf. There's all-day street parking in Jamestown Village between the fire station and town hall; two-hour parking in the wharf parking lot; and overnight park-

Fascinating Fact

This is one of a small number of lighthouses in New England that's available for overnight stays.

ing at the Conanicut Marina Boatyard site at Taylor Point.

From I-95 South, take exit 9 (left exit) to Route 4 South toward North Kingstown. Route 4 South bends to the right and merges into Route 1 South after the second traffic light. Take the next exit to Route 138 East toward Jamestown, and take the last exit on the right to Jamestown, before the Newport Bridge, then follow the directions in the paragraph above.

You can also get a good view from the lighthouse cruises offered by Rhode Island Bay Cruises, leaving from Quonset Point in North Kingstown; see www. rhodeislandbaycruises.com or call 401-295-4040 for the schedule. For more information on transportation to the island or overnight stays at the lighthouse, call the Rose Island Lighthouse Foundation at 401-847-4242 or visit them online at www.roseislandlight house.org.

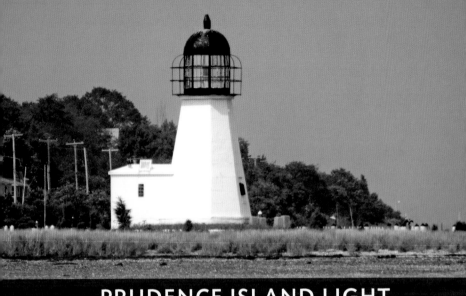

PRUDENCE ISLAND LIGHT
(Sandy Point Light)

Accessibility:

Geographic coordinates:
41° 36' 21" N 71° 18' 13" W

Nearest town: Portsmouth. Located on the east side of 3,600-acre Prudence Island, in the East Passage of Narragansett Bay.

Established: 1852. Present lighthouse built: 1824. Automated: 1972.

Height of tower: 25 feet. Height of focal plane: 28 feet.

Previous optic: Fifth-order Fresnel lens. Present optic: 250 mm

Characteristic: Green flash every 6 seconds.

Prudence Island is approximately 7 miles long and 1½ miles across at its widest point, with a summer population of about 2,000. In 1850, local residents petitioned Congress for a lighthouse at Sandy Point, the island's easternmost extremity, to help mariners passing through Narragansett Bay's East Passage. Instead of building a new lighthouse, the authorities decided to move the disused 1824 stone lighthouse on Goat Island in Newport Harbor to Prudence Island.

{ 94 }

Martin Thompson, originally from Norway, became keeper in 1905 and remained until 1933. In February 1913, Thompson sighted what he believed to be a seal offshore, and his two daughters rowed out to investigate. The girls became frightened when they realized the animal was much larger than the harbor seals usually seen around the island. It also had tusks two feet long. The girls rowed for all they were worth and made it back safely to the island. Walruses were very rare in New England waters by this time.

Keeper George Gustavus

When the calamitous hurricane of September 21, 1938, struck, keeper George T. Gustavus was at home with his wife, Mabel, and the youngest of their ten children, Eddie. Two of their daughters were at school. As the waves and wind steadily rose, a neighboring couple took refuge at the keeper's house. Former keeper Martin Thompson, who lived nearby, came to the light station and told everyone that it was the safest place to be. Gustavus later said that all in the house were "caught like rats in a trap."

The six people in the keeper's house took refuge on the second floor, but the dwelling was soon broken apart by the force of the raging seas. Gustavus woke up at a cottage about a half-mile away. He learned that the five others in the house had all perished. The keeper survived because a wave washed him back to shore, and an island teenager pulled him to safety.

When the Coast Guard cutter *Tahoe* arrived at Prudence Island after the storm, an officer called to someone on shore, "Where are the dead?" The person replied, "All washed to sea." Five people died at Prudence Island in the disaster that killed over 700 across New England.

The light remained active after the hurricane, but the keeper's house was never rebuilt. Several islanders served

Fascinating Fact

The lighthouse here originally stood in Newport Harbor; it's the oldest lighthouse tower in Rhode Island (1824).

Prudence Island Light and fog bell

as "lamplighters" until the light was automated in 1972. In 2001, the Coast Guard granted a license to the non-profit Prudence Conservancy to take over the care of the tower. Volunteers have shored up the foundation and repainted the tower. For more information on the Prudence Conservancy, visit www.prudenceconservancy.org or write the organization at P.O. Box 115, Prudence Island, RI 02872.

Prudence Island can be reached by ferry from the Church Street Wharf in Bristol. The lighthouse is a mildly strenuous walk of about a mile from the ferry landing. The tower is not open to the public. Prudence Island has little to offer tourists, and visitors should be sure to bring their own water and food. (There's just one small store open in summer and one bed and breakfast inn.) You can get the latest ferry schedule by calling 401-253-9808. To reach the Church Street Wharf in Bristol from I-95 in Providence, take I-195 East to 114 South and follow to Bristol. Turn right onto Church Street and continue to the wharf. The old birdcage-style lantern is the one of very few still in use in the United States, and the lighthouse tower is the oldest in the state.

POPLAR POINT LIGHT

In the early 1800s, the wharves of Wickford Harbor were thick with sloops and schooners, many of them built at local shipyards. Congress appropriated $3,000 in 1831 for a light at the entrance to the harbor. Before the end of the year, a wooden dwelling was completed with a wooden lighthouse tower at one end of its roof. Samuel Thomas Jr. was the first keeper at $350 yearly.

Accessibility:

Geographic coordinates:
41° 34' 16" N 71° 26' 21" W

Nearest town: Wickford (a village of North Kingstown). Located on the south side of the entrance to Wickford Harbor, off the west side of Narragansett Bay.

Established: 1831. Present lighthouse built: 1831. Deactivated: 1882.

Height of focal plane: 48 feet.

Previous optic: Fifth-order Fresnel lens.

By 1880, the Lighthouse Board decided that a light located 200 yards offshore from Poplar Point would better serve the local traffic. With the establishment of the new Wickford Harbor Lighthouse on November 1, 1882, the old light at Poplar Point was permanently darkened. The light station property was sold at public auction. (The 1882 Wickford Harbor Lighthouse was demolished in 1930.)

Elmer and Virginia Shippee bought the property in 1966. The Shippees' son, Russell, and his wife, Cathy, later lived in the lighthouse.

The lighthouse and grounds are not open to the public. The building can be viewed from across the harbor at Sauga Point. From Route 1 in Wickford, take Camp Avenue south. Turn right at Shore Acres Road. On Shore Acres, there is a pathway marked with a Private Property sign. The path is actually a public walkthrough. Head down the lane to the beach, then walk west to a breakwater. From the breakwater, the lighthouse can be seen across the harbor. You can also view this lighthouse from cruises offered by Rhode Island Bay Cruises, leaving from Quonset Point in North Kingstown; see www.rhodeislandbaycruises.com or call 401-295-4040 for the schedule.

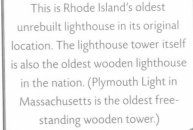

Fascinating Fact

This is Rhode Island's oldest unrebuilt lighthouse in its original location. The lighthouse tower itself is also the oldest wooden lighthouse in the nation. (Plymouth Light in Massachusetts is the oldest free-standing wooden tower.)

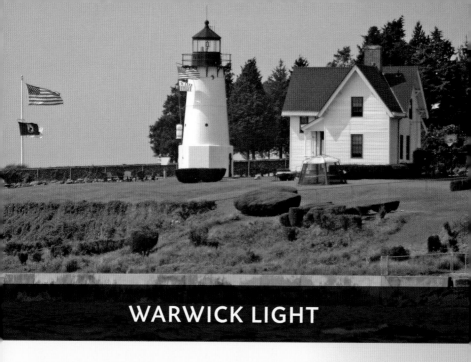

WARWICK LIGHT

Vessels passing through the busy West Passage of Narragansett Bay had to contend with a narrow channel between Warwick Neck and the northern extremity of Patience Island, less than a mile to the southeast. Congress appropriated $3,000 for a lighthouse at the southern end of Warwick Neck to make the passage safer. The first lighthouse, established in 1827, consisted of a 30-foot tower atop a tiny stone dwelling with only two rooms, each about 11 feet square.

Accessibility: 🏛 ⚓

Geographic coordinates: 41° 40' 00" N 71° 22' 42" W

Nearest city: Warwick. Located at the southern end of Warwick Neck, West Passage of Narragansett Bay.

Established: 1826. Present lighthouse built: 1932. Automated: 1985

Height of tower: 51 feet. Height of focal plane: 66 feet.

Previous optic: Fourth-order Fresnel lens. Present optic: 250 mm.

Characteristic: Green light occulting every 4 seconds.

Fog signal: One blast every 15 seconds.

The first keeper at the station, Elisha Case, was provided insufficient living space for himself and his family, and the house was exceedingly damp. Case was replaced in 1831, but he was granted the right to harvest crops he had planted at the lighthouse.

Erosion ate away at the bank over

the years until, by the 1930s, the lighthouse was threatened. A new conical cast-iron tower was built in 1932. A hurricane struck six years later and caused so much erosion that the new lighthouse was in danger of toppling over the cliff. The tower was moved about 50 feet inland with hydraulic jacks.

The last Coast Guard keeper left in 1985 when the light was automated, but the Coast Guard retained the 1889 keeper's house for housing. Because a family lives at the station, the grounds are not usually open to the public.

The lighthouse can be seen at a distance from the locked gate of the station at the end of Warwick Neck Road, but it is better viewed from the water.

Fascinating Fact

The present lighthouse here was one of the last traditional-style lighthouses built in New England (1932).

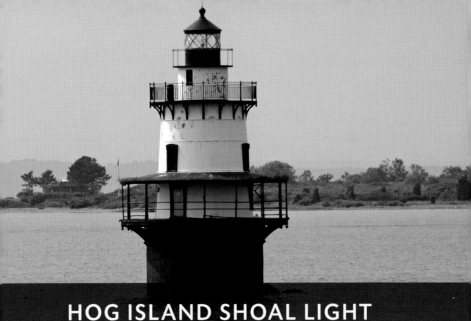

HOG ISLAND SHOAL LIGHT

Two hundred-acre Hog Island is in the middle of the approach to Bristol Harbor, just west of the entrance to Mount Hope Bay. Treacherous shoals extend to the south of the island. In 1866, a small light boat was positioned near the shoals. A larger lightship, the *LV 12*, was stationed there in 1886. Congress approved $35,000 for a lighthouse at the location on March 3, 1899. The 60-foot cast-iron sparkplug-type lighthouse was finished in October 1901.

Accessibility: 🚶 ⛵

Geographic coordinates: 41° 37' 56" N 71° 16' 24" W

Nearest town: Portsmouth. Located at the east side of Narragansett Bay, west of the entrance to Mount Hope Bay.

Established: 1901. Present lighthouse built: 1901. Automated: 1964.

Height of tower: 60 feet. Height of focal plane: 54 feet.

Previous optic: Fifth-order Fresnel lens. Present optic: 250 mm.

Characteristic: 3 seconds white alternating with 3 seconds darkness.

Fog signal: Two blasts every 30 seconds.

The structure has five decks; the second and third levels were the living quarters for the keepers. The light was converted from kerosene to electricity in 1959 with the laying of a submarine cable. It was among the last lights in the nation to be electrified. Automation was completed in 1964, and the last Coast Guard keepers were removed.

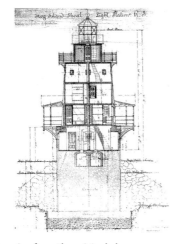

Drawing from the original plans

Fascinating Fact

Shortly before the lighthouse went into service, the keeper of the lightship that preceded it was dismissed for drunkenness.

In 2004, the lighthouse was made available to a new owner under the National Historic Lighthouse Preservation Act of 2000 (NHLPA). There were no applicants within the allotted time period, so the lighthouse was auctioned to the highest bidder under the provisions of the NHLPA. In November 2006, it was announced that the lighthouse had been sold for $165,000 to a couple from South Dakota.

The lighthouse may be seen distantly from many vantage points, including from the Mount Hope Bridge. The Prudence Island ferry from Bristol passes within photographing distance.

BRISTOL FERRY LIGHT

The strait between Bristol and Portsmouth was busy in the 1800s, with vessels passing between Narragansett Bay to the west and Mount Hope Bay to the east. Congress appropriated $1,500 in 1854 for a lighthouse at Ferry Point in Bristol. A brick dwelling was constructed with a square 28-foot lighthouse tower attached to its southern end. The light was first exhibited on October 4, 1855.

Accessibility: 🚗 ⛵

Geographic coordinates: 41° 38' 34" N 71° 15' 37" W

Nearest town: Bristol. Located at the end of Ferry Road in Bristol, just west of the Mount Hope Bridge, at the north side of the entrance to Mount Hope Bay.

Established: 1855. Present lighthouse built: 1855. Automated: 1927.

Height of tower: 34 feet. Height of focal plane: 35 feet.

Previous optic: Sixth-order Fresnel lens. Present optic: none.

Nineteenth-century photo of Bristol Ferry Light

Some keepers' logs from this lighthouse are in the collection of the Bristol Historical Society. Here are some sample entries:

✤ *June 8, 1885 (Keeper Edward P. Hoxsie): Steamer passed by towing a whale 60 ft long.*

✤ *April 22, 1891 (Keeper Edward Sherman): Schooner Hattie Williams carried away—her topmast in front of the lighthouse.*

✤ *August 2, 1903 (Sherman): Rescued two men from overturned boat 4:30 p.m.*

✤ *August 14, 1911 (Sherman): Went to the rescue of two men in an overturned canoe at four p.m.*

The Mount Hope Bridge between Bristol and Portsmouth was completed in 1929, leaving the lighthouse irrelevant as an aid to navigation. The lantern was removed from the tower, and the property was sold into private ownership. The building deteriorated and was in deplorable shape when it was sold to Carol and Bob Lundin in 1991. Thanks to the Lundins, the lighthouse was beautifully renovated. To top off the renovation, a new lantern was fabricated and installed, and the lighthouse once again looked like a lighthouse.

The Lundins sold the property in early 2000. It remains in private ownership and is off limits to the public. It can be seen from the end of Ferry Road in Bristol near the Mount Hope Bridge, but parking is not allowed in the vicinity.

Fascinating Fact

In 1916, this lighthouse's original lantern was replaced by one from the Rondout Lighthouse on the Hudson River in New York.

CONIMICUT LIGHT

The lighthouse established in 1828 at Nayatt Point, on the east side of the entrance to the Providence River, proved insufficient to warn navigators of the dangerous shoal extending out from Conimicut Point across at the west side. An unlighted granite tower was built on the shoal in 1866, and two years later it was converted into a lighted aid to navigation. The early keepers had to make a dangerous one-mile rowboat trip to tend the light. In 1874, a five-room dwelling was built at the light.

Accessibility:

Geographic coordinates:
41° 43' 01" N 71° 20' 42" W

Nearest city: Warwick. Located on Conimicut Shoal at the entrance to the Providence River.

Established: 1868. Present lighthouse built: 1883. Automated: 1963.

Height of tower: 58 feet. Height of focal plane: 55 feet.

Previous optic: Fourth-order Fresnel lens. Present optic: 250 mm.

Characteristic: White flash every 2.6 seconds.

Fog signal: Two blasts every 30 seconds.

Horace W. Arnold was named keeper in 1874. He saved at least five lives during his twelve-year stay. In early March 1875, Arnold was at the dwelling with his young son when drifting ice, driven by strong northeast winds, smashed into the structure. The Arnolds escaped as the house broke apart. They were rescued several hours later by a tugboat captain.

In 1882, the old granite tower was torn down and a new cast-iron spark-plug-style light was built. The keepers' families lived with them at the offshore station. The stress of the isolated location might have proven too much for the thirty-year-old wife of keeper Ellsworth Smith in 1922. Nellie Smith, after about a year of living at the lighthouse, poisoned herself and her two sons. She and one son died, but the other survived.

The lighthouse was a stag station with male keepers only during the Coast Guard era. Coast Guardsman Fred Mikkelsen's scariest experience in his three years at the lighthouse was a 1960 hurricane. At the height of the storm, the surging sea blocked all sunlight through the galley windows on the first level. When he went to the lantern to check the light, Mikkelsen became aware that the lighthouse was moving in the storm. "It would bang you against the wall," he said, "and you had to hang on to the handrail of the ladder."

In 2004, ownership was transferred

Galley (left) and living quarters (right) circa late 1950s

{ CONIMICUT LIGHT }

to the City of Warwick under the provisions of the National Historic Lighthouse Preservation Act of 2000. In early 2005, a new organization, the Conimicut Lighthouse Foundation, was formed. The foundation is responsible for the preservation and operation of the lighthouse. When restoration is completed, there are plans to add furnishings inside the lighthouse to recreate its appearance in the days of resident keepers.

You can get a good view of the lighthouse from Conimicut Point Park in Warwick. From I-95 north or south, take exit 13 to the Airport Access Road. Follow the road onto Route 117 (West Shore Road). The road eventually becomes Bush Avenue. Turn left at Symonds Avenue, then right at Point Avenue and follow to the park. There is a parking fee for the park from July to Labor Day. It is open all year, sunrise to sunset. For more information, call Warwick Parks and Recreation at 401-468-4104.

Fascinating Fact

This was one of the nation's last lighthouses to be converted from kerosene operation to electricity, which occurred in 1960.

{ **107** }

NAYATT POINT LIGHT

Accessibility: 📷 ⛵

Geographic coordinates:
41° 43' 31" N   71° 20' 20" W

Nearest city: Barrington. Located on the east side of the entrance to the Providence River.

Established: 1828. Present lighthouse built: 1856. Deactivated: 1868.

Height of tower: 25 feet. Height of focal plane: 31 feet.

Previous optic: Fourth-order Fresnel lens. Present optic: none.

As Providence became a thriving center of commerce by the early 1800s, it became clear that a lighthouse was needed to guide vessels into the Providence River. Congress appropriated $3,500 for the lighthouse in May 1828. A 23-foot octagonal brick tower was completed along with a five-room, unattached stone dwelling. The tower wasn't built well; the stairs were too narrow and the lantern was too small.

Nineteenth-century view of Nayatt Point Light

A severe storm in 1855 damaged the lighthouse. A new 25-foot, square-brick tower was completed in 1856. The tower exhibited a navigational light for only about a dozen years. A new granite lighthouse was established offshore to mark Conimicut Shoal, and the light at Nayatt Point was extinguished on November 1, 1868.

At first, the keepers lived at the old Nayatt Point dwelling and rowed to the new light. After a lighthouse with integral living quarters was built at Conimicut Shoal in 1883, the property at Nayatt Point was sold to a private owner. Len and Barbara Lesko owned the property in recent years. When severe weather threatened, the Leskos

Fascinating Fact

The keeper's house here is the oldest one in Rhode Island.

sealed up the building with heavy hatch covers over all the doors and windows. They never experienced any major storm damage, but they did find quahog clams on the roof after Hurricane Bob in 1991. The Leskos sold the property in 2001.

The grounds are not accessible to the public. It is possible to get a view by walking about two miles on the Barrington Town Beach. The beach is open to town residents only from June to Labor Day, but it is open to everyone in the off-season. From Route 114, turn south onto Rumstick Road. Turn right at Nayatt Road, then turn left at Bay Road. Continue to the parking area for the beach. Walk west on the beach toward Nayatt Point. You will reach a close side-view of the lighthouse property, and you'll also have a distant view of Conimicut Light offshore.

If you follow the directions above but continue on Nayatt Road to its end, you can get a view of the lighthouse property from the road. The view is somewhat obstructed. If you visit to photograph the lighthouse from the road or from the beach, be sure to respect the privacy of the residents.

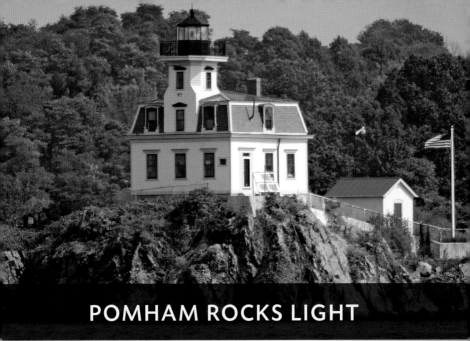

POMHAM ROCKS LIGHT

A pyramidal daymark was erected on Pomham Rocks around 1828, but something more substantial was needed to help ensure the safety of the vessels that passed on the Providence River day and night. Congress appropriated $20,000 in July 1870 for three lights on the river. Of the five lighthouses ultimately established on the river, only Pomham Rocks Light survives.

Accessibility:

Geographic coordinates: 41° 46' 39" N 71° 22' 10" W

Nearest city: East Providence. Located on the east side of the Providence River, about 800 feet offshore from the Riverside section of East Providence.

Established: 1871. Present lighthouse built: 1871. Deactivated: 1974. Relighted: 2006.

Height of tower: 40 feet. Height of focal plane: 54 feet.

Previous optic: Sixth-order Fresnel lens, later fourth-order Fresnel lens. Present optic: 250 mm.

Characteristic: Fixed red.

A wooden dwelling with a mansard roof was built on a granite foundation with a hexagonal lighthouse tower mounted on the front center of the building. The lighthouse was first lighted on December 1, 1871. The first keeper, C. H. Salisbury, had a long twenty-two-year stay. The *Providence Journal* reported in 1891 that the "lovely house" included a parlor with a piano and a hall containing a large library.

Adolph Herman Aronson was keeper for a twenty-nine-year stretch beginning in 1908. The Aronsons brought their furniture to Pomham Rocks in small boats. Their piano was transported on a two-masted schooner, swung between the masts. When the schooner reached the island, the crew all moved to one side, causing the vessel

to tilt, and the piano was lowered gently to the rocks.

During its last years as an active aid to navigation, two Coast Guard keepers, who alternated three days on the island and three days off, staffed the station. The lighthouse was discontinued in 1974 and was replaced by an automatic light on a skeleton tower. In 1980, the property was sold to the Mobil Oil Company, which has a large refinery and terminal nearby. Resident caretakers lived in the lighthouse for some years.

ExxonMobil eventually leased the historic structure at no cost to the American Lighthouse Foundation. A chapter of the foundation, the Friends of Pomham Rocks Lighthouse, was formed in 2005. A restoration of the exterior of the building was completed by Abcore Restoration in early 2006. On July 30, 2006, the navigational light was returned to the lighthouse. In the spring of 2010, Exxon Mobil donated the lighthouse to the American Lighthouse Foundation.

To learn more, you can contact the Friends of Pomham Rocks Lighthouse

Fascinating Fact

A cat named Tommy III, belonging to Keeper Adolph Aronson, became nationally famous for diving into the water and catching fish. Sometimes only the tip of Tommy's tail could be seen above the surface as he did his work.

at P.O. Box 15121, Riverside, RI 02915, or you can visit them online at www.pomhamrockslighthouse.org.

The lighthouse can be easily viewed from the 14.5-mile East Bay Bike Path that borders the Providence River. The path is open to walkers as well as bikers. To reach the bike path, take I-195 to exit 4 to Route 103. Follow about five miles to the Bullocks Point Road parking area for the East Bay Bike Path. The lighthouse can be seen after a short and pleasant walk to the north. Be sure to keep your eyes open; cyclists always have the right-of-way on the path. Call 401-253-7482 for more information on the East Bay Bike Path.

Massachusetts

The Bay State boasts what is arguably the nation's richest lighthouse legacy, with America's oldest light station (Boston Light), the second oldest (Brant Point on Nantucket), the only triple light station on the coast (the Three Sisters of Nauset), and one of the world's most celebrated waveswept towers (Minot's Ledge Light).

Boston's spacious and protected harbor made the city the capital of maritime trade in colonial America, so it's no surprise the continent's first lighthouse was established here in 1716. There were ultimately eight light stations in Boston Harbor, of which only three survive.

With fifteen extant lighthouses, Cape Cod is one of the most heavily lighthouse-saturated areas in the country. The Cape's lighthouse history reaches back to 1797, when Highland Light was established at North Truro. Celebrated by Henry David Throreau in his book *Cape Cod*, it's one of the state's few lighthouses that is open to the public on a regular basis in season. Several others, including Cape Cod's Nauset, Chatham, Nobska, and Race Point, can be toured during scheduled open houses.

Those looking for a taste of real lighthouse life can stay overnight at remote Race Point Light at the tip of Cape Cod. For a less rustic but no less enjoyable stay, try the Lighthouse Inn in West Dennis, which began its life as the Bass River Lighthouse.

One of New England's most enduring and heartwarming lighthouse-related traditions is now based in Massachusetts: the "Flying Santa." The tradition started with Maine pilot Bill Wincapaw in 1929, when he began flying his small plane over lighthouses at Christmastime, dropping gifts for keepers and their families as an expression of gratitude. Today's flights, carried out by helicopter primarily as a thank-you to Coast Guard families, are maintained by the nonprofit Friends of Flying Santa; see www.flyingsanta.org.

Southern Massachusetts Lighthouses

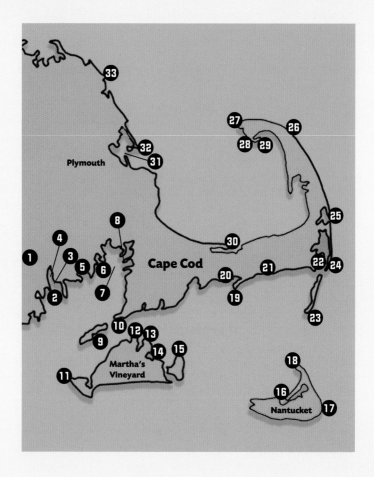

Northern Massachusetts Lighthouses

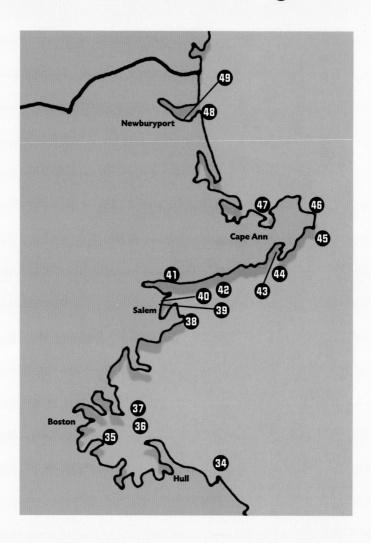

LIGHTHOUSE	PAGE

BORDEN FLATS LIGHT

Accessibility: 🏃

Geographic coordinates:
41° 42' 16" N   71° 10' 28" W

Nearest city: Fall River.
Located at the mouth of the
Taunton River, Mount Hope
Bay.

Established: 1881.
Present lighthouse built:
1881. Automated: 1963.

Height of tower:
50 feet. Height of focal
plane: 47 feet.

Previous optic: Fourth-
order Fresnel lens. Present
optic: VRB-25.

Characteristic: White flash
every 2.5 seconds.

Fog signal: One blast every
10 seconds.

The location of Fall River—famed as the "Textile Capital of the World" in the nineteenth century—at the mouth of the Taunton River allowed easy travel by water to Providence, Newport, and beyond. In June 1880, $25,000 was appropriated for a lighthouse to mark dangerous Borden Flats. The cast-iron tower was erected on a cast-iron caisson, and the light went into service on October 1, 1881. There were five stories above the basement, with two levels serving as living quarters.

On August 3, 1912, two men were passing near the lighthouse in a rowboat. As the men attempted to change places, the boat overturned. Keeper John H. Paul saw the accident and immediately launched his boat. One of the men was unable to swim and was lost in the waves. The other man clung to the overturned boat and was swiftly rescued by Paul.

After the lighthouse was damaged in the hurricane of September 21, 1938, a wider cylindrical caisson was added to provide more protection. The light was electrified in 1957 and automated in 1963. In September 2006, it was announced that the lighthouse would be available for transfer to a suitable applicant under the provisions of the National Historic Lighthouse Preservation Act. No organizations expressed interest, so the lighthouse was sold at auction to the public. The owner is now Nick Korstad of Oregon, who says he plans to eventually offer some degree of public access.

The lighthouse can be seen from the Borden Light Marina at 1 Ferry Street in Fall River. The view is fairly distant, so bring your long camera lens. For more on the marina, call them at 508-678-7547 or visit www.bordenlight.com.

SIDE TRIP: *Marine Museum at Fall River*

This museum houses a diverse collection of marine artifacts and memorabilia, with more than 150 scale models, 30,000 photographs, videos, uniforms, audio recordings, and more. One highlight is a 28-foot model of the *Titanic*. There are exhibits on the Fall River Line, the fleet of luxurious steamships that carried passengers from New York and Boston to Newport.

Marine Museum At Fall River
70 Water Street
Fall River, MA 02721-1515
Phone 508-674-3533
Web site: www.marinemuseum.org

Borden Flats Light in the late 1800s

Fascinating Fact

This lighthouse has had a visible tilt ever since it was battered by the hurricane of September 1938.

SIDE TRIP:
Battleship Cove

Here you can experience firsthand what it was like to serve on board a U.S. Navy warship in World War II. Battleship Cove is home to the battleship USS *Massachusetts*, commissioned in 1942, as well as four other National Historic Landmark ships.

Battleship Cove
Five Water Street
Fall River, MA 02722-011
Phone: 508-678-1100
Web site: www.battleshipcove.org

To reach the marina: From Route 24 South, after you enter Fall River, keep going straight onto Route 79 South. Route 79 forks underneath the Braga Bridge. Stay to the right and follow the sign for Route 138 South, N. Tiverton. This puts you on Broadway. Take the first left at a traffic light onto Columbia Street. Take the first left onto Ponta Delgada Boulevard. Take the first left onto Ferry Street. The marina is at the end of Ferry Street.

From I-195 East, take exit 5 and go to the left. Go right onto Milliken Boulevard and take a right at the first traffic light onto Columbia Street. Take a right onto Ponta Delgada Boulevard and then a left onto Ferry Street. Borden Light Marina is at the end of Ferry Street. From I-195 West, take exit 5 and go to the left following the sign for 138 South, N. Tiverton. When the exit forks again, stay to the right and follow the sign for 138 South. This puts you on Broadway. Take the first left at a traffic light onto Columbia Street. Take the first left onto Ponta Delgada Boulevard. Take the first left onto Ferry Street. The marina is at the end of Ferry Street.

CLARK'S POINT LIGHT

New Bedford's whaling industry flourished in the eighteenth and nineteenth centuries, making the city one of the richest in the world. Clark's Point was an ideal location for a navigational aid to help mariners heading to the city's harbor. Local merchants erected the first wooden lighthouse on the point in 1797. To celebrate the lighthouse, a 100-gallon pot of chowder was prepared.

Accessibility:

Geographic coordinates:
41° 35' 32" N   70° 54' 02" W

Nearest city: New Bedford. Located at Fort Taber Park on the west side of the entrance to the Acushnet River and New Bedford Harbor.

Established: 1797. Present lighthouse built: 1869. Deactivated: 1898. Relighted: 2001.

Height of focal plane: 68 feet.

Characteristic: Fixed white.

The tower burned down about a year later and was promptly rebuilt. Another fire destroyed the tower on August 5, 1803. Congress appropriated $2,500 for a new lighthouse. An octagonal rubblestone tower 38 feet tall was completed in 1804.

In 1857, a new fort began to take shape next to the lighthouse. The walls of the fort blocked the view of the light, so in 1869 a rectangular wooden tower was erected on the northerly wall of the fort. The old stone tower remained standing until 1906, when it was demolished. In 1898, the establishment of Butler Flats Light offshore rendered Clark's Point Light obsolete. The light on the fort was discontinued in April 1898.

After falling victim to neglect and vandalism, the lighthouse was restored in 2000–01. City crews rebuilt the wood-frame upper portion of the light-house, and a new lantern was fabricated. A gala relighting ceremony was held on the evening of June 15, 2001.

Fort Taber Park and the lighthouse are reached by following Route 18 in New Bedford to a traffic light at its southern end. Turn left at the light and continue for two miles to the park entrance at 1 E. Rodney French Boulevard. The fort and lighthouse are not open to the public, but good photo opportunities are available from the grounds.

For more on Fort Taber Park, visit www.newbedford-ma.gov/Tourism/ Attractions/FortTaberPark.html or call 508-979-1487. You can also call the New Bedford Office of Tourism and Marketing for information on tours of the fort: 1-800-508-5353. The Fort Taber Historical Association is a non-profit organization dedicated to the preservation of Fort Taber and its history; you can read about the group at www.forttaber.org.

Fascinating Fact

Edward Howland, who became keeper here in 1835, was taken prisoner during the American Revolution and survived 15 months of captivity in Edinburgh Castle.

BUTLER FLATS LIGHT

This lighthouse replaced the old Clark's Point Light onshore, which had been established in 1797. The tower was designed by F. Hopkinson Smith, who was also an artist and writer. Smith also built the foundation of the Statue of Liberty.

Accessibility: 🏛 ⛵

Geographic coordinates:
41° 36' 12" N 70° 53' 42" W

Nearest city: New Bedford. Located in New Bedford Channel, at the mouth of the Acushnet River.

Established: 1898. Present lighthouse built: 1898. Automated: 1978.

Height of tower: 53 feet. Height of focal plane: 53 feet.

Previous optic: Fifth-order Fresnel lens. Present optic: LED.

Characteristic: White flash every 4 seconds.

The sparkplug-style light has four stories, including living space. Until 1942, when the Coast Guard took over from the civilian Lighthouse Service, the lighthouse had only two keepers: Captain Amos Baker Jr. and his son, Charles A. Baker. Amos Baker Jr. had been in charge at Clark's Point Light for some years earlier, and his father was keeper there before him. The Bakers kept the two lights for about eighty years.

Volunteer Hugh Murray

Some of the logs of Amos Baker are in the possession of the Old Dartmouth Historical Society. The entry for Christmas 1907 reads, "A pleasant Christmas Day . . . Squally in the evening, but we had some music from the phonograph, so we had sunshine inside."

Visitors' signatures in the register while Amos Baker was keeper included President Grover Cleveland.

Charles Baker retired in 1941, and the Coast Guard took over. In 1975, a new automatic light was placed on New Bedford's hurricane barrier. The Coast Guard deemed the lighthouse unnecessary, and it came under the control of the City of New Bedford in 1978. It was automated and became one of the first solar-powered lighthouses in the nation. Local volunteers took responsibility for the maintenance of the light.

On April 30, 1998, more than 600 people attended a celebration of Butler Flats Light's 100th birthday. A new, brighter optic was installed by Hugh Murray, a retired New Bedford wire inspector who in recent years has headed up the preservation efforts.

The lighthouse can be seen distantly from the New Bedford waterfront along East Rodney French Boulevard. A good view can be obtained from the New Bedford–Martha's Vineyard ferry; see www.nefastferry.com or call 866-683-3779 for information. The ferry from New Bedford to Cuttyhunk Island also passes close by; see www.cuttyhunk ferryco.com or call 508-992-0200.

Fascinating Fact

This is said to be the only lighthouse in the United States flying a lighted American flag twenty-four hours a day.

PALMER'S ISLAND LIGHT

New Bedford's whaling industry reached its peak in the mid-1800s, when the city had a fleet of 239 ships. The lighthouse on the northern point of Palmer's Island was first lighted on August 30, 1849, by William Sherman, the first keeper. A walkway connected the rubblestone tower to the higher part of the island.

Accessibility: 🚻 🚶 ⛵

Geographic coordinates: 41° 37' 36" N 70° 54' 36" W

Nearest city: New Bedford. Located on a six-acre island at the entrance to New Bedford Harbor.

Established: 1849. Present lighthouse built: 1849. Deactivated: 1963. Relighted: 1999.

Height of tower: 24 feet. Height of focal plane: 34 feet.

Previous optic: Fifth-order Fresnel lens. Present optic: 250 mm.

Characteristic: White light; 2 seconds on, 6 seconds off.

Palmer's Island Light Station in the late 1800s

Arthur Small, a native of Brockton, Massachusetts, came to Palmer's Island as keeper in 1922, moving with his wife Mabel and two sons from Boston Harbor's Narrows ("Bug") Light. Small was a gifted artist who often painted scenes on Palmer's Island.

On the afternoon of September 21, 1938, the worst hurricane in New England history battered the south-facing coast. Leaving his wife in the oil house on the island's highest ground, Small attempted to walk the 350 feet from the house to the tower to light the lamp. On his way to the tower, Small was struck by a large wave that smashed him against a metal fence. As he managed to get to his feet, he looked back and

Keeper Arthur Small

saw his wife attempting to launch a rowboat to come to his aid. As Mabel Small tried to launch the boat, a wave destroyed the boathouse. Arthur Small lost sight of his wife.

In the morning, neighbors found Arthur Small in the lighthouse and took him to a hospital. Mabel Small had not survived; her body was later found in Fairhaven. Commissioner Harold D. King of the Bureau of Lighthouses called Arthur Small's performance during the storm "one of the most outstanding cases of loyalty and devotion that has come to the attention of this office."

SIDE TRIP: *New Bedford Whaling Museum*

This is the largest museum in America devoted to the history of the American whaling industry, with an extensive collection of art, artifacts, and manuscripts. Among the highlights is the world's largest ship model, a half-scale, 89-foot replica of the whaling ship *Lagoda*. Visitors are invited to climb aboard.

New Bedford Whaling Museum
18 Johnny Cake Hill
New Bedford, MA, 02740-6398
Phone: 508-997-0046
Web site: www.whalingmuseum.org

Fascinating Fact

This lighthouse is on the city seal of New Bedford, along with the motto "Lucem Diffundo," meaning, "I spread the light."

With the construction of a massive hurricane wall in New Bedford Harbor in 1963, the lighthouse was deemed useless. Arsonists burned the tower in 1966. In 1978, ownership went to the City of New Bedford, and local resident Dr. John O'Toole led the way for a renovation of the tower.

The lighthouse again deteriorated until the late 1990s. Welder Jose Pereira rebuilt the lantern. A crew provided by the Bristol County Sheriff Department's Pre-Release Program repainted the tower. A new solar-powered beacon was installed, and the light went back into service on August 30, 1999.

Palmer's Island is accessible at low tide only from New Bedford's hurricane wall. To reach the wall, take exit 15 (Route 18 South/Downtown) from I-195. Travel through three traffic lights. Be sure you're in the left lane before the fourth light. At the fourth light, turn left onto Cove Street, Turn left onto Morton Court, then take your first right onto Gifford Street. Follow Gifford Street to a parking area adjacent to the hurricane barrier. Follow the walking path on the wall for about ten or fifteen minutes, and Palmer's Island will be on your left. To see the lighthouse from the wall, you must walk

---

SIDE TRIP: *New Bedford Whaling National Historic Park*

While in New Bedford, you'll want to explore the cobblestone streets of this historic district. There's a visitor center in the heart of the park and another visitor center on the waterfront; both centers have orientation exhibits and literature. Among the park's attractions are the New Bedford Whaling Museum, the Seaman's Bethel (across from the Whaling Museum on Johnny Cake Hill), and the Rotch-Jones-Duff House and Garden Museum, built in 1834.

New Bedford Whaling National Historic Park
33 William Street
New Bedford, MA 02740
Phone: 508-996-4095
Web site: www.nps.gov/nebe/.

---

past the island. If it's low tide, you can walk across to the island. (BE CAREFUL! The tide comes in fast; if you're not sure about the tide schedule, don't chance crossing to the island.)

Seasonal harbor tours pass by, offering a view from the water; call 508-984-4979 or visit www.whalingcityexpeditions.com for details.

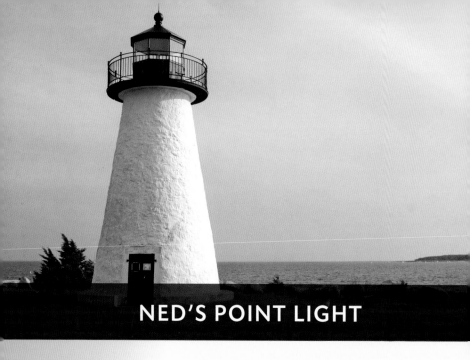

NED'S POINT LIGHT

Accessibility: 🏠

Geographic coordinates:
41° 39' 03" N   70° 47' 44" W

Nearest town: Mattapoisett. Located at the north side of the entrance to Mattapoisett Harbor.

Established: 1838. Present lighthouse built: 1838. Automated: 1923. Deactivated: 1952. Relighted: 1961.

Height of tower: 39 feet. Height of focal plane: 41 feet.

Previous optic: Fifth-order Fresnel lens. Present optic: 250 mm.

Characteristic: White light; 3 seconds white alternating with 3 seconds darkness.

Congress appropriated $5,000 on March 3, 1837, for a lighthouse at Ned's Point. A small stone dwelling was built close to the conical stone lighthouse. The original birdcage-style lantern was replaced by an octagonal lantern at some point before 1888, likely at the same time that a fifth-order Fresnel lens was installed in 1857. The present lantern was installed in 1896.

Zimri Tobias "Toby" Robinson became keeper at Ned's Point in 1912. His granddaughter, Hildegard Saunders, later recalled pushing her doll carriage along the shore at Ned's Point and popping corn on the furnace in the keeper's house.

The Coast Guard decommissioned the light in 1952. In 1958, the site, except the tower itself, was sold to the town of Mattapoisett, and Veterans Memorial Park was developed with the lighthouse as the centerpiece. The light became active again with a new modern optic in 1961. In 1993, the local Coast Guard Auxiliary Flotilla adopted the lighthouse. Auxiliary members renovated the lighthouse in 1995–96. More work was completed on the tower in 2001.

Veterans Memorial Park is open to the public daily. Thanks to Coast Guard Auxiliary volunteers, the lighthouse has been open to the public on a limited basis. In 2011, the lighthouse was open in July on Thursdays, 10 a.m. to noon, and in August on Thursdays, 4 to 6 p.m., ending on August 18. Contact Bert Theriault at nedspointlight@comcast.net for the latest information.

To reach Veterans Memorial Park from Route 6 East, turn right onto Main Street at a traffic light. Main

Ned's Point Light in the early 1900s

Street becomes Water Street, then Beacon Street as it continues uphill and bends right. Follow to Ned's Point Road and follow to the parking area. From Route 6 West, where the road forks and Route 6 continues to the right, continue straight on Marion Road. Follow Marion Road to Ned's Point Road and follow to the park. For further information on Veterans Memorial Park, call the Town of Mattapoisett at 508-758-4121.

Fascinating Fact

In 1923, the keeper's house at this station was loaded on a barge and floated across Buzzards Bay to Wing's Neck Light in Bourne, where it is now a private home.

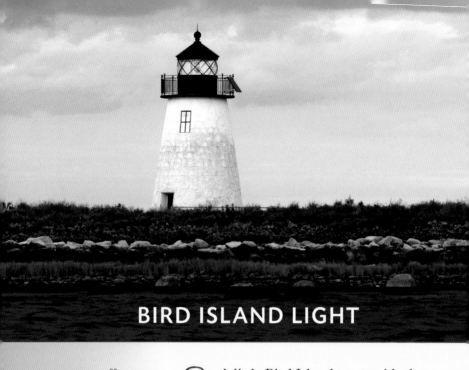

BIRD ISLAND LIGHT

Accessibility:

Geographic coordinates:
41° 40' 12" N 70° 42' 58" W

Nearest town: Marion. Located on a two-acre island at the entrance to Sippican Harbor.

Established: 1819. Present lighthouse built: 1819. Deactivated: 1933. Relighted: 1997.

Height of tower: 31 feet. Height of focal plane: 37 feet.

Previous optic: Fourth-order Fresnel lens. Present optic: 300 mm.

Characteristic: White flash every 6 seconds.

Stark little Bird Island was an ideal place to establish a lighthouse that would serve to guide mariners to Sippican Harbor and points north. A conical rubblestone tower was constructed with an accompanying stone dwelling; a covered walkway connected the house and tower. William S. Moore, a veteran of the War of 1812, was appointed as the first keeper, and the light went into operation on September 1, 1819.

The Light's 300 mm optic

Local legend claims that Keeper Moore was a pirate and that he was banished to Bird Island as punishment. Some accounts claim that Moore murdered his wife at the lighthouse and disappeared soon after. These stories are not true, but his wife did die on the island, and there are those who say it has been haunted or cursed ever since. According to a newspaper article, legend has it that "the ghost of a hunched-over old woman, rapping at the door during the night," frightened some later keepers.

Keeper Zimri Tobias "Toby" Robinson brought a cow to the island while he was keeper (1895–1912). According to his brother's grandson, Robinson attached a rope to the cow and tied it to his skiff, then rowed to the island with the cow swimming behind.

The light was taken out of service on June 15, 1933, and it turned out to be a lucky decision for the last keeper, George Gustavus, and his family. The hurricane of September 21, 1938, swept away every building on the island except the lighthouse tower.

The town of Marion has owned the property since 1966. In 1994, a restoration effort was launched when the Bird Island Lighthouse Preservation Society was formed, led by Chairman Charles Bradley. The society raised funds privately and secured a federal grant, and International Chimney Corporation of Buffalo, New York, restored the lighthouse tower. Then, at 9:00 p.m. on July 4, 1997, with 3,000 people gathered onshore, Bird Island Light was relighted as a private aid to navigation.

For more information or to help with the ongoing preservation of this lighthouse, contact the Bird Island Lighthouse Preservation Society, 2 Spring Street, Marion, MA 02738.

Bird Island Light can be seen distantly from shore. From Route 6 in Marion, head south on Creek Road. Follow to the end and turn right on Point Road. Follow Point Road to its end at a golf course. The lighthouse can be seen from a seawall. Be sure to bring a long lens or binoculars for a closer view.

Fascinating Fact

Tiny Bird Island is one of the most important nesting sites on the East Coast for the endangered roseate tern.

CLEVELAND LEDGE LIGHT

Accessibility: 🏛

Geographic coordinates:
41° 37' 51" N 70° 41' 39" W

Nearest town: Bourne. Located in the Cleveland Ledge Channel in Buzzards Bay, about two miles offshore.

Established: 1943. Present lighthouse built: 1943. Automated: 1978.

Height of tower: 70 feet. Height of focal plane: 74 feet.

Previous optic: Fourth-order Fresnel lens. Present optic: 190 mm.

Characteristic: White flash every 10 seconds.

Fog signal: One blast every 15 seconds.

This unique concrete tower was one of the last lighthouses built in New England. It was established to help guide shipping traffic through the Cape Cod Canal, which opened in 1914. The sleek architecture is classified as Art Moderne, a trendy style of the 1930s and 1940s.

The new lighthouse was put through a grueling test a little over a year after it went into service. On September 14, 1944, a hurricane battered Buzzards Bay. A Coast Guard crew of nine men was in the lighthouse. At the height of the storm, at about 12:30 a.m., a skylight dislodged, and seawater flooded the engine room. When the seas subsided slightly, two of the men, with lifelines around their waists, made it to the broken skylight and managed to plug the break with oil drums, mattresses, and planking.

The last Coast Guard crew departed when the light was automated in 1978. In April 2007, it was announced that the lighthouse would be available to a suitable new owner under the National Historic Lighthouse Preservation Act. No organization showed interest, so the lighthouse was auctioned to the general public. It sold for a high bid of $190,000 in December 2010.

Cleveland Ledge Light can be seen very distantly from Old Silver Beach off Route 28A in North Falmouth. Be sure to bring your binoculars. There's a parking fee for the beach from late May to Labor Day. To get a closer look, you'll have to arrange a charter cruise or flight.

Fascinating Fact

Cleveland Ledge is named for President Grover Cleveland, who frequented the area to fish in the days when his summer White House was at the Gray Gables mansion in Bourne.

Undated aerial view

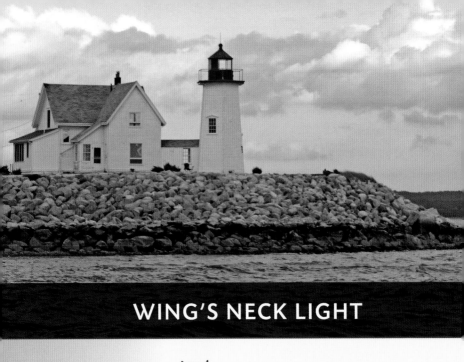

WING'S NECK LIGHT

Accessibility: 🖼 🚹 🛏

Geographic coordinates:
41° 40' 48" N 70° 39' 42" W

Nearest town: Pocasset
(a village of Bourne). Located
at the tip of the Wing's Neck
peninsula on the east side of
Buzzards Bay.

Established: 1849.
Present lighthouse built:
1890. Deactivated: 1945.

Height of focal plane:
44 feet.

Previous optic: Fourth-
order Fresnel lens. Present
optic: none.

The land where this lighthouse is located was once swampy and mosquito-infested. There was plentiful iron ore in the swampy terrain, and several foundries were established by the mid-1800s. As maritime traffic in the vicinity increased, Congress appropriated $3,500 for a lighthouse in August 1848. The first lighthouse consisted of a wooden hexagonal tower and lantern atop a stone dwelling. The first keeper was Edward D. Lawrence. John Maxim, keeper in the 1850s, was killed at the Battle of Gettysburg during the Civil War.

The building was in poor condition by the 1870s, and a fire did further damage in 1878. The station was finally rebuilt in 1890, with a new wood-frame dwelling and a hexagonal wooden lighthouse tower.

George Addison Howard became keeper in 1921. His brother, William, was his assistant. The Howard brothers gained widespread fame as lifesavers. In one instance, on July 14, 1931, a small boat overturned with a man and four young boys on board, and William went out in the station's boat and rescued all five. "I wish they wouldn't go off here fishing or cruising in such small craft. If it comes up a quick blow, there's sure to be trouble," William Howard once said.

The light was discontinued in 1945, and the property was later bought by Frank and Irene Flanagan of Boston. Irene Flanagan lived at the lighthouse until recent years; she died in 1999 at the age of 96.

The lighthouse is now available as a vacation rental; for more information contact Christina Stevens, P.O. Box 694, South Chatham, MA

02659. Phone: 508-430-8685. Web site: www.wingsnecklighthouse.com.

The lighthouse is on private property at 1 Lighthouse Lane, and the grounds are not accessible to the public. It can be viewed from a gate about 100 yards from the lighthouse. From Route 28, take Barlow's Landing Road to the west. Turn right onto Wing's Neck Road. Continue for about two miles to the gate at the end of the road, where you can stop briefly to take photos. For closer views, you'll need to charter a flight or cruise.

Fascinating Fact

William Howard, an assistant keeper here, was credited with thirty-seven lives saved during his career.

TARPAULIN COVE LIGHT

Accessibility:

Geographic coordinates:
41° 28' 08" N   70° 45' 27" W

Nearest town: Gosnold.
Located on the east side of
Naushon Island, a 5,000-acre
island in the Elizabeth Island
chain.

Established: 1817.
Present lighthouse built:
1891. Automated: 1941.

Height of tower:
48 feet. Height of focal
plane: 78 feet.

Previous optic: Fifth-order
Fresnel lens. Present optic:
300 mm.

Characteristic: White flash
every 6 seconds.

Naushon Island is a chain of sixteen islands that extend about 16 miles westward from Falmouth on Cape Cod. The waters of Vineyard Sound were among the busiest in the world in the early 1800s. The federal government established a lighthouse on the west side of Tarpaulin Cove in 1817. A rubblestone tower went into service in October 1817. John Hayden, the first keeper, remained for at least twenty-five years. He complained in 1843 that the tower was "leaky from top to bottom."

In 1891, a new 38-foot brick lighthouse tower was built. A 1,200-pound fog bell was installed in a separate tower with striking machinery. The bell tower was destroyed in the hurricane of September 1938.

The light was automated in 1941, and the keeper's house was torn down in 1962. The Cuttyhunk Historical Society now maintains the lighthouse. For information, you can write the society at P.O. Box 165, Cuttyhunk, MA 02713. Phone: 508-971-0932 (summer only).

Naushon Island is privately owned and is off limits to the public. No regular cruises pass by the lighthouse; a private charter cruise or flight is needed for a good view.

Fascinating Fact

An early navigational light was established at Tarpaulin Cove in 1759 by tavern owner Zaccheus Lumbert.

Nineteenth-century view of Tarpaulin Cove Light and bell tower to the right

NOBSKA POINT LIGHT

Accessibility:

Geographic coordinates:
41° 30' 57" N 70° 39' 18" W

Nearest town: Woods Hole (a village of Falmouth). Located at the entrance to Woods Hole Harbor at the southwestern corner of Cape Cod.

Established: 1829. Present lighthouse built: 1876. Automated: 1985.

Height of tower: 40 feet. Height of focal plane: 87 feet.

Optic: Fourth-order Fresnel lens.

Characteristic: White flash every 6 seconds with a red sector.

Fog signal: Two blasts every 30 seconds.

Woods Hole, with its deep harbor, developed a substantial whaling fleet in the early 1800s. A stream of vessels crossing through Vineyard Sound passed Nobska Point in Woods Hole. In 1829, the year the lighthouse was established, it was reported that more than 10,000 vessels passed through the area.

The first lighthouse built here in 1828 consisted of an octagonal lantern on top of the keeper's house. In 1876, the lighthouse was rebuilt as a 40-foot cast-iron tower lined with brick. The individual sections of the lighthouse were cast in Chelsea, Massachusetts. A second dwelling for an assistant keeper and his family was added in 1907.

Oliver A. Nickerson had the longest stay of any keeper in the station's history, from 1874 to 1911. For some years his daughter, Florence, was the official "observer" at Nobska Point, keeping track of all the vessels passing by in daylight hours. Florence also kept house at the station and tended a flock of chickens.

George Cameron was the keeper in August 1911 when the Boston-bound steamer *Bunker Hill*, with more than 300 passengers, ran aground close to the light station on a clear night in calm seas. "If the pilot or captain, whoever was in charge of the steamer, was trying to hit Nobska Lighthouse," wrote one passenger, "he was a very poor shot, as he didn't come within 100 feet of it, and if he was trying to avoid hitting it he was equally a poor shot, as he had plenty of water in the broad Vineyard sound to escape striking the beacon, the rays of

which must nearly have blinded him as he was running his vessel toward it." The passengers were safely unloaded.

The Coast Guard took over the

SIDE TRIP: Woods Hole Oceanographic Institution

The Woods Hole Oceanographic Institution (WHOI), located in the Woods Hole village in Falmouth on Cape Cod, is dedicated to research and education to advance understanding of the ocean. Founded in 1930, WHOI has grown from a summer laboratory into a thriving, year-round, major research operation.

During the summer, WHOI volunteers guide visitors on free walking tours through the WHOI dock area and other restricted village facilities. The tours begin at 93 Water Street in the center of Woods Hole village and take approximately one hour and fifteen minutes. Tours run from late June through early September, Monday through Friday at 10:30 a.m. and 1:30 p.m. Call 508-289-2252 for reservations.

Woods Hole Oceanographic Institution
Woods Hole, MA 02543
Phone: 508-289-2252
Web site: www.whoi.edu

Fascinating Fact

One a single day in 1864, Keeper Frederick Ray counted 188 vessels—including 175 schooners—passing Nobska Point.

management of lighthouses in 1939, but civilian keepers remained at Nobska Point Light until November 1973. The light was automated in 1985, but the Coast Guard retained the station for family housing.

This scenic lighthouse has been "adopted" by the members of the Coast Guard Auxiliary Flotilla 11-02, and there are occasional public open houses in season. Children must be at least six years old and 45 inches tall to enter. For more information, visit www.a01311. uscgaux.info/lighthouse_tours.html online.

There's a small parking area near the lighthouse, and the grounds are open to the public until dusk every day. You can also get good views from the beach across the road. To reach the light station, follow Route 28 into Falmouth. Head south on Woods Hole Road, following the signs for the Woods Hole ferry terminal. Turn left on Church Street and follow to the lighthouse.

The ferries leaving Woods Hole for Martha's Vineyard pass by, offering an excellent view from the water. You can call the Steamship Authority at 508-477-8600 or visit www.steamship authority.com.

GAY HEAD LIGHT
(Aquinnah Light)

The name "Gay Head" for this location was in common usage by the 1660s, after the varied coloring of the clay in the cliffs here. In 1998, the name of the town of Gay Head was changed to Aquinnah, which roughly means "end of the island," to better reflect the heritage of its residents.

Accessibility: ⚓ + 🚗 🏠

Geographic coordinates: 41° 20' 54" N 70° 50' 06" W

Nearest town: Aquinnah. Located at the western tip of Martha's Vineyard, Vineyard Sound.

Established: 1799. Present lighthouse built: 1856. Automated: 1960.

Height of tower: 51 feet. Height of focal plane: 170 feet.

Previous optic: First-order Fresnel lens. Present optic: DCB 224.

Characteristic: Alternating white and red flash every 15 seconds.

Late 1800s view

The passage through Vineyard Sound past the cliffs was treacherous because of the long underwater obstruction called Devil's Bridge. The first lighthouse here was an octagonal wooden tower. The first keeper, Ebenezer Skiff, was the first white man to live in the town of Gay Head, which was populated by Wampanoag Indians. Skiff remained keeper for twenty-nine years, also serving for a while as a teacher for local children. In 1829, his son, Ellis Skiff, became keeper at $350 per year. Ellis Skiff remained keeper until 1845, ending close to a half century of the Skiffs at Gay Head.

The extant brick tower was built in 1855–56 to hold an enormous first-order Fresnel lens, which contained 1,008 prisms.

The worst shipwreck in the vicinity occurred in the early morning of January 19, 1884, when the passenger steamer *City of Columbus* ran aground on Devil's Bridge. Within twenty minutes, 100 persons had drowned. Some managed to hold onto the rigging long enough for lighthouse keeper Horatio N. Pease to arrive with a crew of Gay Head Indians in a lifeboat. A number of people were saved by this crew and by the crew of the Revenue Cutter *Dexter*.

The light was automated in 1956, and the dwelling was soon razed. Since 1994, the lighthouse has been managed by the Martha's Vineyard Historical Society. The lighthouse is in need of some work, and the society is raising funds for a full restoration.

The lighthouse is opened by the Martha's Vineyard Historical Society for an extensive schedule of open houses. For information on the open houses, contact the Martha's Vineyard Historical Society, Box 827, Edgartown, MA 02539. Phone 508-627-4441. Web site: www. marthasvineyard history.org.

There is an extensive schedule of open houses at the lighthouse from mid-June to mid-September. See www. mvmuseum.org/lighthousetours.php or call 508-627-4441 for the schedule. To reach Martha's Vineyard, you can take a passenger and vehicle ferry from Woods Hole to Vineyard Haven (Steamship Authority, 508-477-8600, www.steamshipauthority.com), a passengers-only ferry from Hyannis to Oak Bluffs (Hy-Line Cruises, 508-778-2600, www.hy-linecruises.com), a passengers-only ferry from Falmouth to Oak Bluffs (Island Queen, 508-548-4800, www.islandqueen.com), a passengers-only ferry from Falmouth to Edgartown (Falmouth-Edgartown Ferry, 508-548-9400, www.falmouth ferry.com), a passengers-only ferry from New Bedford to Oak Bluffs or Vineyard Haven (New England Fast Ferry, 866-683-3779, www.mvexpress ferry.com), or a passengers-only ferry from North Kingstown, RI, to Oak Bluffs (Vineyard Fast Ferry, 401-295-4040, www.vineyardfastferry.com).

The best views of the lighthouse and cliffs are from a scenic lookout near the small strip of shops and restaurants at Aquinnah. If you bring your own car on the ferry to Vineyard Haven, follow State Road to the west; it eventually becomes North Road. Turn left onto Menemsha Cross Road (becomes South Road), then turn right onto State Road and follow to the parking area at the end.

If you don't bring your own car, you can rent a car or moped, or you can take a taxi. Contact the Martha's Vineyard Chamber of Commerce at 508-693-0085 or visit www.mvy.com for listings. The island also has its own year-round bus system, the Martha's Vineyard Regional Transit Authority. VTA service is accessible from all ferry terminals and the MV Airport, and it provides service to all six of the island's towns. For more information, visit www.vineyardtransit.com or call 508-693-9440.

Tours are available that will take you to Aquinnah; contact the Martha's Vineyard Chamber of Commerce at 508-693-0085 or visit www.mvy.com for current offerings.

Fascinating Fact

It's said that keeper Charles Vanderhoop, a Wampanoag Indian, and his assistant, Max Attaquin, took about one-third of a million visitors to the top of the lighthouse between 1910 and 1933.

WEST CHOP LIGHT

Accessibility: ⛵ + 🚗

Geographic coordinates:
41° 28' 51" N 70° 35' 59" W

Nearest town: Tisbury. Located at the west side of the entrance to Vineyard Haven Harbor, Martha's Vineyard.

Established: 1817. Present lighthouse built: 1891. Automated: 1976.

Height of tower: 45 feet. Height of focal plane: 84 feet.

Optic: Fourth-order Fresnel lens.

Characteristic: White light occulting every 4 seconds with a red sector.

Two areas of land known as East Chop and West Chop protect the harbor at Vineyard Haven. To aid vessels heading in and out of the harbor as well as coastal traffic passing through Vineyard Sound, Congress appropriated $5,000 for a light station in March 1817. The first lighthouse, a 25-foot rubblestone tower, was erected along with a stone dwelling. James Shaw West, a Tisbury native, became the first keeper at $350 per year.

West, still keeper in 1843, reported that the inside of the tower was coated with ice in winter. The keeper also pointed out that the bluff on which the lighthouse stood had eroded to within 37 feet of the tower's base.

The station was rebuilt in 1846, with a round stone tower and a

West Chop's fourth-order Fresnel lens

stone house that were about 1,000 feet southeast of the old location. The 1846 tower was later enclosed in shingled wooden sheathing.

By the early 1890s, West Chop had become a summer resort, and the proliferation of large houses in the area began to obscure the light. In 1891, a new 45-foot brick tower, painted red, replaced the 1846 tower. The tower was painted white in 1896.

In 1976, West Chop Light became the last Martha's Vineyard lighthouse to be automated. Two keeper's houses still stand; the house closest to the lighthouse now serves as living quarters for the officer in charge of Coast Guard Station Menemsha. The other house is a vacation home for people in the military.

The grounds are closed to the public, but the lighthouse can be seen from West Chop Road and is also easily viewed from the ferries to and from Vineyard Haven. To reach the light station, follow Main Street north from the ferry dock in Vineyard Haven. It's about a two-mile walk from the ferry. The station is just past Minnesota Street on the right and just before Oneida Street on the left.

For information on getting to Martha's Vineyard and transportation on the island, see the section on Gay Head Light.

Fascinating Fact

Charles West became keeper in 1847. His son, also named Charles, took over in 1868 and remained until his retirement in 1909, ending a sixty-two-year father/son dynasty.

EAST CHOP LIGHT

Accessibility: ⚓ + 🚗

Geographic coordinates: 41° 28' 13" N   70° 34' 03" W

Nearest town: Oak Bluffs. Located at the east side of the entrance to Vineyard Haven Harbor, Martha's Vineyard.

Established: 1878. Present lighthouse built: 1878. Automated: 1933.

Height of tower: 40 feet. Height of focal plane: 79 feet.

Previous optic: Fourth-order Fresnel lens. Present optic: 300 mm.

Characteristic: 3 seconds green alternating with 3 seconds darkness.

There had been a lighthouse at West Chop, across the entrance to the harbor at Holmes Hole (the name was officially changed to Vineyard Haven in 1871) since 1817. A local mariner, Silas Daggett, took it upon himself to erect a lighthouse at East Chop in 1869. Daggett's lighthouse burned down in 1871 and was rebuilt as a light on top of a house. In March 1875, Congress finally appropriated $5,000 for a proper lighthouse.

A conical cast-iron lighthouse tower was erected in 1878, along with a keeper's house. For many years, the tower was painted a reddish-brown color that earned it the nickname "the Chocolate Lighthouse."

George Walter Purdy, keeper in the 1920s and '30s, was a former lobsterman who had lost an arm in an accident in the engine room of a lighthouse tender. Purdy's daughter, Alice Purdy Ray, later remembered that the house was built so solidly that you were always comfortable regardless of the weather outside. The family had a cow and a vegetable garden.

In 1934, when the light was being automated, the Purdy family was offered the chance to stay in the house for $100 a month rent. They refused the offer, so the keeper's house was demolished. In 1957, the Coast Guard sold the land surrounding the lighthouse to the town of Oak Bluffs for use as a park.

The lighthouse is now cared for by the Martha's Vineyard Historical Society. The grounds around the lighthouse are beautifully maintained, and a $140,000 renovation of the tower was completed in 2007. Sunset tours of the lighthouse are offered on Sundays only from mid-June to mid-September.

Tours are available from 90 minutes prior to sunset to 30 minutes after. For information on the open houses, contact the Martha's Vineyard Historical Society, Box 827, Edgartown, MA 02539. Phone 508-627-4441. Web site: www.marthasvineyardhistory.org.

To reach the lighthouse from Vineyard Haven, follow Beach Road toward Oak Bluffs. After a right turn, the road becomes Eastville Avenue. Turn left after a short distance onto Temahigan Avenue. At the end of the road, turn left onto Highland Drive and continue to the lighthouse, on your left.

For more information on transportation to Martha's Vineyard and tours on the island, see the section for Gay Head Light.

Fascinating Fact

The area where the lighthouse stands is known as Telegraph Hill. A semaphore station once operated here. A tower displaying a series of raised and lowered arms and flags linked the site with stations in Nantucket, Woods Hole, Plymouth, Duxbury, and Boston, among others.

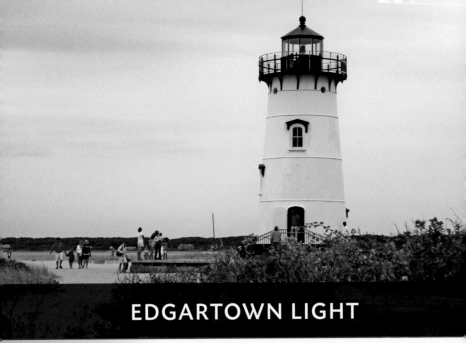

EDGARTOWN LIGHT

Accessibility: ⛵ + 🚗 🚶

Geographic coordinates:
41° 23' 27" N   70° 30' 11" W

Nearest town: Edgartown.
Located in Edgartown
Harbor, on the east coast
of Martha's Vineyard.

Established: 1828.
Present lighthouse built:
1881. Automated: 1933.

Height of tower:
45 feet. Height of focal
plane: 45 feet.

Previous optic: Fourth-
order Fresnel lens. Present
optic: 250 mm.

Characteristic: Red flash
every 6 seconds.

Edgartown's spacious harbor is bounded by Chappaquiddick Island to the south and east. By the 1800s, more than 100 Edgartown men were captains of whaling ships. Congress appropriated $5,500 in 1828 for the purpose of establishing a lighthouse at the entrance to Edgartown Harbor. A two-story house with a lantern on the roof was soon constructed. The first keeper, Jeremiah Pease, was also an accountant and surveyor.

At first, the lighthouse was slightly offshore and could be reached only by boat. In 1830, a wooden causeway was added. The causeway became known as the "Bridge of Sighs," because men about to leave on whaling voyages would walk there with their wives or girlfriends.

The dwelling and walkway were repaired often through the years. The hurricane of September 21, 1938, did great damage to the old building. After the Coast Guard took over the Lighthouse Service in 1939, they quickly demolished the dilapidated structure. Plans to erect a beacon on a skeleton tower were objected to by residents, so the Coast Guard instead decided to relocate an 1881 cast-iron tower from Ipswich.

Over the decades, sand gradually filled in the area between the lighthouse and the mainland, making the structure more easily accessible. The lighthouse is now under the care of the Martha's Vineyard Museum. A memorial was established at the base of the lighthouse in 2001. The Martha's Vineyard Children's Lighthouse Memorial consists of stones engraved with the names of children who have died, along with part of a poem by Tomas Napoleon titled "A

Fascinating Fact

This lighthouse tower was originally erected on a beach in Ipswich, Massachusetts, in 1881. It was disassembled and moved by barge to Edgartown in 1939.

Remembrance of an Unforgotten Vineyard Summer."

For information or to donate to the Martha's Vineyard Children's Lighthouse Memorial, write to Children's

Lighthouse Memorial, P.O. Box 827, Edgartown, MA 02539. Web site: www.childrenslighthousememorial.org.

In 2007, the Martha's Vineyard Museum received funds for a resto-ration of the lighthouse. The renovations included the installation of new windows with glass panes and a spiral staircase to the top of the tower. Previously, there had been only a ladder. The grounds around the lighthouse at Lighthouse Beach are open year-round. The lighthouse is open for an extensive schedule of open houses from late May to mid-October; see www.mvmuseum.org/lighthousetours.php or call 508-627-4441 for details.

To drive to the lighthouse from Vineyard Haven, follow Edgartown Road, which becomes Vineyard Haven Road after about 3.3 miles. Continue for about 3.5 miles; the road becomes Main Street in Edgartown. Turn left onto North Water Street, and then turn right onto Starbuck Neck Road. A walking path leads from the road to the beach and lighthouse. Street parking in the vicinity can be hard to come by in the heart of the summer season. There is also a free parking lot off Main Street as you enter Edgartown.

For information on how to reach Martha's Vineyard and island tours, see the section on Gay Head Light.

SIDE TRIP: *Martha's Vineyard Historical Society Museum*

The collections of the island's largest museum include more than 30,000 items relating to all aspects of life on Martha's Vineyard: paintings, prints and sculpture, hunting and fishing and shellfishing tools, fossils and botanical samples, maritime-related tools, Wampanoag tools, and much more. Of chief interest to lighthouse buffs is the old first-order lens from the Gay Head Lighthouse, which is displayed in a replica lantern on the museum grounds. The museum also boasts a 5,000-book research library with a vast paper collection dating back to the 1600s.

Martha's Vineyard Historical Society
P.O. Box 1310
Edgartown, MA 02539
Street Address: 59 School Street
(Pease House) Corner of Cooke and
School Streets
Phone: 508-627-4441
Web site: www.mvmuseum.org

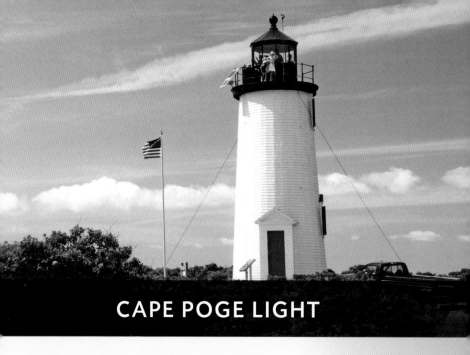

CAPE POGE LIGHT

With Edgartown's whaling business flourishing in the early 1800s, Congress recognized the need for a navigational light at Cape Poge on Chappaquiddick Island to help direct traffic to the Edgartown Harbor. A 35-foot octagonal wooden lighthouse tower was completed in November 1801, along with a small keeper's house.

The 1844 lighthouse

Accessibility: ⛵ + 🚌 🏠

Geographic coordinates: 41° 25' 10" N   70° 27' 08" W

Nearest town: Edgartown. Located at the northern tip of Chappaquiddick Island, at the entrance to Edgartown Harbor on Martha's Vineyard.

Established: 1802. Present lighthouse built: 1893. Automated: 1943.

Height of tower: 35 feet. Height of focal plane: 65 feet.

Previous optic: Fourth-order Fresnel lens. Present optic: 300 mm.

Characteristic: White flash every 6 seconds.

Matthew Mayhew was the first keeper at $200 a year. Mayhew and his wife had eight children, several of them born during their years at the station. In 1825, Mayhew reported the loss of two acres of land at the station due to erosion. The house was moved before the ocean could claim it. The tower was moved back from the edge of the eroding bluff in 1838.

A new tower was built in 1844 at a cost of $1,600. A new, larger dwelling was built, farther from the shore, in 1880. The extant wooden tower, 40 feet inland from the previous one, was built in 1893. The tower has been moved four times, the first time in 1907. The most recent move was in 1987, when the tower was lifted by a U.S. Army helicopter and relocated 500 feet inland.

The light was automated in 1943, and the last keeper was removed. In 1954 the keeper's house was sold and torn down for the lumber. The lighthouse now stands in the Cape Poge Wildlife Refuge, managed by the Trustees of Reservations. Annual vehicle permits are available for qualified vehicles, providing access to 14 miles of dune roads.

Seasonal tours, led by expert naturalists, allow other visitors to explore Cape Poge and the lighthouse. The 90-minute lighthouse tour leaves from the Mytoi (Japanese garden) parking area on Chappaquiddick and runs from Memorial Day to Columbus Day weekend, with three departures daily. The limit is twelve people per tour. Reservations are strongly recommended; call 508-627-3599.

To reach the parking area for the tours, take the ferry (the "On Time") from Edgartown, which leaves from the foot of Dagget Street. It makes frequent crossings with cars and passengers year round. For questions on the ferry, call 508-627-9427. After reaching Chappaquiddick, take Chappaquiddick Road 2.5 miles. At a sharp right curve, continue straight onto Dike Road (dirt road) and follow for 0.3 miles to the parking area on the left. For more on the tours, visit www.thetrustees.org.

Fascinating Fact

Vineyard Gazette editor Henry Beetle Hough recorded walking over the ice from Edgartown to Cape Poge—close to three miles—during a stretch of severe cold in 1933.

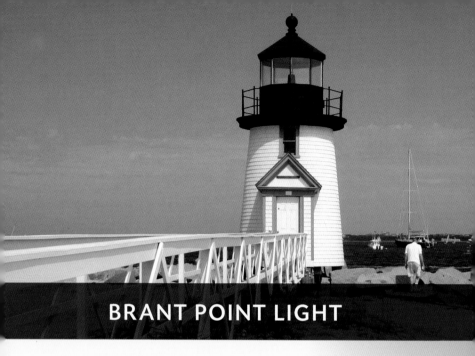

BRANT POINT LIGHT

At a town meeting in January 1746, the merchants and mariners of Sherburne, as the town on Nantucket was then called, voted to erect a lighthouse at Brant Point. The island's whaling business was booming by this time. No detailed description survives of the first wooden lighthouse, which burned down in 1757. The second lighthouse, also made of wood, was destroyed in a violent storm in March 1774. A third Brant Point Light was paid for by a tax on shipping coming into the area.

Accessibility: ⛵

Geographic coordinates: 41° 17' 24" N 70° 05' 25" W

Nearest town: Nantucket. Located at the west side of the entrance to Nantucket Harbor.

Established: 1746. Present lighthouse built: 1901. Automated: 1965.

Height of tower: 26 feet. Height of focal plane: 26 feet.

Previous optic: Fifth-order Fresnel lens. Present optic: 250 mm.

Characteristic: Red light occulting every 4 seconds.

Fog signal: One blast every 10 seconds.

In 1783, the lighthouse burned down again. A new light was erected—no more than a lantern hoisted up between two spars. This structure burned down in 1786. The fifth lighthouse lasted only two years before it was destroyed by a storm. The next lighthouse, built in 1788, was ceded to the federal government in 1795. Yet another new lighthouse was built in 1825 at a cost of

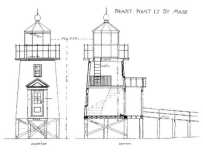

Plans for the 1901 tower

$1,600. The tower was situated on top of the keeper's house.

In 1856, the station was rebuilt; this time a 47-foot brick tower was built along with a new keeper's house. This lighthouse still stands, west of the presently active lighthouse, minus its lantern. It's part of U.S. Coast Guard Station Brant Point.

Because of shifts in the channel, the 1856 lighthouse was discontinued in 1900. The present tower was built 596 feet east of the previous one in 1901. Soon after it was built, the sea threatened the new tower, so 500 tons of riprap was placed around the beach.

In the fall of 2000, the Coast Guard and Campbell Construction Group completed an overhaul of the light-

house. The six-week project entailed removing the lead paint from the lantern and replacing all the lantern glass, reshingling the tower, repainting the entire structure, and replacing the interior stucco.

You can reach Nantucket by vehicle and passenger ferry from Hyannis (Steamship Authority, 508-477-8600, www.steamshipauthority.com), or passengers only from Hyannis (Steamship Authority, 508-495-3278, www.steamship authority.com or Hy-Line Cruises, 508-778-2600, www.hy-linecruises.com). There's also a seasonal passengers-only ferry from Harwichport on Cape Cod (Freedom Cruise Line, 508-432-8999, www.nantucketislandferry.com).

One of the best opportunities to photograph the lighthouse is from the deck of the ferry as you enter the harbor. The lighthouse will be on your right as you arrive at Nantucket.

The beach around this pretty little lighthouse—one of the most photographed in New England—is open year round. It's possible to walk to the lighthouse from the ferry landing at Steamboat Wharf. Walk west (away from the water) on Broad Street, and turn right (north) on South Beach Street. Turn

right again on Easton Street and follow to the end. You'll pass the 1856 lighthouse tower at Station Brant Point on the way to the beach. The walk is a little less than a mile. Parking is very limited, so you probably won't want to drive there. If you bring your car to the island, you can park near the wharf or in town and walk to Brant Point. Bike rentals are available near Steamboat Wharf.

Ara's Tours offers 90-minute van tours with personalized guided commentary. The tours include Brant Point Light. Call 508-221-6852 or visit www.arastours.com online. Gail's Tours also includes this lighthouse in seasonal van tours; call 508-257-6557 or visit www.nantucket.net/tours/gails/. Nantucket Adventures offers sailboat rides that can pass all of the island's lighthouses; call 508-228-6365 or visit www.nantucketadventures.com.

Fascinating Fact

This is the second oldest light station in America, and it has been rebuilt more than any other; the present tower is the ninth at Brant Point.

SANKATY HEAD LIGHT

Accessibility: ⚓ + 🚗

Geographic coordinates:
41° 17' 01" N   69° 57' 54" W

Nearest town: Siasconset (a village of Nantucket). Located on the east shore of Nantucket.

Established: 1850. Present lighthouse built: 1850. Automated: 1965.

Height of tower: 70 feet. Height of focal plane: 158 feet.

Previous optic: Second-order Fresnel lens. Present optic: DCB 224.

Characteristic: White flash every 7.5 seconds.

In 1843, engineer I.W.P. Lewis pointed out the need for a lighthouse at Sankaty Head. "By establishing a powerful light on the southeastern elbow of Nantucket Island," he wrote, "all the vessels that now feel their dubious way around the South shoal . . . could coast the south shore of the island, and pass . . . in a deep safe channel." The brick and granite lighthouse was built on a 90-foot bluff in 1850 at a cost of $10,330. The first keeper was Alexander Bunker, who had been a merchant ship captain for twenty-five years.

The lighthouse received a second-order Fresnel lens from Paris and soon became known as New England's most powerful light, reportedly seen as far as 40 miles away. The lighthouse became a popular attraction. The keepers made an accommodation to the styles of the period: the small opening to the lantern had to be enlarged to allow women with hoop skirts to pass through.

The light was converted to electric operation in 1933. The Fresnel lens was removed in 1950; it was replaced by modern rotating aerobeacons. The old lens can now be seen at the Nantucket Whaling Museum. In 1953, the keeper's house was razed and replaced by ranch-style housing, which itself has been removed. The Coast Guard removed the lantern in 1969. There were many complaints until a new aluminum lantern, similar in appearance to the old one, was installed.

The lighthouse was increasingly threatened by the steady erosion of the bluff. A move took place in the fall of 2007, as International Chimney and Expert House Movers relocated the tower 390 feet to the northwest to a spot adjacent to the Sankaty Head Golf Club.

For information on getting to Nan-

Nineteenth-century view

SIDE TRIP: *Nantucket Whaling Museum*

This museum's collection includes scrimshaw, lightship baskets, a 46-foot sperm whale skeleton, a spermaceti candle factory, and the second-order Fresnel lens from Sankaty Head Lighthouse. The museum is open daily from mid-May to mid-October, 10:00 a.m. to 5:00 p.m., Thursdays to 8:00 p.m. (until Labor Day only). From mid-October to mid-December, the museum is open Thursday through Monday, 11:00 a.m. to 4:00 p.m. There's also a museum shop with a wide selection of fine gifts. The museum, which is operated by the Nantucket Historical Association, is at 15 Broad Street, a short walk from Steamboat Wharf.

Nantucket Historical Association
P.O. Box 1016
Nantucket, MA 02554
Phone 508-228-5785
Web site: www.nha.org/sites/

tucket, see the section on Brant Point Light. The "Two Out of Three Lighthouses on Nantucket" tour offered by the Trustees of Reservations includes climbs of the Sankaty Head and Great Point lighthouses. For more information, visit www.thetrustees.org online or call 508-228-6799.

To reach the lighthouse from the

Sankaty Head Light circa early 1900s

center of town, follow the signs TO AIRPORT, SIASCONSET. From the Nantucket Rotary, pick up Milestone Road and follow about 6.5 miles to Siasconset ('Sconset). From the rotary in Siasconset, take a left across from the 'Sconset Market and head out of the village on Center Street. Follow north until it merges into Broadway and then Shell Street. Continue north on Shell, which merges into Sankaty Road. Continue for approximately 1 mile until you reach Bayberry Lane and take a right. Bayberry dead-ends at Baxter Road. Take a left and follow to end of the road. For information about the preservation of Sankaty Head Light, contact the 'Sconset Trust (508-228-9917, www.sconsettrust.org).

Fascinating Fact

This was the first lighthouse in the United States to have a Fresnel lens as part of its original equipment.

GREAT POINT LIGHT

The area between between Nantucket and Monomoy Island to the north was one of the busiest sections of the Atlantic Coast for many years. In 1784, the General Court of Massachusetts agreed to erect a lighthouse at Great Point, and a wooden tower was completed by the following year. Former whaleman Captain Paul Pinkham was the first keeper at a salary of $166.66 per year. A few years later, Pinkham published the era's best chart of Nantucket Island and its surrounding shoals.

Accessibility: ⛵ + 🚗 🏠

Geographic coordinates:
41° 23' 25" N   70° 02' 54" W

Nearest town: Nantucket. Located at the northernmost point of the island of Nantucket.

Established: 1784. Present lighthouse built: 1986.

Height of tower:
60 feet. Height of focal plane: 71 feet.

Previous optic: Third-order Fresnel lens. Present optic: VRB-25.

Fascinating Fact

When the present tower was built in 1986, some of the stone from the earlier tower—destroyed in a 1984 storm—was incorporated into its construction.

The first tower was destroyed by fire in 1816. A new 60-foot stone tower was finished in 1818. The lantern was fitted with a third-order Fresnel lens in 1857. That same year, the tower was lined with brick, and an assistant keeper's house was built.

Archford Haskins became keeper at Great Point in 1937. His daughter Jeanette Lee Haskins (now Jeanette Killen) later wrote about her years at Great Point. "I used to love to walk in the brisk wind along the beach and feel the sting of the sand," she wrote. As a girl, Jeanette sometimes helped her father light the lighthouse's lamp, an act she said

Assistant keeper John Taylor, left, and keeper Frank Grieder, right, circa 1930s

made her feel like she was "helping God" guide mariners to safe harbor.

The light was automated in the 1950s. In 1966, a suspicious fire razed the keeper's house. Erosion gradually brought the seas perilously close to the lighthouse. Then, in March 1984, a storm destroyed the 1818 tower. The storm had broken through the barrier beach, temporarily turning the point into an island.

Federal funds were appropriated for the building of a tower. A replica, 300 yards west of the site of the old tower, was finished in 1986 at a cost of over a million dollars. Senator Edward M. Kennedy smashed a bottle of champagne against the tower at the dedication and announced, "Great Point is alive and well again."

Great Point is now part of Coskata-Coatue Wildlife Refuge, managed by the Trustees of Reservations. The Trustees offer several tours that include a visit to the lighthouse, including a daily natural history tour, sunset tours, and birding tours. The "Two

Out of Three Lighthouses on Nantucket" tour includes climbs to the tops of both Great Point and Sankaty Head lights. Reservations are required; call 508-228-6799. For more information, visit www.thetrustees.org online.

For information about getting to Nantucket, see the section on Brant Point Light. Cap'n Tobey's Native Water Taxi can also take you to Great Point; call 508-221-1059 or visit www.tobey leskeinc.com for more information.

SIDE TRIP: *Nantucket Lifesaving Museum*

This museum at Folger's Marsh at 158 Polpis Road tells the story of the U.S. Life-Saving Service and the U.S. Coast Guard. Of special interest is the old third-order Fresnel lens from Great Point Lighthouse, which is on display in a replica lantern on the grounds. The museum is open daily from 9:30 a.m. to 4:00 p.m., June 15 through Columbus Day weekend in October.

Nantucket Lifesaving Museum
158 Polpis Road
Nantucket, MA 02554
Phone: 508-228-1885
Web site: www.nantucketlife
savingmuseum.com

The old third-order Fresnel lens on display at the Nantucket Lifesaving Museum

POINT GAMMON LIGHT

Accessibility: ⛵

Geographic coordinates: 41° 36' 35" N 70° 15' 58" W

Nearest town: West Yarmouth. Located at the southern tip of Great Island, south side of Cape Cod, Nantucket Sound.

Established: 1816. Present lighthouse built: 1816. Deactivated: 1858.

Height of focal plane: 70 feet.

Present optic: none.

Point Gammon is east of the entrance to Lewis Bay and Hyannis Harbor and a little over two miles north of the dangerous ledges known as Bishops and Clerks. As Hyannis grew in importance, a navigational aid was needed to help mariners negotiate the area. The 20-foot-tall (not including the lantern) conical stone lighthouse went into service on November 21, 1816, with seven lamps and reflectors exhibiting a fixed white light.

The first keeper, Samuel Adams Peak, died in 1824. His young son, John, took over and remained keeper until 1858, when the light was discontinued. John Peak and his wife raised nine children at the lighthouse, two of whom became lighthouse keepers. John Peak complained in 1843 that the house was "extremely leaky . . . so that we always have to move our beds during an easterly rain, and also to mop up bucketfuls of water."

The lighthouse was eventually deemed inadequate, and a lightship was stationed close to the Bishops and Clerks ledges. In 1858, the lightship was replaced by a lighthouse on the ledges, and John Peak became the first keeper. The 65-foot-tall granite Bishop and Clerks Lighthouse was demolished in 1952.

In 1882, Great Island was sold to Charles B. Cory, a wealthy ornithologist from Boston, and the island became one of the nation's earliest bird sanctuaries. Cory added a taller structure in place of the original lantern, designed to facilitate the use of the tower as a viewing platform. The station's stone dwelling was dismantled in the 1930s and rebuilt as a private home elsewhere on the island.

Fascinating Fact

The point's name comes from an old term used in the game of backgammon. Mariners trying to pass between the point and the offshore ledges were sometimes deceived, or "gammoned," which often resulted in disaster.

Malcolm G. Chace, a banker from Rhode Island, purchased the property in 1914. Most of Great Island remains in the ownership of the Chace family. The island is closed to the public. The lighthouse can be viewed distantly from the Hyannis-Nantucket ferry. Marcus Sherman offers sails from Hyannis on the 34-foot catboat *Eventide*, with a distant view of the lighthouse. If you let him know of your interest, Captain Sherman might be able to sail closer. Call 508-775-0222 or visit www.catboat.com online.

HYANNIS HARBOR LIGHT

Accessibility: 🏠 🚶 ⛵

Geographic coordinates:
41° 38' 10" N 70° 17' 19" W

Nearest town: Hyannis
(a village of Barnstable).
Located in Hyannis
Harbor on the south
side of Cape Cod.

Established: 1849.
Present lighthouse built:
1849. Deactivated: 1929.

Height of tower:
19 feet (to the base of the
lantern). Height of focal
plane: 43 feet.

Previous optic: Fifth-order
Fresnel lens. Present optic:
none.

Hyannis grew into a busy fishing and trade port in the 1800s. A local man, Daniel Snow Hallett, provided the first light in the harbor—a simple shack on the beach with a lamp that hung in a window. His son, Daniel Bunker Hallett, assisted Hallett in his lightkeeping duties. Young Daniel would sometimes spend the night in the shack with his dog and then return home for breakfast before going to school.

In 1848, Congress authorized the building of a proper lighthouse at South Hyannis. A conical brick tower was built, and the light went into service on May 7, 1849.

Keeper John Lothrop circa 1870s

Capt. John A. Peak, part of a family dynasty of local lighthouse keepers, took over as keeper in 1899 and remained until 1915. Peak let local children help with lighthouse chores, such as polishing the brass parts of the tower.

The light was discontinued in 1929. The property was sold at auction; it has since passed through several hands. The present owners, Janice Hyland and Alan Granby, who are antique dealers, completed a full renovation and built a new top for the tower. It's not a traditional lantern, but it reportedly provides a great view at sunset. For more on Hyland Granby Antiques, visit www.hylandgranby.com online.

The lighthouse is difficult to see from nearby Harbor Road. You can get a better view by walking east from the parking lot at Keyes Beach on Sea Street in Hyannis. For information on the beach, call the Barnstable Recreation Division at 508-790-6345. Captain Marcus Sherman's outings on the 34-foot catboat *Eventide* provide a view of the lighthouse. If you let him know of your interest, Captain Sherman might be able to sail closer than usual. Call 508-775-0222 or visit www.catboat.com online.

Fascinating Fact

Keeper John A. Peak positioned a mirror in his bedroom so he could keep an eye on the light without leaving his bed.

Nineenth-century view of Hyannis Harbor Light Station

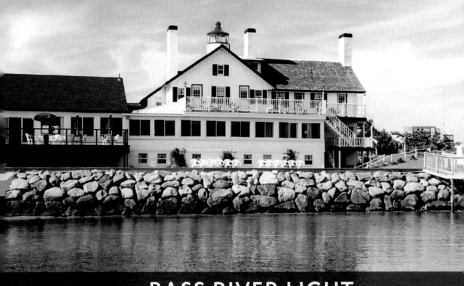

BASS RIVER LIGHT
(The Lighthouse Inn)

Accessibility:

Geographic coordinates:
41° 39' 07" N   70° 10' 08" W

Nearest town: Dennis. Located east of the mouth of the Bass River, West Dennis, on the south side of Cape Cod.

Established: 1855. Present lighthouse built: 1855. Deactivated: 1914. Relighted: 1989.

Height of tower: 44 feet. Height of focal plane: 44 feet.

Previous optic: Fifth-order Fresnel lens. Present optic: 300 mm.

Characteristic: White flash every 6 seconds.

For some years prior to the building of a lighthouse near the mouth of the Bass River, a local man named Warren Crowell kept a lantern burning in the attic window of his house to aid local mariners. In 1850, Congress appropriated $4,000 for a proper lighthouse. Oxen hauled building materials across the local marshes, and when the lighthouse was finished in 1855, Warren Crowell became the first keeper. The station consisted of a two-story dwelling with a lantern on the roof.

The government considered the lighthouse unnecessary with the advent of the Cape Cod Canal and the installation of a nearby automatic beacon, the Bass River West Jetty Light. The lighthouse was extinguished in 1914, and the property was sold at auction. Car dealer Harry K. Noyes used it as a summer residence for a while. In 1938, it was bought by State Senator Everett Stone. The Stones began to have overnight guests at the lighthouse, and it became so popular that they soon opened it as the Lighthouse Inn. Many additions and improvements have been made to the property over the years.

Stone's son, Bob, eventually took over the management of the inn. Bob's wife, Mary, later recalled that American planes bombed the rocks near the inn for practice during World War II. The guests would gather on the beach and cheer the show. A 1944 hurricane destroyed the dining room and the oil house, but the Stones continued to expand.

In 1989, the Stone family had their lighthouse relighted as a private aid to navigation. The light, officially designated the West Dennis Light, now operates each summer.

The cozy Lighthouse Inn features 700 feet of private beach, with 61 rooms and cottages and a waterfront dining room offering a five-course dinner every evening. The building is vastly changed, but you can still make out the 1855 lighthouse in the middle of the main building. If you stay at the inn, you might also be able to arrange a tour of the lighthouse and lantern room.

For more information, contact the Lighthouse Inn (508-398-2244, www.lighthouseinn.com). To reach the inn, take Route 6 East on Cape Cod. Take Exit 8 (Dennis) and turn right onto Station Avenue. At the third traffic light, turn left onto Route 28. After about a mile, turn right onto School Street. Follow School Street for a half-mile, and then turn right onto Lighthouse Road. Follow Lighthouse Road for 0.2 miles, and then turn left onto Lighthouse Inn Road.

Fascinating Fact

Warren Crowell, the light's first keeper, was wounded and taken prisoner in Virginia during the Civil War.

STAGE HARBOR LIGHT

Accessibility: 👣

Geographic coordinates:
41° 39' 31" N   69° 59' 02" W

Nearest town: Chatham. Located on Harding's Beach, at the west side of the entrance to Stage Harbor, near the southeast corner of Cape Cod.

Established: 1880. Present lighthouse built: 1880. Deactivated: 1933.

Height of tower: 48 feet.

Previous optic: Fifth-order Fresnel lens. Present optic: None.

Chatham's Stage Harbor (named for racks used for drying fish) developed into a busy fishing port. Congress appropriated $10,000 for a light station at the harbor's entrance, and a 48-foot cast-iron tower with a fifth-order Fresnel lens went into service on July 15, 1880. Enoch Eldredge, the first keeper, was paid $560 per year.

In 1918, keeper Mills Gunderson died, and his son, Stanley, took over as keeper. In 1933, an automated light on a skeleton tower replaced the lighthouse. Stanley Gunderson complained to the *Boston Post*: "To save money, they put in something that is far more expensive and less

Keeper Alfred Howard

reliable and all that economy and put another employee on the unemployment list. Rather a poor way to reduce unemployment and surely no help toward better times."

The government removed the lantern, and the property passed into private hands. The same family that first bought the property, the Hoyts, still owns it. There has never been electricity at the station and no plumbing except a single pump. Henry Sears Hoyt once told *Yankee* magazine about his first visit to the lighthouse in the 1930s: "A more desolate spot would be hard to imagine. . . . A howling gale, whistling around angry sea, but nevertheless a grand place."

The lighthouse can be reached after a one-mile hike on Harding's Beach in Chatham. Please keep in mind that the house and tower are private property, and respect the privacy of the residents. To reach the beach from Route 28 in Chatham, take Barn Hill Road south to a right on Harding's Beach Road. Follow to the parking area. A fee is charged in summer. For more information on Harding's Beach, you can call Chatham Parks and Recreation at 508-945-5175.

The lighthouse can also be viewed across the water from the town landing at the end of Sears Road in Chatham. The Monomoy ferry passes the lighthouse; see the next entry for details.

Fascinating Fact

In 1914, Keeper Alfred Howard was praised for rescuing a horse that was stuck in the mud in a nearby marsh. In the following year, he was commended for coming to the aid of the passengers of a disabled pleasure boat.

MONOMOY POINT LIGHT

Accessibility: ⛵ 🚶

Geographic coordinates:
41° 33' 33" N   69° 59' 38" W

Nearest town: Chatham. Located at the southern end of South Monomoy Island, off the southeastern corner of Cape Cod.

Established: 1823. Present lighthouse built: 1849. Deactivated: 1923.

Height of tower: 40 feet. Height of focal plane: 47 feet.

Previous optic: Fourth-order Fresnel lens. Present optic: None.

Monomoy was once a peninsula extending southward from the elbow of Cape Cod's bending arm. It's now two islands, North Monomoy and South Monomoy. South of the islands is Pollock Rip, a region of unusually strong tidal currents. A lightship was stationed in the treacherous area for many years.

Cape Cod's fifth lighthouse was built for $3,000 in 1823 at Monomoy Point, near the southern end of the peninsula. It was a so-called Cape Cod–style lighthouse with a wooden tower and iron lantern on the roof of a brick dwelling. The present cast-iron brick-lined tower was built in 1849, making it one of the oldest cast-iron lighthouses in the country. The lighthouse was painted red in 1882, making it more visible by day. In 1892, iron trusses were added to prevent vibration.

James P. Smith, a native of Copenhagen, became keeper in 1899. His oldest daughter, Annie, acted as housekeeper and tended the light when her father was away. In 1904, a reporter asked if life at the lighthouse was lonely. Annie replied, "Oh, no! We don't have time to be lonesome. There is always something to do, with the housekeeping and the light."

The light was discontinued in 1923, and the property passed into private hands. The property came under the management of the U.S. Fish and Wildlife Service (USFWS) in the 1970s. North and South Monomoy and part of Morris Island constitute the Monomoy National Wildlife Refuge.

In 1988, a federal grant paid for a

Fascinating Fact

This lighthouse was once close to the water's edge, but the shifting contours of the island have left acres of sand between the tower and the shore.

refurbishing of the lighthouse, but the tower and house deteriorated in the ensuing years. In May 2010, it was announced that a $1.24 million contract from Recovery Act funding had been awarded to the Campbell Construction Group for the restoration of the keeper's house and lighthouse tower. The extensive work was carried out in 2010–11.

The best way for the public to visit this remote and historic lighthouse is with Captain Keith Lincoln aboard the 32-foot (20-passenger) Monomoy Island ferry. Trips depart from the Monomoy National Wildlife Refuge in Chatham. To reach the refuge, take Route 28 South to Chatham Center. At the rotary, continue straight on Main Street. Go past the Chatham Lighthouse and Coast Guard Station (on the right). Bear left at a fork in the road. Take your first right (Morris Island Road). Look for a sign saying: Rip Ryder Monomoy Island Ferry. Follow this road until you see a brown sign for the USFWS Headquarters (Tisquantum Road). Take your first left (Wikis Way). The ferry is located at the bottom of the stairs. Look for the red shuttle van for parking instructions. For more information, call 508-945-5450 or visit www.monomoyislandferry.com.

CHATHAM LIGHT

The waters off Chatham were a menace to coastal shipping traffic, with strong currents and dangerous shoals. In April 1806, Congress appropriated funds for Cape Cod's second light station. In order to distinguish Chatham from Highland Light to the north, it was decided that the new station would have two fixed white lights. Two octagonal wooden towers were erected along with a small dwelling.

Keeper Josiah Hardy

Accessibility: 🚗 🏠

Geographic coordinates:
41° 40' 17" N   69° 57' 01" W

Nearest town: Chatham. Located in Chatham Harbor at the southeastern corner of Cape Cod.

Established: 1808. Present lighthouse built: 1877. Automated: 1982.

Height of tower: 48 feet. Height of focal plane: 80 feet.

Previous optic: Fourth-order Fresnel lens. Present optic: DCB 224.

Characteristic: Two white flashes every 10 seconds.

Two new brick towers, each 30 feet tall, were completed in the summer of 1841. Collins Howe, a Cape Cod fisherman who had lost a leg in an accident, became keeper shortly before the new towers were built. The house had such a poor foundation that rats had burrowed in and infested the cellar. A storm in October 1841 broke seventeen panes of glass in the lanterns, which Keeper Howe blamed on poor construction.

Captain Josiah Hardy served as keeper from 1872 to 1900. In 1875, Hardy counted 16,000 vessels passing the lighthouse. By 1877, the light towers stood only 48 feet from the brink. The authorities took note of the rampant erosion and moved quickly to rebuild the station much farther from the edge of the bluff. Two 48-foot, conical cast-iron towers were erected in 1877, along with dwellings for the principal keeper, the assistant keeper, and their families.

By the early 1900s, the Lighthouse Board began phasing out twin light stations. The north light was moved up the coast to Eastham to replace the survivor of the "Three Sisters" in 1923, ending 115 years of twin lights at Chatham.

In 1969, the Fresnel lens and the lan-

SIDE TRIP: *Atwood House Museum*

Chatham's gambrel-roofed Atwood House, built in 1752, was acquired by the Chatham Historical Society in 1926. Museum galleries have been added to the original structure; there are now eight galleries with permanent exhibits (paintings, decorative arts, maritime artifacts, and more), plus a large special exhibit gallery. There's also a gift shop. On the grounds is a display that includes the old lantern and fourth-order Fresnel lens from Chatham Light. The museum is open June to mid-October, Tuesday through Saturday. You can view the Chatham Lighthouse display even when the museum is closed.

Chatham Historical Society/Atwood House Museum
347 Stage Harbor Road
P.O. Box 381
Chatham, MA 02633
Phone: 508-945-2493
Web site: www.chathamhistorical society.org

Fascinating Fact

On a single day in the 1880s, Keeper Josiah Hardy counted 365 ships passing the lighthouse.

Nineteenth-century view of Chatham Light Station

tern were removed. Modern aerobeacons were installed, and a new, larger lantern was constructed to accommodate the larger apparatus. The old lantern and lens were later put on display on the grounds of the Atwood House Museum on Stage Harbor Road, just a few minutes from the lighthouse.

The station is still staffed by the Coast Guard. The lighthouse and grounds aren't open to the public except during open houses. For information on open houses and group tours offered by the Coast Guard Auxiliary, visit www.a01311.uscgaux.info/lighthouse_tours.html online.

When there's not an open house scheduled, you can still get a good view from the fence around the station. To reach the lighthouse, take Route 28 South to Chatham Center. At the rotary, continue straight on Main Street. The lighthouse and Coast Guard station will be on the right. There's a parking lot just across the road. (The official address 37 Main Street, Chatham.)

NAUSET LIGHT
and the Three Sisters of Nauset

Accessibility:

Geographic coordinates: 41° 51' 36" N   69° 57' 12" W

Nearest town: Eastham. Located on Nauset Light Beach, on the east coast of Cape Cod.

Established: 1838. Present lighthouse built: 1877 (originally in Chatham). Automated: 1955.

Height of tower: 48 feet.

Previous optic: Fourth-order Fresnel lens. Present optic: DCB 224.

Characteristic: Alternating red and white flash every 5 seconds.

In 1836, twenty-one residents of Eastham wrote to the Boston Marine Society asking for a lighthouse on the Atlantic shore of the Cape, halfway between Highland Light and the twin lights at Chatham. Many vessels had been wrecked on the Nauset Bars offshore. To distinguish the location from the single light in North Truro and the double lights at Chatham, it was determined that there would be three lighthouses. The trio acquired a famous nickname, the "Three Sisters of Nauset."

{ 178 }

Erosion eventually threatened to claim the original towers. Three new shingled wooden lighthouses, 22 feet high, were built 30 feet west of the old towers in 1892. By 1911, the cliff had eroded to within eight feet of the northernmost tower, and the authorities decided to change the station to a single light. The center tower was given a flashing white light and was attached to the 1876 keeper's house.

In 1918, the two defunct "Sisters" were sold to a private owner. By 1923, the remaining Sister was in poor condition. Meanwhile, Chatham Light Station was changed from two lights to a single light. The discontinued 48-foot cast-iron north tower from Chatham was transported to Eastham. The last of the wooden Sisters was sold and incorporated into a residence.

In the 1960s and 1970s, the National Park Service purchased the 1892 Three Sisters towers from their private owners. A restoration of the Three Sisters was completed in 1989, and their new site—about 1,800 feet from the beach—was opened for tours.

Erosion threatened Nauset Light by the 1990s. The Nauset Light Preservation Society (NLPS) was soon formed to save the lighthouse. After much debate,

Fascinating Fact

This was the only place in the country where the government decided to build three lighthouses at a single location. The present tower, moved here in 1923, was painted white until the early 1940s, when the upper half was painted red to increase its daytime visibility. It has become a Cape Cod icon, gracing countless postcards, calendars, and potato chip bags.

a new site was chosen for the tower in 1996. The team of International Chimney and Expert House Movers was contracted for the relocation.

On November 15, 1996, workers lifted the tower and transferred its weight to two heavy-duty dollies hitched

The 1892 Three Sisters in their original location

to a truck. The tower was moved to the edge of the road before the end of the day. The move was completed the next day when the truck hauled the lighthouse across the road to its new home, 336 feet from the old site. On October 27, 1998, the keeper's house was moved to a new foundation near the lighthouse.

SIDE TRIP: *Salt Pond Visitor Center*

The Salt Pond Visitor Center is conveniently located on Route 6 in Eastham, at the intersection with Nauset Road. This is the Cape Cod National Seashore's main visitor facility. There are educational exhibits and an excellent bookstore. There are walking trails on the grounds, including the quarter-mile Buttonbush Trail, featuring a guide rope and signs printed in large lettering and Braille.

Of special interest to lighthouse fans is the fourth-order Fresnel lens that was removed from Nauset Light in 1981. The center is open daily all year, with increased hours in the summer.

Salt Pond Visitor Center

Route 6

Eastham, MA

Phone: 508-255-3421

Web site: www.nps.gov/caco/ planyourvisit/visitorcenters.htm

The Cape Cod National Seashore now owns the lighthouse. NLPS operates the lighthouse as a private aid to navigation and is responsible for all maintenance. The group also holds lighthouse open houses from May through October. For more information, contact the Nauset Light Preservation Society, (508-240-2612, www. nausetlight.org.)

To reach the lighthouse from Route 6, turn right onto Brackett Road. (Heading north, Brackett Road is at the third traffic light from the Eastham/ Orleans rotary). Continue to the end of Brackett Road and turn left onto Nauset Road. Take the first right onto Cable Road. At the end of Cable Road, turn left onto Ocean View Drive to the parking lot. (In season, there's a fee to park in the Cape Cod National Seashore lot.) Walk along the path to the lighthouse.

There's also a sign at the parking lot pointing out the walking trail (about 0.3 miles) that leads to the Three Sisters lighthouses on Cable Road. The National Park Service offers occasional tours of the site. Call 508-255-3421 for the schedule and details. There are also a small number of parking spaces—including handicapped spaces—close to the Three Sisters on Cable Road.

HIGHLAND LIGHT
(Cape Cod Light)

A dangerous spot called Peaked Hill Bars, graveyard of many ships, lies about a mile off the northeast coast of Cape Cod. With maritime traffic increasing in the area, the federal government acquired 10 acres of land on a high bluff in Truro from Isaac Small. A 45-foot wooden lighthouse, Cape Cod's first, was built in 1797.

Accessibility:

Geographic coordinates:
42° 02' 21" N 70° 03' 44" W

Nearest town: Truro. Located on the Cape Cod National Seashore, on the northeast coast of Cape Cod.

Established: 1797. Present lighthouse built: 1857. Automated: 1986.

Height of tower: 66 feet. Height of focal plane: 170 feet.

Previous optic: First-order Fresnel lens. Present optic: VRB-25.

Characteristic: White flash every 5 seconds.

A new brick lighthouse was erected close to the site of the first one in 1833. Naturalist Henry David Thoreau visited Highland Light several times in the 1850s. Thoreau found the lighthouse "a neat building, in apple-pie order."

The keeper's dwelling was rebuilt in 1856. A new round brick lighthouse tower, 66 feet tall, was built in 1857 for $15,000. It was equipped with an enormous first-order Fresnel lens from Paris. This made Highland Light, the highest on the New England mainland, one of the coast's most powerful lights. It was, for many years, the first glimpse of America seen by many immigrants from Europe.

An even larger Fresnel lens, rotating on a bed of mercury, was installed in 1901. After an electric light was put inside this lens in 1932, the 4,000,000-candlepower light could reportedly be seen for 45 miles. The giant lens was removed in the early 1950s, replaced by modern aerobeacons. The light was automated in 1986, but the station's radio beacon remained in service, and the keeper's dwelling continued to be used as Coast Guard housing.

When the first lighthouse was built in 1797, it was over 500 feet from the

Fascinating Fact

One of the duties of the keeper was to count the vessels passing the light. In an eleven-day period in July 1853, Keeper Enoch Hamilton counted 1,200 craft passing his station. As many as 600 vessels were counted in a single day in 1867.

edge of the cliff. By the early 1990s, the forces of erosion left the lighthouse just over 100 feet from the edge. A group within the Truro Historical Society began raising funds for the relocation of the tower. In 1996, these funds were combined with federal funds and state funds to pay for the move of the 404-ton lighthouse to a site 450 feet back from its former location.

The operation got under way in June 1996, under the direction of International Chimney Corporation of Buffalo, with the help of subcontractor Expert House Moving of Maryland. Thousands of sightseers came to catch a glimpse of the rare move. The move took eighteen days. The relocated lighthouse stands close to the seventh fairway of the Highland Golf Links.

The lighthouse is now open daily to visitors, mid-May through October. There are exhibits and a gift shop in the keeper's house. An admission fee is charged, and children must be 51 inches tall to climb the lighthouse. For more information, call 508-487-1121 or visit www.capecodlight.org.

To get to the lighthouse from Route 6, exit at Highland Road in North Truro. Bear right onto Highland Road and follow to the end. Turn right onto South Highland Road and continue a short distance, then turn left onto Lighthouse Road and the parking lot for the lighthouse and the Highland House Museum. There are signs directing you to the site from Route 6.

SIDE TRIP: *Highland House Museum*

This building, located close to Highland Lighthouse, was originally built in 1907 as a summer hotel. The museum's eclectic collection includes paintings, shipwreck mementoes, and fishing and whaling gear. Upstairs rooms have Victorian furniture, old sea chests, and a collection of antique clothing. The museum is open daily from June 1 to September 30; call or check online for the hours.

Highland House Museum
P. O. Box 486
Truro, MA 02666
Phone: 508-487-3397
Web site: www.trurohistorical.org

RACE POINT LIGHT

Accessibility: 🚗 🚶 🏠 🛏️

Geographic coordinates:
42° 03' 45" N 70° 14' 35" W

Nearest town: Province-town. Located on the Cape Cod National Seashore near the northern tip of Cape Cod.

Established: 1816. Present lighthouse built: 1876. Automated: 1972.

Height of tower:
45 feet. Height of focal plane: 41 feet.

Previous optic: Fourth-order Fresnel lens. Present optic: VRB-25.

Characteristic: White flash every 10 seconds.

Fog signal: Two blasts every 60 seconds.

This was Cape Cod's third light station, after Highland Light and Chatham's twin lights. The original rubblestone tower, first lighted on November 5, 1816, was one of the earliest revolving lights in an attempt to differentiate it from the other lighthouses on Cape Cod.

Race Point Light Station in the late 1800s

By 1875, the original lime mortar in the tower had disintegrated, and the lighthouse was covered with shingles in an attempt to stop leaks. The stone tower was replaced in 1876 by a 45-foot cast-iron lighthouse, lined with brick. A new dwelling was also built.

Three keepers and their families lived at the lighthouse in two keeper's houses. The children had to walk more than two miles across soft sand to school each day. In the 1930s, Keeper James Hinckley made the trip much quicker by customizing an early Ford into a dune buggy. The trip that took 75 minutes on horseback was shortened to 30 minutes. Keeper Hinckley once commented on the wind in winter at the station: "The sand is bad enough, cutting into your skin, but a combination of sand and snow is almost unbearable."

In 1960, the larger keeper's house was torn down and the other house was modernized. The light was automated in 1972. After years of abandonment, the property was leased to the American Lighthouse Foundation (then known as the New England Lighthouse Foundation). The five-bedroom house was restored inside and out, largely by volunteer labor.

The keeper's house is open for over-

SIDE TRIP: *Province Lands Visitor Center*

This Cape Cod National Seashore center on Race Point Road offers orientation films, exhibits, a bookstore, and an observation deck. Ranger-guided walks based here explore the surrounding dunes. Call 508-487-1256 for information.

night stays. Guests must bring their own bedding, and the kitchen is shared with other guests. The restored fog signal building (or "whistle house") also has

two bedrooms and is rented on a weekly basis. For information on stays in the keeper's house or whistle house at Race Point, call 508-487-9930 or visit www.racepoint lighthouse.net online.

Volunteers of the Cape Cod Chapter of the American Lighthouse Foundation also conduct light-

house tours. Check www.racepoint lighthouse.net for the schedule.

You can park at Race Point Beach and walk about 45 minutes (a little over two miles in very soft sand) to the lighthouse. To get to the beach parking area, take Race Point Road off Route 6 in Provincetown. You can also use your own four-wheel-drive vehicle with the proper permit, or you can contact Art's Dune Tours, a Provincetown tour operator (508-487-1950, www.arts dunetours.com). Volunteers of the Cape Cod chapter of the American Lighthouse Foundation may provide transportation during special events, such as an open house during Cape Cod Maritime Week in late May.

SIDE TRIP:
Old Harbor Museum

This old lifesaving station, now on Race Point Beach, was originally established on Cape Cod at the entrance to Chatham Harbor in 1897. It was deactivated in 1944. It was then moved to Race Point Beach in 1977 and is now a museum featuring rescue equipment. There are demonstrations by National Park Service rangers in summer. Call 508-349-3785 for details.

Fascinating Fact

Race Point's name comes from the strong crosscurrent, known as a "race," which made this area a nightmare for mariners.

WOOD END LIGHT

With Provincetown flourishing as a fishing port, it was determined that a lighthouse was needed at Wood End, the southernmost extremity of the curving spit of land that protected the harbor. Congress appropriated $15,000 for the lighthouse in June 1872.

Wood End Light circa late 1800s

Accessibility: 🚗 🚶 ⛵

Geographic coordinates: 42° 01' 16" N   70° 11' 37" W

Nearest town: Provincetown. Located on the Cape Cod National Seashore, west of the entrance to Provincetown Harbor.

Established: 1872. Present lighthouse built: 1872. Automated 1961.

Height of tower: 39 feet. Height of focal plane: 45 feet.

Previous optic: Fifth-order Fresnel lens. Present optic: VRB-25.

Characteristic: Red flash every 10 seconds.

Fog signal: One blast every 30 seconds.

The 38-foot square brick tower was painted brown at first. A keeper's dwelling was built about 50 feet northeast of the lighthouse. The first keeper, Thomas Lowe, remained at the station for twenty-five years.

During a stretch of severe cold in February 1935, keeper Douglas Shepherd was marooned at the light station for weeks. Ordinarily, Shepherd made a daily trip into town. He had no worries despite his isolation, as the Coast Guard kept him in touch with the mainland.

The lighthouse was automated in 1961, and the keeper's house was destroyed. The light was converted to solar power in 1981. The Cape Cod Chapter of the American Lighthouse Foundation is now licensed by the Coast Guard to maintain the property. Volunteer work parties have periodically repainted the tower and oil house.

You can walk to the lighthouse from the western end of Provincetown's Commercial Street. It's a fairly strenuous walk of around a mile each way across a granite breakwater and then across a stretch of soft sand to the lighthouse. There are limited parking spaces available near the start of the walk; it's an additional walk of around 20 to 30 minutes from the center of town.

The lighthouse can also be seen from some of the excursion boats out of Provincetown. One option is the harbor tours offered by Viking Princess Cruises, leaving daily in summer from MacMillan Pier in Provincetown. The cruises provide a good view, but the distance can vary according to the tides. (508-487-7323, www.capecodecotours. com)

For more information or to donate to the restoration of Wood End Light, contact the Cape Cod chapter of the American Lighthouse Foundation, P.O. 570, North Truro, MA 02652. Web site www.lighthousefoundation.org.

Fascinating Fact

In December 1927, the Navy submarine S-4 and the Coast Guard cutter *Paulding* collided a half mile south of here. Forty men on the S-4 died in the disaster. The S-4 was raised and later was used to help devise greater safety measures for future submarines.

LONG POINT LIGHT

The first lighthouse established at Long Point in 1826 consisted of a lantern on top of the keeper's house. The first keeper, Charles Derby, was still at the station in 1843. He complained that while he had a boat, there was no boathouse or landing place at the station. He had lost a boat the previous year due to the lack of a proper slip.

Long Point Light Station circa early 1900s

Accessibility: ⚓ 🚻

Geographic coordinates: 42° 01' 59" N   70° 10' 07" W

Nearest town: Provincetown. Located on the Cape Cod National Seashore at the entrance to Provincetown Harbor.

Established: 1826. Present lighthouse built: 1875. Automated 1952.

Height of tower: 38 feet. Height of focal plane: 36 feet.

Previous optic: Fifth-order Fresnel lens. Present optic: 300 mm.

Characteristic: Fixed green.

Fog signal: One blast every 15 seconds.

SIDE TRIP: *Pilgrim Monument and Provincetown Museum*

If you enjoy climbing the stairs inside lighthouses, you'll really love ascending to the top of the world's tallest all-granite structure, the Pilgrim Monument. The Pilgrims spent five weeks exploring the tip of Cape Cod before they went on to Plymouth, and the Cape Cod Pilgrim Memorial Association built the monument to honor the Pilgrims' first landing. The view from the top of the 252-foot tower (350 feet above sea level) is not to be missed.

A museum was opened at the base of the monument to educate the public about Provincetown's role in American history. Permanent exhibits tell the story of the arrival of the Pilgrims and highlight the town's rich maritime history as well as the early days of modern American theater in Provincetown. The museum and monument are open daily from early April through October and limited weekend hours into early December.

Pilgrim Monument and Province-
town Museum
High Pole Hill Road
Provincetown, MA
Phone: 508-487-1310
Web site: www.pilgrim-monument.
org

Long Point once had a thriving village. Henry David Thoreau reported circa 1850 that lobsters were plentiful here and were caught to be sold to the New York market for two cents apiece. By the Civil War, there were very few people left. Many of the houses at Long Point were floated across the harbor to Provincetown's West End.

A new 38-foot-tall square brick lighthouse and a new keeper's house were built in 1875. A 1,200-pound fog bell was also installed.

In 1933, during a thick fog, the mechanism that rang the station's fog bell broke down. Keeper Thomas L. Chase rang the bell by hand for over nine hours straight, pulling the rope with his right hand every 30 seconds. After a few hours of sleep he had to sound the bell for several more hours, this time with his left hand. He said he felt like "a baseball pitcher who has twirled a couple of doubleheaders without rest."

The light was automated in 1952 and converted to solar power in 1982. The Cape Cod chapter of the American Lighthouse Foundation has been licensed by the Coast Guard to restore and maintain Long Point Light.

You can see the lighthouse distantly

A floating playpen created by keeper Joseph Poindexter in 1949

from MacMillan Wharf in Province-town. It's possible to walk across Wood End and all the way to Long Point from the western end of Commercial Street in Provincetown, but this strenuous hike is not recommended.

A much easier way to get to Long Point is to take the seasonal shuttle boat run by a company called Flyer's. The shuttle leaves from MacMillan Pier in Provincetown and lets you off a short distance from the lighthouse. Call 508-487-0898, extension 205, or visit www.flyersrentals.com for more information. The harbor tours offered by Viking Princess Cruises (508-487-7323, www.capecodecotours.com), leaving daily in summer from MacMillan Pier, also provide a good view.

Fascinating Fact

During the Civil War, a Confederate warship was seen near Provincetown. In anticipation of a possible attack, two small forts were built at Long Point close to the lighthouse. Local residents called the batteries "Fort Useless" and "Fort Ridiculous."

For more information or to donate to the restoration of Long Point Light, contact the Cape Cod chapter of the American Lighthouse Foundation, P.O. 570, North Truro, MA 02652. Web site www.lighthousefoundation.org.

SANDY NECK LIGHT

Accessibility: 🚶‍♂️ ⛵

Geographic coordinates:
41° 43' 22" N 70 16 51 W

Nearest town: Barnstable.
Located at the eastern end
of the Sandy Neck peninsula
at the entrance to Barnstable
Harbor, on the north coast of
Cape Cod.

Established: 1826.
Present lighthouse built:
1857. Deactivated 1931.

Height of tower:
38 feet. Height of focal
plane: 36 feet.

Previous optic: Fifth-order
Fresnel lens. Present optic:
LED.

Characteristic: White flash
every 6 seconds.

The eastern tip of six-mile-long Sandy Neck marks the entrance to Barnstable Harbor as well as the approach to the small harbor at Yarmouthport. Congress appropriated $3,500 for a lighthouse at the eastern tip of the peninsula, a site known as Beach Point, in May 1826. The first lighthouse consisted of a wooden lantern on the roof of a brick dwelling.

The 48-foot brick tower that still stands replaced the original lighthouse in 1857. The distinctive pair of iron hoops and six staves that surround the lighthouse were added in 1887 as part of an effort to shore up cracks.

One bitterly cold day, keeper Thomas Baxter headed for Barnstable in his dory, alternately rowing, pulling, and pushing the vessel through the icy harbor. He caught his leg between the dory and the ice, suffering an injury that led to gangrene and eventually his death in 1862. Baxter's wife, Lucy Hinckley Baxter, succeeded him as keeper and raised three children at the station.

The lighthouse was decommissioned in 1931. The lantern was removed, and the property was sold at auction. In 1944, the property was sold to Fred Lang, a radio personality. Lang sold the property to the Hinckley family in 1950. Ken Morton and Kee Hinckley today manage the property for the family.

In 2004, Morton began working with the Cape Cod chapter of the American Lighthouse Foundation to have a replica lantern installed on the tower in time for its 150th birthday in 2007. A new chapter of the American

Fascinating Fact

After a storm in 1898, George A. Jamieson discovered that his chicken coop and forty chickens had apparently been washed away to their doom. As it turned out, the coop had washed safely ashore in Barnstable. The chickens were fine, although they did exhibit some strange symptoms that were attributed to seasickness.

Lighthouse Foundation was formed to help restore a lantern on the tower: Sandy Neck Restoration Committee, P.O. Box 147, Barnstable, MA 02630. The installation of a new lantern was completed in 2007; in October, the lighthouse was relit as a private aid to navigation, with a modern LED optic.

The lighthouse can be seen distantly from Millway Beach in Barnstable, but it is best seen by boat. Hyannis Whale Watcher Cruises from Barnstable Harbor provide a good view. Call 508-362-6088 or visit www.whales.net.

DUXBURY PIER LIGHT
(Bug Light)

Accessibility:

Geographic coordinates:
41° 59' 15" N   70° 38' 55" W

Nearest town: Plymouth. Located in Duxbury Bay, in the main channel to Plymouth Harbor.

Established: 1871. Present lighthouse built: 1871. Automated: 1964.

Height of tower: 47 feet. Height of focal plane: 35 feet.

Previous optic: Fourth-order Fresnel lens. Present optic: 250 mm.

Characteristic: Two red flashes every 5 seconds.

Fog signal: One blast every 15 seconds.

This lighthouse was established to mark a dangerous shoal off Saquish Head in Plymouth Bay. The 47-foot cast-iron tower was filled with concrete to a height of 25 feet. Two levels inside the structure served as living quarters for the resident keepers.

Original plans for Duxbury Pier Light

The first keeper was William Atwood. In early February 1875, after about six weeks of being imprisoned because of ice around the tower, Atwood and his wife ran out of food and were living on a pint of water a day. A steamer cut a path through the ice, and food and supplies were delivered.

Frank Grieder became keeper in 1930. His son later recalled the huge fog bell: "You'd wind it up and all of a sudden it'd go *whammo,* and the whole tower would shake. When the fog cleared and they shut the bell off, you woke up— 'Why is it so quiet?'"

A hurricane in 1944 washed away the fog bell mechanism, the station's boat, and the privy (referred to by Coast Guardsman Harry Salter as "our favorite reading room").

The station was automated and destaffed in 1964, and it soon fell victim to vandalism and nesting birds. It deteriorated to the point that the Coast Guard considered replacing it with a fiberglass pole in early 1982. Concerned local residents started a group called Project Bug Light, and the Coast Guard reconsidered their plans. Some restoration was completed in the 1980s, thanks to a cooperative effort by the Coast Guard and Project Bug Light.

Another preservation effort was mounted in the 1990s. The nonprofit group Project Gurnet and Bug Lights now care for this lighthouse and Plymouth ("Gurnet") Light. A renovation was carried out in 2001; more than 1,200 pounds of rust was removed. The group is now working to raise funds for another repainting and other restoration.

The lighthouse can be seen very distantly from the waterfront in Plymouth. One of the best ways to see it is on the sightseeing cruises from Plymouth offered by Captain John Boats (508-747-3434, www.plymouthharbor cruises.com).

For more on the lighthouse's preservation, contact Project Gurnet and Bug Lights, P.O. Box 2167, Duxbury, MA 02331. Web site: www.buglight.org.

Fascinating Fact

This was the first offshore cast-iron caisson lighthouse in the United States. Its appearance has been likened to a coffee pot.

PLYMOUTH LIGHT
(Gurnet Light)

Accessibility:

Geographic coordinates:
42° 00' 13" N 70° 36' 02" W

Nearest town: Plymouth. Located at Gurnet Point in Plymouth Bay.

Established: 1768. Present lighthouse built: 1843. Automated: 1986.

Height of tower: 34 feet. Height of focal plane: 104 feet.

Previous optic: Fourth-order Fresnel lens. Present optic: 190 mm.

Characteristic: Three white flashes every 30 seconds with a red sector.

Fog signal: One blast every 15 seconds.

The peninsula known as the Gurnet is a seven-mile-long sand spit at the northern border of Plymouth Bay. With burgeoning trade in Plymouth and shipbuilding in neighboring Duxbury and Kingston, the Gurnet was an ideal place for a lighthouse to help guide the local traffic.

Plymouth Light Station with two towers circa early 1900s

The first lighthouse, established in 1768, was a wooden dwelling with two lanterns on its roof, one at each end—America's first "twin" lights. It was felt that mariners wouldn't confuse the double lights with the single light at Boston. The first keeper was John Thomas, a doctor from Marshfield, Massachusetts. He became a major general and led troops at Quebec during the American Revolution. When Thomas contracted smallpox and died in 1776, his wife, Hannah, became the new keeper.

The original building was destroyed by fire in 1801. A pair of 22-foot towers was built, 30 feet from each other. Joseph Burgess was keeper for 39 years beginning in 1812. His sixteen-year-old daughter, Eunice, jumped from the bluff to her death when her father wouldn't consent to her marriage to a soldier from the neighboring fort.

New octagonal wooden towers were built in 1843, along with a large dwelling. A fog bell with striking machinery was added in 1907. In 1924, as part of the effort to phase out twin light stations as an unnecessary expense, the northeast tower was discontinued and torn down.

The old keeper's house was destroyed, and a four-bedroom ranch

Fascinating Fact

This is the oldest free-standing wooden lighthouse in the U.S., and the station had the nation's first woman keeper (Hannah Thomas).

Coast Guardsmen skateboarding down the drive in 1964.

house was built for the Coast Guard crew in 1962. During the Coast Guard era, the crew was an important link to the mainland for Gurnet residents. The station had the Gurnet's only telephone and the only full-time electric power.

The light was automated and destaffed in 1986. By the 1990s, the lighthouse stood only 45 feet from the edge of the bluff, which was losing at least a foot each year to erosion. The thirteen-ton tower was moved 140 feet to a new location in December 1998.

Project Gurnet and Bug Lights, the same group that cares for Duxbury Pier ("Bug") Light, now manages the property. Volunteers have painted the tower, and a window has been replaced. The former keepers' house can be rented by the week or by the month. Rents vary depending upon the month and season. For more information, see www.buglight.org.

The Gurnet is accessible by four-wheel-drive vehicle from Duxbury Beach, but the road to the lighthouse is not open to the general public. There are occasional open houses, including one each year during Duxbury's Opening of the Bay festival in late May. For more information, contact Project Gurnet and Bug Lights, P.O. Box 2167, Duxbury, MA 02331. Web site: www.buglight.org. The group has also sponsored an annual lighthouse cruise in June.

The sightseeing cruises from Plymouth offered by Captain John Boats (508-747-3434, www.plymouthharborcruises.com) offer a view, but it may be distant. The Friends of the Boston Harbor Islands (781-740-4290, www.fbhi.org) have offered occasional cruises from Boston to Plymouth, including a view of the lighthouse.

SCITUATE LIGHT

Scituate's small but protected harbor developed a flourishing fishing fleet by the early 1800s. The town's selectmen convinced Congress to appropriate $4,000 for a lighthouse in 1810. The 25-foot stone lighthouse went into service in April 1812. The first keeper was Simeon Bates, who stayed at the station until his death in 1834. During the War of 1812, Bates once fired a cannon at a British warship as it departed from the harbor.

Accessibility:

Geographic coordinates: 42° 12' 18" N 70° 42' 57" W

Nearest town: Scituate. Located at Cedar Point at the north side of the entrance to Scituate Harbor.

Established: 1811. Present lighthouse built: 1812. Deactivated: 1860. Relighted: 1991.

Height of tower: 50 feet. Height of focal plane: 70 feet.

Present optic: 250 mm.

Characteristic: White flash every 15 seconds.

On September 1, 1814, most of the Bates family was away. The keeper's daughters, twenty-one-year-old Rebecca and fifteen-year-old (or seventeen-year-old according to some accounts) Abigail were left in charge. The sisters saw a British warship anchored in the harbor. Fearing an attack on the town, they thought quickly. Rebecca grabbed her fife, and Abigail got her drum. Being sure to stay out of sight, the sisters played "Yankee Doodle." Thinking the music signaled the arrival of the town militia, the British retreated. The durable legend of the "Lighthouse Army of Two" was born.

In 1827, a 15-foot brick extension and a new lantern were added to the tower. When the second tower offshore at Minot's Ledge was completed in 1860, it was decided that the light at Scituate was no longer needed. The light was deactivated in November 1860. For some years, keepers in charge of a light on a nearby jetty lived in the old Scituate keeper's house, but the jetty light was automated in 1924.

The lighthouse tower, its lantern removed, fell to ruin. It was sold to the

Fascinating Fact

This is the oldest extant lighthouse tower and keeper's house combination in the country.

Town of Scituate in 1917. A replica lantern was installed in 1930. In 1968, the Scituate Historical Society took over the care of the lighthouse and keeper's house. The lighthouse was relighted in 1991, but the light was visible from land only. Three years later, the lighthouse became a private aid to navigation, with a flashing white light.

The keeper's house is rented to an individual, and the rent helps fund the maintenance of the site. In recent years, educational exhibits have been developed in the covered walkway between the house and tower. The Scituate Historical Society had the tower restored in 2004; the outer layer of bricks on the upper part of the tower was replaced.

To reach the lighthouse from Route 3, take exit 13 onto Route 53 North. At the intersection with Route 123, turn right onto Route 123 North. Continue for about six miles to the intersection with Route 3A. Cross Route 3A onto Old Country Way. Turn right onto Stockbridge Road, then turn right onto First Parish Road and continue to the end. Turn left onto Front Street. Turn right onto Jericho Road, and then turn right onto Lighthouse Road. Follow to the parking lot for the lighthouse. The grounds are open all year. Contact the Scituate Historical Society (781-545-1083, www.scituatehistoricalsociety. org) for more information.

Some of the cruises offered by the Friends of the Boston Harbor Islands (781-740-4290, www.fbhi.org) might provide views.

SIDE TRIP: *Hull Lifesaving Museum*

This museum, formerly the Point Allerton Life Saving Station, preserves the region's lifesaving tradition. There are dramatic views of Boston Harbor and its lighthouses from the building. The station was once the home of Joshua James and his crews, the most celebrated lifesavers in the world. The Keeper's Room celebrates the amazing life and deeds of Joshua James. The upstairs Edward Rowe Snow Room features lighthouse models, exhibits about Boston Harbor, a research collection, and a fourth-order Fresnel lens from Plymouth Light. The museum is open year round; call for the current hours.

Hull Lifesaving Museum
1117 Nantasket Avenue
Hull, MA 02045
Phone 781-925-5433
Web site: www.lifesavingmuseum.
org

MINOT'S LEDGE LIGHT

Accessibility: ⛵ 🏚

Geographic coordinates:
42° 16' 12" N 70° 45' 30" W

Nearest towns: Scituate
and Cohasset. Located at
the Cohasset Rocks, on the
southern approach to Boston
Harbor.

Established: 1850.
Present lighthouse built:
1860. Automated: 1947.

Height of tower:
114 feet. Height of focal
plane: 85 feet.

Earlier optics: Second-
order Fresnel lens (1860),
Third-order Fresnel lens
(1947). Present optic:
300 mm.

Characteristic: Flashing
white (1-4-3)

The Cohasset Rocks are about a mile off-shore, near the South Shore towns of Cohasset and Scituate. The ledges were the scene of many shipping disasters, and there were repeated requests for a lighthouse in the vicinity. Congress appropriated funds for a lighthouse in 1847. Capt. William H. Swift, in charge of the project, designed a spidery 70-foot-tall iron pile lighthouse, with living quarters and a lantern atop piles drilled into the rock. Construction began in the summer of 1847.

The lighthouse went into service on January 1, 1850. The first keeper was Isaac Dunham. During one storm, Dunham wrote in his log that the tower reeled "like a drunken man." Believing the tower was unsafe, Dunham resigned after ten months. His successor was John Bennett, a veteran of the British navy. Bennett also came to believe the tower was in danger of falling in a storm. "I fear something awful will happen," he wrote.

The keepers' boat was lost in a gale on April 9, 1851. Bennett went to Boston to see about procuring a new boat, leaving two young assistants—twenty-year-old Joseph Wilson and twenty-five-year-old Joseph Antoine—in charge. A tremendous storm swept into the area before Bennett could return. The storm of April 16–17 would be remembered as the Minot's Light Gale.

Around 1:00 a.m. on April 17, near high tide, residents on shore heard the frantic ringing of the fog bell at the lighthouse. By morning, the tower was gone. The two young keepers had dropped a note in a bottle into the sea. It read, "The lighthouse won't stand over to-night. She shakes 2 feet each way now." The bodies of Antoine and Wilson were later found.

Fascinating Fact

This lighthouse was recognized as an American Society for Civil Engineering Landmark in 1997.

A lightship served near the ledges for a time. Congress appropriated $80,000 for a new lighthouse in 1852; the project would ultimately cost about $244,000. General Joseph G. Totten of the Lighthouse Board designed the second tower. Lieutenant Barton S. Alexander of the Army Corps of Engineers, who also supervised the construction, modified the design.

The building of the granite tower took about five years. The cutting and assembling of the granite (from Quincy, Massachusetts) took place at Cohasset's Government Island. At the ledge, the blocks were dovetailed to each other and doweled to each other with iron pins. The workers were required to be good swimmers, and there were no deaths or serious injuries during the construction process. The tower went into service on November 15, 1860.

The first 40 feet of the tower are solid granite, topped by space for storage and living quarters. Generally, three men were assigned; two men were at the tower at a time, with one on shore leave. Keeper Milton Reamy once said, "The trouble with life here is that we have too much time to think." There was reportedly at least one attempted suicide by a keeper. The keepers' families lived at a shore station at Government Island in Cohasset, with two houses.

The light was automated and the keepers removed in 1947. The light was converted to solar power in 1983. Since 1894, the light has had a distinctive 1-4-3 flash. Someone suggested that the characteristic stands for "I love you," so Minot's Ledge Light became popularly known as the "I Love You Light," or the "Lover's Light."

You can visit Government Island to see a replica of the lantern with part of a third-order Fresnel lens once used in the lighthouse. There's also a gran-

ite memorial to the two assistant keepers who died in the 1851 storm. To reach Government Island in Cohasset, take Route 3 South from Boston to Route 228. Take exit 14 onto Route 228 North. Continue as Route 228 becomes East Street, then North Main Street. Turn left onto Summer Street and then turn right onto Border Street. Immediately after crossing a bridge, turn left onto Government Island.

The lighthouse can be seen distantly from various locations in Hull (including Nantasket Beach), Scituate, and Cohasset. The best mainland view is from Minot Beach in Scituate. To get there, follow Route 3A into Scituate. Turn left on Gannett Road and continue as it becomes Glades Road. The beach is on the right, opposite Bailey's Causeway. There's a small parking lot, open to residents only in summer. If you're there in summer, you should be able to pull over on the road near the beach to photograph the lighthouse. A more distant view is possible from Sandy Beach on Atlantic Avenue in Cohasset. (The parking lot is open to residents only during summer.) Some of the cruises offered by the Friends of the Boston Harbor Islands (781-740-4290, www.fbhi.org) might provide views.

Drawing of the first tower at Minot's Ledge

LONG ISLAND HEAD LIGHT

Long Island, at 214 acres, is the largest of Boston Harbor's 34 islands. In the early 1800s, countless vessels passed by the island as they entered the harbor from Broad Sound. Congress appropriated funds for a lighthouse at the northern end of the island in March 1819. The original lighthouse was a 20-foot stone tower topped by a 7-foot-tall lantern. A stone dwelling was attached to the tower. The first keeper was Jonathan Lawrence, who had been wounded in the War of 1812.

Accessibility:

Geographic coordinates:
42° 19' 48" N   70° 57' 30" W

Nearest city: Boston. Located at the northern end of Long Island in Boston Harbor.

Established: 1819. Present lighthouse built: 1901. Automated: 1929. Deactivated: 1982. Relighted 1985.

Height of tower: 52 feet. Height of focal plane: 120 feet.

Earlier optics: Fourth-order Fresnel lens. Present optic: 250 mm.

Characteristic: White flash every 2.5 seconds.

SIDE TRIP: *Boston Harbor Islands National Park Area*

Boston's spacious harbor is sprinkled generously with islands, many of them rich in history and lore. Park ferries regularly serve Georges Island and four other islands (in season), and park tour boats visit several others. Thirty-nine-acre Georges Island, home of Fort Warren, is the transportation hub of the islands. The island has picnic grounds, open fields, paved walkways, and a snack bar. Guided tours of historic Fort Warren are offered. Georges is also the site of a memorial to historian Edward Rowe Snow, who maintained the "Flying Santa" gift-giving flights to New England lighthouse families for more than forty years. (See www.flyingsanta.org for more on this continuing tradition.) From the island, you can see Boston Light and Graves Light in the distance.

Another highlight of the park is 105-acre Spectacle Island, featuring a marina, visitor center, café, a beach, and 5 miles of walking trails.

Boston Harbor Islands Partnership
408 Atlantic Avenue, Suite 228
Boston MA 02110-3350
Phone: 617-223-8666
Web site: www.bostonislands.org

A new cast-iron tower, 34 feet tall, was built in 1844. That tower was replaced by another cast-iron lighthouse in 1881, and a new wood-frame dwelling was built at the same time.

Keeper John B. Carter was interviewed during a stretch of bad weather in the winter of 1895. "I have a cow and some fowl, and I don't care how hard it blows," said Carter. "My daughter has her piano, and we manage to take lots of comfort here, gale or no gale."

The island's Fort Strong was enlarged around 1900, and the light station had to be relocated. A new 52-foot cylindrical brick tower was built, and the other buildings were all moved to the new location. The lighthouse was converted to automatic acetylene gas operation in 1929. The keeper's house and outbuildings have been destroyed.

The Coast Guard discontinued the light in 1982 and then decided to reactivate it three years later. The Coast

Fascinating Fact

The lighthouse tower built here in 1844 was the first cast-iron lighthouse in the United States.

Long Island Head Light in the early 1900s

Guard hired the Campbell Construction Group of Beverly, Massachusetts, for a renovation in 1998. Some of the original brick and iron were replaced, and the tower was repainted.

Ownership of the lighthouse was transferred to the National Park Service in June 2011. The tower and grounds are not accessible to the public. (A bridge to Long Island from the city of Quincy was built in 1951, but the bridge is not open to the public.) The lighthouse can be seen from many of the sightsee-ing cruises in Boston Harbor, including those offered by the Friends of the Boston Harbor Islands (781-740-4290, www.fbhi.org), Boston Harbor Cruises (617-227-4321, www.bostonharbor cruises.com), the New England Aquarium (617-973-5200, www.neaq.org).

The 1844 tower at Long Island Head

BOSTON LIGHT

Accessibility: 🏛 ⚓ 🏠

Geographic coordinates:
42° 19' 42" N   70° 53' 24" W

Nearest town: Hull. Located on Little Brewster Island in outer Boston Harbor.

Established: 1716. Present lighthouse built: 1783.

Height of tower: 89 feet. Height of focal plane: 102 feet.

Optic: Second-order Fresnel lens.

Characteristic: White flash every 10 seconds.

Fog signal: One blast every 30 seconds.

Boston's spacious harbor helped it become the commercial center of America in colonial days. Early in 1713, a prominent Boston merchant and selectman named John George, representing the business community of the city, proposed to the General Court the "Erecting of a Light Hous & Lanthorn [sic] . . . for the Direction of Ships & Vessels in the Night Time bound into the said Harbour." The General Court of Massachusetts passed the Boston Light Bill, and a stone tower was soon built.

The first keeper, forty-three-year-old George Worthylake, moved to the island with his family. An African slave named Shadwell also lived at the lighthouse. Worthylake lighted the lighthouse for the first time on Friday, September 14, 1716.

On November 3, 1718, Worthylake went with his wife and their daughter Ruth to Boston to collect his pay. A family friend joined the party for the return trip. The sloop returned a little past noon, and Shadwell paddled out in a canoe to transfer the party to the island. The canoe capsized and all five people drowned. Benjamin Franklin, twelve years old at the time, wrote a poem called *The Lighthouse Tragedy* and hawked copies on the streets of Boston.

A cannon, America's first fog signal, was placed on the island in 1719. Today, the venerable cannon sits on a new carriage in the base of the lighthouse tower.

In July 1775, Boston Harbor and the lighthouse were under the control of the British. On July 20, American troops

"Storm child"
Georgia Norwood

under Major Joseph Vose landed at the lighthouse and burned the wooden parts of the tower. As the British worked to repair the tower, 300 American soldiers under Major Benjamin Tupper landed at the island on July 31. They easily defeated the British guard and again burned the lighthouse. As the British forces left the area on June 13, 1776, one of their final acts was to set off a timed charge on Little Brewster, completely destroying the lighthouse. A new 75-foot rubblestone tower was built in 1783.

A 1,375-pound fog bell replaced the old cannon in 1851. In 1859, the tower was raised to its present height of 89 feet, and a new lantern was installed

Fascinating Fact

This is the oldest light station in North America and the only one in the United States that still has an official keeper.

Inside Boston Light's second-order Fresnel lens

along with a second-order Fresnel lens.

For many years, three keepers and their families lived on the tiny island (about 1 acre). In the 1930s, Little Brewster was home to as many as nineteen children. Summers were lively with rowboat races and pie-eating contests versus the children who summered on nearby Great Brewster. The older children made money by lobstering. Games of all sorts were played, even baseball.

In 1932, Josephine Norwood, wife of assistant keeper Ralph Norwood, was expecting their seventh child. The birth seemed imminent the night of a terrible storm. A doctor made the trip to Little Brewster from Hull, but it was a false alarm. Mrs. Norwood had her child in calm weather a week later. Nevertheless, a legend was born. Author Ruth Carmen wrote a novel called *Storm Child*, a highly fictionalized version of the Norwoods' story.

By 1989, the Coast Guard had automated every lighthouse in the United States, and Boston Light was scheduled to be the last in this process. Pres-

ervation groups appealed to Congress, and funding was appropriated to keep Coast Guard staff on Little Brewster, making the island a living museum of lighthouse history. Coast Guard Auxiliary (volunteer) personnel have worked on the island since 1980. In September 2003, Sally Snowman was appointed as the new civilian keeper. Little Brewster Island is part of the Boston Harbor Islands National Recreation Area, and National Park Service rangers are also present during the days the island is open from June to October.

You can see Boston Light from the shores of Hull (from Nantasket Beach, Fort Revere, and the Hull Lifesaving Museum), and more distantly from Revere Beach and Winthrop Beach.

The Friends of the Boston Harbor Islands (781-740-4290, www.fbhi.org) run several special trips to the lighthouse every summer.

The National Park Service runs trips to the lighthouse from Boston in season. Trips depart the Moakley United States Courthouse at Fan Pier in the South Boston Seaport District. Fan Pier is convenient to public transportation, and parking is available. The program includes a narrated harbor tour and views of Graves Light and Long Island Head Light. Participants get to climb Boston Light's 76 stairs for a magnificent view and a close look at the lens. For the current days and times, call 800-979-3370 or visit www.boston harborislands.com/tour-lighthouse.

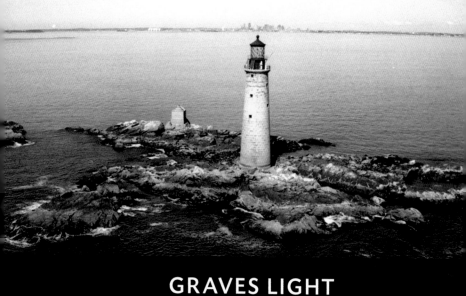

GRAVES LIGHT

Accessibility: 🚢 ⛵

Geographic coordinates:
42° 21' 54" N 70° 52' 09" W

Nearest town: Winthrop. Located in outer Boston Harbor at the entrance to the Broad Sound Channel.

Established: 1905. Present lighthouse built: 1905.

Height of tower:
113 feet. Height of focal plane: 98 feet.

Earlier optic: First-order Fresnel lens. Present optic: VRB-25.

Characteristic: Two white flashes every 12 seconds.

Fog signal: Two blasts every 20 seconds.

An iron bell buoy was placed near the Graves Ledges in outer Boston Harbor in 1854. It was later replaced by a whistling buoy beyond the northeast end of the ledges; the sound of the buoy was described in a newspaper as a "shriek of despair."

Keepers Fitzpatrick and Reamy circa 1935

A shipping channel into Boston Harbor, the Broad Sound Channel, was improved in the early 1900s, necessitating a lighthouse at the Graves Ledges. Congress appropriated funds in 1902. Construction began in 1903. The huge granite blocks for the tower were cut on Cape Ann and transported to Lovell's Island in Boston Harbor. A steam vessel carried workers and materials from Lovell's to the Graves Ledges.

The light went into operation on September 1, 1905. The giant first-order Fresnel lens rotated on a bed of mercury. Entrance to the tower was at the top of a 30-foot ladder, and three levels inside the tower served as living quarters for the keepers. The bottom 42-foot section of the tower is filled with concrete, with space left for a cistern.

Elliot C. Hadley was the first keeper. He reported that storms never shook the tower; the only vibrations were from the firing of practice shots from nearby forts. "The way we found out first was by having all our dishes broken," he told a reporter.

The light was automated, and the keepers were removed in 1976. The light was converted to solar power in 2001. The lighthouse is still owned and operated by the Coast Guard. You can see it distantly from Winthrop Beach and Revere Beach to the north and from Nantasket Beach in Hull to the south.

Better views are available from some of the lighthouse cruises offered by the Friends of the Boston Harbor Islands (781-740-4290, www.fbhi.org) and Boston Harbor Cruises (617-227-4321, www.bostonharborcruises.com).

Fascinating Fact

The most famous shipwreck in this vicinity was in April 1938, when the 419-foot British freighter *City of Salisbury* hit an uncharted rock with a cargo of exotic zoo animals. Most of the animals—and all of the humans—were rescued successfully.

MARBLEHEAD LIGHT

Accessibility: 🚗

Geographic coordinates:
42° 30' 18" N   70° 50' 00" W

Nearest town: Marblehead. Located at the northern tip of Marblehead Neck, at the entrance to Marblehead Harbor.

Established: 1835. Present lighthouse built: 1896. Automated: 1960

Height of tower:
105 feet. Height of focal plane: 130 feet.

Earlier optic: Sixth-order Fresnel lens. Present optic: 300 mm.

Characteristic: Fixed green.

Marblehead's large harbor became an important center for trade and fishing by the early 1800s. After citizens of the town petitioned for a lighthouse, Congress appropriated funds in 1834. A 23-foot tower went into service on October 10, 1835.

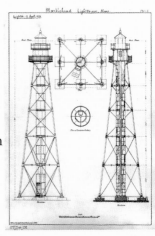

Plans for the 1896 tower

James S. Bailey was keeper from 1872 to 1892. An 1889 article stated that Bailey had saved seventeen lives in the vicinity of the lighthouse. On one occasion, he rescued two drunken men who fell into the harbor while dancing in their rowboat. Bailey said simply, "It is a duty for me to save my fellow men."

Henry T. Drayton was keeper from 1893 to 1928. His daughter Mary later recalled that the family kept a cow and chickens at the station. Mary took a ferry to town each day to attend school.

Surrounding summer cottages eventually dwarfed the first tower. A taller tower was in order, so the extant 105-foot cast-iron skeletal tower was erected in 1896. The lighthouse is the only one of its type in New England, but there are similar towers in the mid-Atlantic and in Florida.

The lighthouse is now part of Marblehead's 3.74-acre Chandler Hovey Park. The town of Marblehead is licensed to care for the tower, which is still owned by the Coast Guard. The grounds are open all year.

Marblehead Neck is attached to the rest of Marblehead by a causeway (Ocean Avenue). To reach the lighthouse from Route 114 (Pleasant Street) or Route 129 (Atlantic Avenue) in Marblehead, head east on Ocean Avenue. At the end of the causeway, bear left onto Harbor Avenue. Follow almost a mile until the road reconnects with Ocean Avenue. Turn left onto Follett Street and follow to the free parking area for Chandler Hovey Park. The park has benches, picnic tables, and restrooms. For more on the park, call 781-631-3350.

Views are also available from some of the lighthouse cruises offered by the Friends of the Boston Harbor Islands (781-740-4290, www.fbhi.org) and Boston Harbor Cruises (617-227-4321, www.bostonharborcruises.com). Mahi Mahi Cruises, with excursions leaving from Salem Willows Park in Salem, offers occasional lighthouse cruises that pass by this lighthouse; see www.mahi cruises.com or call (800) 992-MAHI.

Fascinating Fact

Ezekiel Darling, the first keeper, was a former gunner on the U.S.S. *Constitution*.

DERBY WHARF LIGHT

Accessibility: 🚗 🚶 ⛵

Geographic coordinates:
42° 31' 00" N   70° 53' 01" W

Nearest city: Salem. Located at the end of Derby Wharf in Salem Harbor.

Established: 1871. Present lighthouse built: 1871. Deactivated: 1977. Relighted: 1983.

Height of focal plane: 25 feet.

Earlier optic: Fifth-order Fresnel lens (1871); Fourth-order Fresnel lens (1906); Sixth-order Fresnel lens (1910). Present optic: 155 mm.

Characteristic: Red flash every 6 seconds.

This square brick lighthouse at the end of Derby Wharf went into service in January 1871. The light never had a keeper's house. Instead, Salem residents were hired to serve as caretakers.

Early photo of Derby Wharf Light

A disastrous fire swept Salem in 1914. The caretaker of the light, William Osgood, was preoccupied with saving his own home, so his wife went to light the lighthouse for the evening. She narrowly escaped as the flames engulfed the wharf. After that, Osgood had to travel to the lighthouse by rowboat.

The National Park Service began the restoration of the wharf in 1937. Derby Wharf is now part of the Salem Maritime National Historic Site, which includes twelve buildings on the waterfront. The Coast Guard deactivated the lighthouse in 1977, and ownership subsequently went to the National Park Service. The Friends of Salem Maritime convinced the authorities to relight the lighthouse as a private aid to navigation in 1983.

The wharf and grounds around the diminutive lighthouse are open all year. It's an easy walk to the lighthouse at the end of the wharf. The tall ship *Friendship*—a replica of a 1797 Salem East Indiaman—is an added attraction at Derby Wharf.

Follow Route 114 into Salem and continue as the road becomes North Street, then Summer Street. Turn left onto Norman Street and stay straight through a traffic light onto Derby

Fascinating Fact

Across the street from the foot of Derby Wharf is Salem's 1818 Custom House, where Nathaniel Hawthorne once worked as a clerk.

SIDE TRIP: *Peabody Essex Museum*

This world-class museum, founded in 1799, recently underwent a $194 million expansion. The galleries contain a vast array of Asian art and maritime art collections. The American decorative art, folk art, and costume collection represents more than 300 years of New England art and culture. Don't miss the fascinating Yin Yu Tang house, a late Qing Dynasty home relocated from southwestern China. The museum is open daily; call or check online for the hours.

Peabody Essex Museum
East India Square
Salem, MA 01970
Phone: 978-745-9500
(Toll Free) 866-745-1876
Web site: www.pem.org

Street. Follow Derby Street through the traffic light straight past the Beverly Cooperative Bank to the next intersection. There's a parking garage at this corner, the best place to park for Derby Wharf. From the garage, walk east on Derby Street for a few minutes to the wharf. There's an orientation center near the foot of the wharf. For more on the Salem Maritime National Historic Site, call 978-740-1660 or visit www. nps.gov/sama/.

Views are available from some of the lighthouse cruises offered by the Friends of the Boston Harbor Islands (781-740-4290, www.fbhi.org) and Boston Harbor Cruises (617-227-4321, www.bostonharborcruises.com), and Mahi Mahi Cruises (800-992-MAHI, www.mahicruises.com).

FORT PICKERING LIGHT
(Winter Island Light)

 This is one of three new lights established in 1871–72 to help mariners approaching Salem Harbor. Fort Pickering Lighthouse, a cast-iron tower lined with brick, went into service on January 17, 1871. A six-room keeper's house was built on Winter Island, and a 52-foot wooden walkway connected the lighthouse to shore.

Keeper's house circa late 1800s

Accessibility: 🚗 ⛵

Geographic coordinates:
42° 31' 36" N   70° 52' 00" W

Nearest city: Salem. Located at the southeast corner of 20-acre Winter Island, at the north side of the entrance to Salem Harbor.

Established: 1871. Present lighthouse built: 1871. Deactivated: 1969. Relighted: 1983.

Height of focal plane: 28 feet.

Earlier optic: Fifth-order Fresnel lens. Present optic: 300 mm.

Characteristic: White flash every 4 seconds.

John Harris, a native of Ipswich, Massachusetts, became keeper in 1882. When he retired at age seventy-five in 1919, it was noted that he had been absent from the lighthouse for only five days in thirty-seven years. Until his retirement, Harris never saw Salem after dark, and he never rode in a car. "It will take some time for us to learn how to act among people," he told a reporter when he retired.

A Coast Guard air station was commissioned on Winter Island in 1935. The Coast Guard left the island in 1969, and the lighthouse was deactivated. The tower soon fell to ruin. Concerned local citizens formed the Fort Pickering Light Association in the early 1980s. The lighthouse was restored, largely with volunteer labor. It was reactivated as a private aid to navigation in 1983 and converted to solar power in 1994.

Winter Island, attached to the mainland by a causeway, offers camping, a beach, a boat launch, walking trails, and the remains of old Fort Pickering. The grounds near the lighthouse are open year round; there's a substantial fee for nonresidents to park on the island in summer. To reach Winter Island, take Route 114 into Salem and connect onto Route 107 North. At a traffic light, turn right onto Webb Street. Webb Street becomes Fort Avenue as it bends to the left. You'll pass a power plant on your right. About one-third mile after the plant, you'll see a sign on the right for Winter Island. Turn right and continue to the island. For more information, contact Winter Island Marine Park, 50 Winter Island Road, Salem, MA 01970. Phone: 978-745-9430. Web site: www.salemweb.com/winterisland/.

Views are also available from some of the lighthouse cruises offered by the Friends of the Boston Harbor Islands (781-740-4290, www.fbhi.org), Boston Harbor Cruises (617-227-4321, www.bostonharborcruises.com), and Mahi Mahi Cruises (800-992-MAHI, www.mahicruises.com).

SIDE TRIP: *Salem Willows Park*

This pretty park, a short distance from Winter Island at the end of Fort Avenue, is named for the European white willow trees planted in 1801 to provide shade for patients at the small-pox hospital that was located here. The area later developed into a park with a carousel and other entertainment and a popular "Restaurant Row." It's claimed that the E.W. Hobbs Company at Salem Willows invented the ice cream cone in 1906. Today, there are arcades, food concessions, and ample picnic grounds by the water. From the park's pier, you can see Hospital Point Light in Beverly and, in the distance, Baker's Island Light.

Salem Willows Park

Phone 978-744-9444

Web site: www.salemwillowspark.com.

Fascinating Fact

Winter Island in Salem was home to the first official air and sea Coast Guard rescue station on the eastern seaboard, designated in 1944. The island was also the birthplace of the famed navy frigate *Essex*, built in 1799.

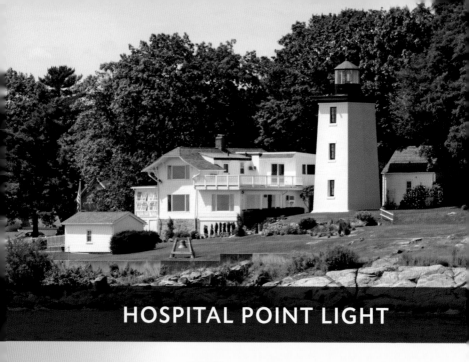

HOSPITAL POINT LIGHT

Accessibility: 👥 ⚓

Geographic coordinates:
42° 32' 47" N 70° 51' 23" W

Nearest city: Beverly.
Located on the north side of
the channel to Salem Harbor.

Established: 1872.
Present lighthouse built:
1872. Automated: 1947.

Height of tower:
45 feet. Height of focal
plane: 70 feet.

Optic: Three-and-one-half-
order Fresnel lens.

Characteristic: Fixed white.

The lighthouse here was one of three aids established in 1871–72 (the lights at Fort Pickering and Derby Wharf were the others) to help mariners headed for Salem Harbor. The 45-foot square brick lighthouse received a three-and-one-half-order Fresnel lens, which is still in service. It also has a very rare component called a condensing panel. Because of the panel, the light diminishes in intensity if a mariner veers from the main channel.

Beverly Cove Light House, Beverly, Mass.

Hospital Point Light circa early 1900s

In 1927, the lighthouse officially became the Hospital Point Range Front Light. A rear range light was established in the steeple of Beverly's First Baptist Church, about a mile from the lighthouse. Incoming mariners lined up the light seen from a window in the steeple above the light in the lighthouse.

After the light was automated in 1947, the Coast Guard retained the station to serve as the home of the commander of the First Coast Guard District and his or her family. The grounds around the lighthouse and the tower itself are not open to the public except during an annual open house that's part of Beverly's Homecoming Week in late July or early August. For more information on this event, visit www.beverly homecoming.com. To drive to the lighthouse, take Route 1A north from Salem into Beverly. Bear right onto Cabot Street. Turn right at Dane Street and follow onto Hale Street (Route 127). Turn right onto East Corning Street. Follow straight onto Bayview Road, which leads to a cul-de-sac near the lighthouse. The view of the tower from the road is largely obstructed by the keeper's house.

You can also see the lighthouse distantly across the water from the pier at Salem Willows Park in Salem. Better views are available from some of the lighthouse cruises offered by the Friends of the Boston Harbor Islands (781-740-4290, www.fbhi.org), Boston Harbor Cruises (617-227-4321, www. bostonharborcruises.com), and Mahi Mahi Cruises (800-992-MAHI, www. mahicruises.com).

The First Baptist Church, which serves as a rear range light, is at 221 Cabot Street in Beverly. For more on the church, call 978-922-3295 or visit www.fbcbeverly.org.

SIDE TRIP: *Lynch Park*

This 16-acre park in Beverly has two beaches and a formal rose garden. President William Howard Taft leased the Stetson cottage here and made it his summer White House. The park is open all year; there's a fee for nonresidents from Memorial Day to Labor Day. In summer, there's a Sunday evening concert series and numerous special events. At low tide, it's possible to walk from the park to the shoreline in front of Hospital Point Lighthouse. To reach the park from Route 127 in Beverly, head south on East Corning Street and turn right onto Neptune Street. At the top of the hill, you will see a stone wall. The second entrance on the left leads to the parking lot.

Lynch Park
55 Ober Street
Beverly, MA 01915
Phone: 978-921-6067
Web site: www.bevrec.com/lynchpark.html

Fascinating Fact

A rear range light that works in tandem with this lighthouse is shown from the steeple of Beverly's First Baptist Church. It's the only church in the country that's also an official aid to navigation.

BAKER'S ISLAND LIGHT

aker's Island is about three miles east of the entrance to Salem Harbor. With Salem's foreign trade booming by the late 1700s, aids to navigation were needed to ensure the safety of the heavy shipping traffic. An unlighted beacon was placed on Baker's Island in 1791. In 1796, President Washington signed an appropriation of $6,000 for a lighthouse on the island.

Accessibility: 🚶 ⛵

Geographic coordinates: 42° 32' 11" N 70° 47' 09" W

Nearest city: Beverly. Located on a 55-acre island on the approach to Salem Harbor.

Established: 1798. Present lighthouse built: 1820. Automated: 1972.

Height of tower: 59. Height of focal plane: 111 feet.

Earlier optic: Fourth-order Fresnel lens. Present optic: VRB-25.

Characteristic: Alternating white and red flashes every 20 seconds.

Fog signal: One blast every 30 seconds.

The first structure was a two-story dwelling with two towers about 40 feet apart on the roof. The first keeper was George Chapman, He later became blind, which was blamed on the brightness of the lighthouse lamps. Joseph Perkins, a former harbor pilot who became keeper in 1815, kept cows, pigs, rabbits, and sheep at the light station.

In 1816, the station was reduced from two lights to one. There were complaints that it was hard to tell the light

apart from Boston Light, so two lights were restored to service in 1820. The extant conical rubblestone tower was built that year. It stood about 40 feet from a shorter 25-foot octagonal stone tower that had been built in 1816. The two towers were nicknamed the "Mr. and Mrs." lighthouses.

In March 1825, keeper Nathaniel Ward and his assistant, a Mr. Marshall, went to the mainland to pick up supplies in a small boat. They were caught in a storm on the return trip, and both died after their boat capsized. The forty-nine-year-old Ward left a large family.

The shorter lighthouse was discontinued in June 1926, and it was demolished a short time later. The light in the taller tower was automated in 1972; the old Fresnel lens is now at the Maine Lighthouse Museum in Rockland, Maine. The tower underwent an extensive restoration in 1993.

The Baker's Island Association, which manages the island, held a license to use the two keeper's houses for some years. In April 2005, U.S. Secretary of the Interior Gale Norton recommended that ownership of the light station be transferred to the Essex National Heritage Commission (ENHC) under the provisions of the National Historic Lighthouse Preservation Act of 2000. For more information, contact the Essex National Heritage Commission, 221 Essex Street, Suite 41, Salem MA 01970. Phone 978-740-0444. Web site: www.essexheritage.org.

The island is not accessible to the general public. You can see the lighthouse distantly from points in Manchester-by-the-Sea, Beverly, Salem, and Marblehead, but it's best seen by boat. Views are available from some of the lighthouse cruises offered by the Friends of the Boston Harbor Islands (781-740-4290, www.fbhi.org), Boston Harbor Cruises (617-227-4321, www.bostonharborcruises.com), and Mahi Mahi Cruises in Salem (800-992-MAHI, www.mahicruises.com).

Fascinating Fact

When Walter Scott Rogers of Beverly became an assistant keeper in 1872, he was in ill health and weighed only 101 pounds. It was reported that by the time he left in 1881, his health had improved and he weighed 226 pounds.

TEN POUND ISLAND LIGHT

Accessibility: 🏃 ⛵

Geographic coordinates:
42° 36' 06" N 70° 39' 54" W

Nearest city: Gloucester. Located on a small island on the east side of Gloucester Harbor.

Established: 1821. Present lighthouse built: 1881. Deactivated: 1956. Relighted: 1989.

Height of tower: 30 feet. Height of focal plane: 57 feet.

Earlier optic: Fifth-order Fresnel lens. Present optic: 250 mm.

Characteristic: 3 seconds red alternating with 3 seconds darkness.

Fog signal: Two blasts every 20 seconds.

Congress appropriated funds in May 1820 for a lighthouse to help mariners entering Gloucester's inner harbor. A small 20-foot conical stone tower went into service in October 1821. The famed American artist Winslow Homer boarded at the light station during the summer of 1880, and he painted about fifty scenes of Gloucester Harbor.

The station was rebuilt in 1881 with a cast-iron tower lined with brick and a wood-frame keeper's house. In 1956, the light was replaced by an automated optic on the old fog bell tower, later moved to a skeleton tower. (The Fresnel lens is now at the Maine Lighthouse Museum in Rockland, Maine.) The keeper's house has been removed.

In the late 1980s, the Lighthouse Preservation Society initiated the restoration of the lighthouse. The tower was relighted as an active aid to navigation on August 7, 1989, which was Lighthouse Bicentennial Day.

The lighthouse can be seen from points along the Gloucester waterfront, including the area near the famous fisherman statue on Stacey Boulevard. Closer views are available from tour boats that pass through the harbor. Harbor Tours, Inc. (www.capeann harbortours.com, 978-283-1979) offers a cruise that circumnavigates Cape Ann, passing all five of the cape's lighthouses. Seven Seas Whale Watch (888-283-1776, www.7seas-whalewatch. com) offers a "Lighthouse & Lobstering Cruise" that includes this lighthouse and Eastern Point Light. The 65-foot schooner *Thomas Lannon* (978-281-6634, www.schooner.org) sails out of Glouces-

ter Harbor, passing Ten Pound Island daily in season. Some of the fundraising cruises held by the Thacher Island Association (www.thacherisland.org) also provide views.

Fascinating Fact

Some say Ten Pound Island is named for the amount of money paid to the local Indians for the property, but the more likely origin is the number of sheep pens (or pounds) kept on the island by the early settlers.

Undated aerial view

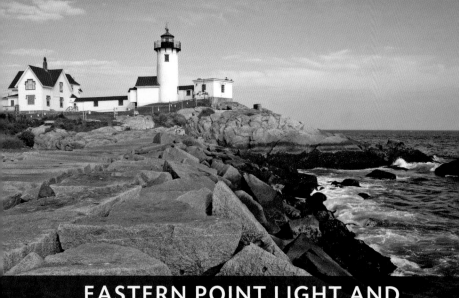

EASTERN POINT LIGHT AND GLOUCESTER BREAKWATER LIGHT

Accessibility:

Geographic coordinates:
42° 34' 49" N   70° 39' 52" W

Nearest city: Gloucester. Located on the east side of the entrance to Gloucester Harbor.

Established: 1832. Present lighthouse built: 1890. Automated: 1985.

Height of tower: 36 feet. Height of focal plane: 57 feet.

Earlier optic: Fourth-order Fresnel lens. Present optic: DCB 24.

Characteristic: White flash every 5 seconds.

Fog signal: One blast every 10 seconds.

To aid fishermen and others entering Gloucester Harbor, an unlighted stone beacon was placed at Eastern Point in 1829. Two years later, the stone beacon was converted into a lighthouse with the addition of a wrought-iron and copper lantern. The first keeper was a local fisherman, Samuel Wonson. A new 34-foot brick tower was built in 1848. Panes of brilliant red French plate glass in the lantern produced the fixed red light. A fog bell with striking machinery was added in 1857.

A 2,250-foot granite breakwater was built next to the light station between 1894 and 1905. A new light, Gloucester Breakwater Light, was established at the end of the breakwater. For many years, the keepers had the added duty of maintaining the breakwater light, a dangerous task when ice covered the granite blocks.

The light was automated in 1985, but the Coast Guard retained the station for family housing. Scott W. McClain was living at the station with his family during the infamous "Perfect Storm" of October 30, 1991. McClain drilled holes in the covered walkway between the house and tower to keep it from collapsing from the weight of the water that was crashing into it. The McClains escaped the house around midnight when the tide was low, and rode out the rest of the night at the nearby yacht club.

The grounds of the station are closed to the public, but there's a parking lot and the breakwater is open all year, with good views of the lighthouse. (There are private road signs posted in the Eastern Point neighborhood, but visitors are permitted to drive to the lighthouse.) To reach the lighthouse from Route 128 North, follow 128 all

Fascinating Fact

A rock formation at the light station is said to resemble a reclining woman and is known as "Mother Ann." A whistling buoy offshore, which produces a low groan, has been dubbed "Mother Ann's Cow."

Gloucester Breakwater Light

the way to the end. Continue straight past a traffic light onto East Main Street, which eventually becomes Eastern Point Road and then Eastern Point Boulevard. Follow the road through a gate and all the way to the parking lot at the end.

Good views are available from tour boats in the area. Harbor Tours, Inc. (www.capeannharbortours.com, 978-283-1979) offers a lighthouse cruise

SIDE TRIP: *Cape Ann Historical Museum*

This museum in downtown Gloucester has a wonderful permanent art collection, featuring the work of maritime luminist Fitz Henry Lane (formerly known as Fitz Hugh Lane) and portrait artist Gilbert Stuart, among others. The decorative arts collection includes eighteenth- and nineteenth-century American furniture, Paul Revere silver, and much more. The old fourth-order Fresnel lens from Eastern Point Light is also on display here. The museum is open Tuesday through Sunday, year round, except for the month of February and major holidays.

Cape Ann Historical Museum
27 Pleasant Street
Gloucester MA 01930
Phone: 978-283-0455
Web site: www.capeannhistorical
museum.org

that passes all five of the cape's lighthouses. Seven Seas Whale Watch (888-283-1776, www.7seas-whalewatch.com) offers a "Lighthouse & Lobstering Cruise" that includes this lighthouse and Ten Pound Island Light. The 65-foot schooner *Thomas Lannon* (978-281-6634, www.schooner.org) sails out of Gloucester Harbor daily in season. Some of the fundraising cruises held by the Thacher Island Association (www.thacherisland.org) provide views. Some of the lighthouse cruises offered by the Friends of the Boston Harbor Islands (781-740-4290, www.fbhi.org) and Boston Harbor Cruises (617-227-4321, www.bostonharborcruises.com) also pass by.

THACHER ISLAND TWIN LIGHTS

Fifty-acre Thacher Island—less than a mile off the east coast of Cape Ann—was named for Anthony Thacher, an Englishman whose vessel, the *Watch and Wait*, was wrecked in a ferocious storm near the island in 1635 on its way to Marblehead from Ipswich. Thacher and his wife, Elizabeth, were the only survivors of the wreck in which twenty-one people died.

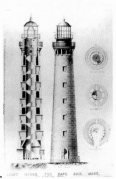

Plans for the 1861 towers

{ 233 }

Accessibility: 🔭 ⛵ 🏠 🛏

Geographic coordinates:

North Light: 42° 38' 24" N 70° 34' 30" W

South Light: 42° 38' 12" N 70° 34' 30" W

Nearest town: Rockport.

Established: 1771. Present lighthouses built: 1861. North light deactivated 1932, relighted as a private aid in 1989. South light automated in 1980.

Height of both towers: 124 feet. Height of focal plane: 166 feet

Optics: First-order Fresnel lenses. Present optics: VRB-25 (south light), 200 mm (north light).

Characteristic: Flashing red every 5 seconds (south light); fixed yellow (north light)

Fog signal: Two blasts every 60 seconds.

Two 45-foot stone lighthouse towers on Thacher Island, about 300 yards apart, were lighted for the first time on December 21, 1771. The twin lights were soon nicknamed "Ann's Eyes." Local patriots branded the first keeper, James Kirkwood, a Tory. In 1775, Minutemen arrived and removed Kirkwood, who managed to escape to Canada.

It was eventually decided that taller towers were needed. Twin towers, 124 feet high, were built in 1861. New Hampshire granite was used instead of local Cape Ann granite, which drew much criticism from locals. The lighthouses were fitted with enormous first-order Fresnel lenses, first illuminated on October 1, 1861.

Alexander Bray, a Civil War veteran, became principal keeper in 1864. On December 21, 1864, one of the assistant keepers fell ill with a fever. Keeper

Bray left for the mainland to take the ailing man to a doctor. The keeper's wife, Maria, was left in charge of the station. A heavy snowstorm blew in later that day, making it impossible for Alexander Bray to return to the island. Maria Bray braved the high winds and heavy snow to light the lamps in both towers. Each tower had 148 steps to the top, and Maria had to repeat the trip three times that night to keep the lamps supplied with oil and the lantern room panes free of soot. A second night passed before Alexander Bray could return to the island, and not once did Maria allow either light to go out. It was a happy Christmas when the Brays were reunited.

The north light was extinguished in 1932. The south light and the fog signal were automated in 1980, and the Coast Guard moved off the island. The first-order Fresnel lens was removed from the south tower; it's now on display at the Coast Guard Academy Museum in New London, Connecticut.

Concerned citizens of Cape Ann formed the Thacher Island Association in the 1980s. In 1989, the north light was restored and opened to visitors. It has since been relighted as a private aid to navigation. The town of Rockport's Thacher Island Committee, in partnership with the Thacher Island Association, now maintains and operates the island, under agreements with the Coast Guard and the U.S. Fish and Wildlife Service.

The twin lights can be seen from a few locations on shore in Rockport, including Marmion Way, Eden Road, Penzance Road and Emerson Point, and distantly from Long Beach on the Rockport/Gloucester line (on Route 127A). The Thacher Island Association (www.thacherisland.org) holds occasional lighthouse cruises that sometimes provide views. Harbor Tours, Inc. (978-283-1979), offers a lighthouse cruise that passes all five of the cape's lighthouses. Some of the lighthouse cruises offered by the Friends of the Boston Harbor Islands (781-740-4290, www.fbhi.org) and Boston Harbor Cruises (617-227-4321, www.bostonharborcruises.com) also include Thacher Island.

Members of the Thacher Island Association (www.thacherisland.org) can visit the island on Saturday and Wednesday mornings from July through the end of August (weather permitting) d. You must make reservations in advance by calling 617-599-2590. The Thacher Island launch only accommodates 12 passengers, and there are only three trips each Saturday morning and one on Wednesday morning.

You can also visit using your own small rowboat or kayak; larger boats cannot land on the ramp.Only small rowboats and kayaks are allowed to land on the ramp. Two guest moorings are available about 50 yards offshore. If you'd like to use one of these moorings, you must call the caretaker in advance at 617-599-2590. Bring a dinghy to land on the ramp. For more information about visiting the island, visit the Thacher Island's web site at www.thacherisland.org. A small campground (July to mid-September, small nightly fee) is available on the island. You must reserve by calling 617-599-2590.

Fascinating Fact

The original twin lighthouse,s built here in 1771 were the first in America to mark a dangerous spot (the Londoner Ledge to the southeast) rather than a harbor entrance. They were also the last lighthouses built under British rule in the colonies.

STRAITSMOUTH ISLAND LIGHT

Accessibility: 🚶‍♀️⛵

Geographic coordinates:
42° 39' 42" N   70° 35' 18" W

Nearest town: Rockport. Located a short distance off the northeast coast of Cape Ann.

Established: 1835. Present lighthouse built: 1896. Automated: 1967.

Height of tower: 37. Height of focal plane: 46 feet.

Earlier optic: Sixth-order Fresnel lens. Present optic: 250 mm.

Characteristic: Green flash every 6 seconds.

Fog signal: One blast every 15 seconds.

The town of Rockport grew up around an indentation in the northeastern part of Cape Ann known as Sandy Bay. It was determined that Straitsmouth Island, at the bay's southeastern end, would be an ideal place for a lighthouse to guide vessels toward the busy harbor at Pigeon Cove. Congress appropriated $5,000 for the lighthouse in 1834. A 19-foot lighthouse tower and a keeper's dwelling, both made of brick, were built on Straitsmouth Island in 1835. The first keeper was Benjamin Andrews.

A 24-foot octagonal stone tower at the northeast point of the island replaced the original lighthouse in 1851. A new wood-frame keeper's house was built in 1878, and the present 37-foot brick lighthouse replaced the 1850 tower in 1896.

The light was converted to automatic operation by the 1930s. The island, except for the lighthouse tower, was sold into private hands in 1941. The island was donated to the Massachusetts Audubon Society in 1967.

The abandoned house rapidly deteriorated. In the early 1980s, a local man did some renovation of the dwelling only to have his work immediately ruined by vandals. The house has continued to deteriorate, and there appears to be no hope that it will be saved. The "Perfect Storm" of October 1991 destroyed the old entryway to the tower, and the Coast Guard built a smaller entryway during the following year.

In July 2009, it was announced that ownership of the lighthouse tower would be conveyed to the Thacher Island Association, in accordance with the National Historic Light-house Preservation Act. The island is not accessible to the public. The lighthouse can be seen distantly from a breakwater at the end of Rockport's Bearskin Neck, a popular section with quaint studios, shops, and restaurants. The Thacher Island Association (www.thacherisland.org) holds occasional lighthouse cruises that might provide views. Harbor Tours, Inc. (978-283-1979, www.capeann harbortours.com), offers a lighthouse cruise that passes all five of Cape Ann's lighthouses.

Fascinating Fact

William Francis Gibbs, a naval architect who directed the production of cargo-carrying Liberty ships during World War II, was owner of Straitsmouth Island for a time.

ANNISQUAM LIGHT

Accessibility:

Geographic coordinates:
42° 39' 43" N 70° 40' 53" W

Nearest town: Gloucester. Located at Wigwam Point on the east side of the northern entrance to the Annisquam River.

Established: 1801. Present lighthouse built: 1897. Automated: 1974.

Height of tower: 41. Height of focal plane: 45 feet.

Earlier optic: Fifth-order Fresnel lens. Present optic: VRB-25.

Characteristic: White flash every 7.5 seconds with red sector.

Fog signal: Two blasts every 60 seconds.

The Annisquam River is actually an estuary that's open to the ocean at both ends. The northern end opens into Ipswich Bay, and the southern end connects to Gloucester Harbor via the Blynman Canal. Annisquam village, on the east side of the river's northern end, grew into a fishing and shipbuilding center that rivaled Gloucester Harbor in its early days.

Congress appropriated $2,000 in April 1800 for a lighthouse at the northwesterly point of Annisquam village. The first lighthouse was a 32-foot wooden tower. The original wood-frame keeper's house still stands today, enlarged and altered over the years.

On August 17, 1818, a newspaper reported, "The famous Sea Serpent, was seen on the 16th inst. near Squam Light House, by many persons, some of whom were within twenty feet of him." The serpent was said to be more than 130 feet long.

James Day, a Gloucester native, was named the first keeper. In 1805, President Thomas Jefferson approved the appointment of George Day to succeed his elderly father. George Day remained keeper for a remarkable 45 years.

He complained about the condition of the station in 1843: "Two years ago, the walk or bridge leading from the house to the tower was swept away by a heavy sea only a few minutes after I crossed it. I expect every storm that comes, the tower will be destroyed."

A new 40-foot octagonal wooden lighthouse tower was built in 1851. The lighthouse was rebuilt again in 1897 when the extant brick tower was erected on the same foundation as its predecessor. The lighthouse was automated in 1974. During a major restoration in 2000, about 3,000 bricks in the tower were replaced along with metal support beams.

A Coast Guard family lives at the station. Although there has been some limited access to the station in the past, there is no longer any public access. The road to the lighthouse is private, and there is no parking.

The lighthouse can be seen distantly from Gloucester's Wingaersheek Beach, across the river. Harbor Tours, Inc. (978-283-1979, www.capeann harbortours.com) offers a lighthouse cruise that passes all five of Cape Ann's lighthouses, and the Thacher Island Association (www.thacherisland.org) holds occasional lighthouse cruises that might provide views.

Fascinating Fact

Wigwam Point, the location of this lighthouse, is named for the longtime use of the spot as a summer gathering place for local Indians.

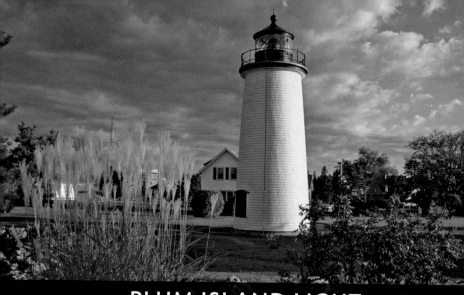

PLUM ISLAND LIGHT
(Newburyport Harbor Light)

Accessibility:

Geographic coordinates:
42° 48' 54" N 70° 49' 06" W

Nearest city: Newburyport. Located at the northern end of Plum Island, at the entrance to the Merrimack River.

Established: 1788. Present lighthouse built: 1898. Automated: 1951.

Height of tower:
35 feet. Height of focal plane: 50 feet.

Optic: Fourth-order Fresnel lens.

Characteristic: Green light occulting twice every 15 seconds.

Plum Island is a 9-mile-long barrier island off the northern coast of Massachusetts; the island's northern end is part of the city of Newburyport. The entrance to Newburyport's harbor was dangerous with shifting channels at the mouth of the Merrimack River. The General Court of Massachusetts authorized the building of two small wooden lighthouses in 1787, and they were completed in the following year.

The original two towers were built on movable foundations, so their positions could be changed easily as the sandbars around Plum Island shifted. After an 1808 tornado knocked both lighthouses to the ground, the towers were soon rebuilt. Congress appropriated $4,000 for the rebuilding of the lighthouses in July 1838, but it isn't clear if the towers were rebuilt or simply altered or repaired.

In 1855, a strange-looking small tower called the "Bug Light" was added, and one of the lighthouses was destroyed by fire a short time later. The shifting sands left the remaining lighthouse and the "Bug" too far inland. They were moved several times between 1870 and 1882. In 1898, the extant wooden lighthouse was built next to the old one.

The lighthouse is now cared for by the Friends of Plum Island Light. The grounds are open year round, and the lighthouse is open to the public on some summer weekend days. For information on open houses, contact the Friends of Plum Island Light, Inc., P.O. Box 381, Newburyport, MA 01950; www.lighthouse.cc/plumisland/

To reach the lighthouse from Route I-95, take exit 57 and follow Route 113 East for 3.8 miles. At a traffic light in Newbury, turn left onto Rolfe's Lane. After 0.6 miles, at the end of Rolfe's Lane, turn right onto the Plum Island Turnpike. After crossing the bridge onto Plum Island, take the second left onto Northern Boulevard. The lighthouse is near the end of Northern Boulevard, on your left. Curbside parking is available and there's a parking lot across the street (fee charged for the lot in summer). From downtown Newburyport, follow Water Street on to the Plum Island Turnpike and follow the directions above.

Fascinating Fact

The original lights here were fueled by whale oil. Keeper Lewis Lowell lit a charcoal fire under the lantern one cold night in 1823 to keep the oil from congealing. He was overcome and died at his post of asphyxiation.

NEWBURYPORT HARBOR RANGE LIGHT

Accessibility: 🚗

Geographic coordinates (rear range tower): 42° 48' 39" N 70° 51' 56" W

Nearest city: Newburyport. Located on Water Street in downtown Newburyport.

Established: 1873. Present lighthouses built: 1873. Deactivated: 1961.

Height of tower (rear tower): 53 feet. Height of tower (front tower): 15 feet.

Present optics: none.

The Lighthouse Board established a range light station in Newburyport Harbor in June 1873, with a conical cast-iron front range light on Bayley's Wharf and a square brick rear range tower. There was not a keeper's dwelling; the lights were serviced by local caretakers and later by the keepers at Plum Island.

The rear tower was raised to its present height of 53 feet in 1901. The range lights were discontinued in 1961. In 1964, the front range tower was moved a short distance to the grounds of Coast Guard Station Merrimack River. After its decommissioning, the rear range tower was bought by a private party.

In 1999, the Lighthouse Preservation Society launched a fundraising campaign to renovate the front range tower. Some renovation and painting of the tower has taken place in recent years. The society hopes to establish a memorial park at the lighthouse, commemorating Newburyport's role as the birthplace of the Coast Guard.

The Lighthouse Preservation Society also offers gourmet dinners at the top of the rear range tower. To make a reservation, contact the Lighthouse Preservation Society, 11 Seaborne Drive, Dover, NH 03820-4551. Phone: 603-740-0055 or 1-800-727-BEAM. Web site: www.lighthousepreservation. org.

Downtown Newburyport is easily accessible by taking I-95 exit 57 and following Route 113 to the east. Turn left on Fruit Street, and then turn right on Water Street. The rear tower is on Water Street, between Federal and Independent streets. There's street parking and parking lots nearby. The presence of numerous power lines makes it difficult to get a good photo. The parking lot for the Starboard Galley restaurant (55 Water Street) is just behind the lighthouse—a good place to stop for a meal while in Newburyport.

The front tower is just down the street on the grounds of Coast Guard Station Merrimack River. The grounds are not open to the public, but you can see the lighthouse through the fence from the restaurant parking lot. Another way to see both range lights is from seasonal harbor cruises aboard the *Yankee Clipper* (603-682-2293, www. harbortours.com), offering eco-tours and seal-watching tours on the Merrimack River. You also get a distant view of the lighthouse at Plum Island.

Fascinating Fact

Newburyport is considered the birthplace of the U.S. Coast Guard. The nation's first revenue cutter was launched here in 1791.

New Hampshire

New Hampshire has an abbreviated coastline (only 18 miles) but two very historic lighthouses. Portsmouth Harbor Light, established in 1771, was the first lighthouse north of Boston in the American colonies. The present (1878) tower is worth visiting during summer open houses. At other times, you can get excellent views of the lighthouse from adjacent Fort Constitution, along with a wide panorama of the mouth of the Pistacaqua River.

A great way to see this region and to learn about its legends and lore is to take advantage of the scenic cruising opportunities from Portsmouth and Rye. If you take a cruise to photograph White Island Light, you'll be pleased to discover that the rest of the islands are equally fascinating.

The two coastal lighthouses are the state's only official ones built by the federal government, but New Hampshire has some interesting lake lights established by private interests. The three wooden lighthouses on Lake Sunapee add to the considerable beauty of the lake, which you can soak in from the decks of the sightseeing vessel *Mt. Sunapee II*.

The state's largest lake, 72-square-mile Lake Winnipesaukee, has a small privately owned stone tower known as the Spindle Lighthouse. It was built as an observatory and not for navigation, but a distant view is available from scenic cruises on the M/V *Mount Washington*. The tall, wide tower near the lake on Brickyard Mountain that looks like a blue-and-white-striped lighthouse is actually a water tower and cell phone tower.

Prominent Whaleback Lighthouse is sometimes referred to as a New Hampshire attraction, but it's just over the border in Maine at the mouth of the Pistacaqua River.

New Hampshire Lighthouses

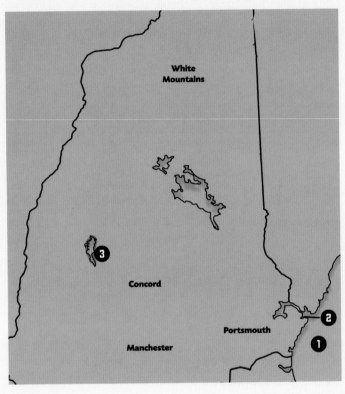

LIGHTHOUSE	PAGE
❶ White Island	247
❷ Portsmouth Harbor	249
❸ Lake Sunapee	252

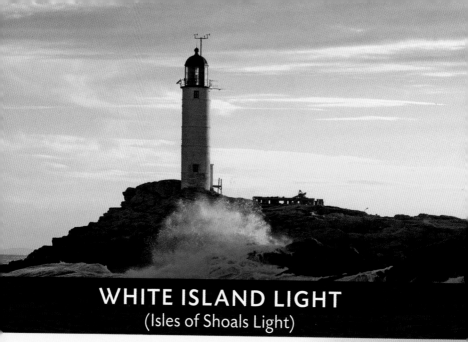

WHITE ISLAND LIGHT
(Isles of Shoals Light)

The Isles of Shoals are a cluster of nine islands located about six miles off the coast of New Hampshire and southern Maine. The islands were once home to a thriving fishing community. The first lighthouse on White Island, established in 1821, was a stone tower, later encased in wood.

Nineteenth-century view

Accessibility: ⛵

Geographic coordinates: 42° 58' 02" N 70° 37' 24" W

Nearest town: Rye. Located on the southern-most of the Isles of Shoals.

Established: 1821. Present lighthouse built: 1859. Automated: 1986.

Height of tower: 58 feet. Height of focal plane: 82 feet

Earlier optic: Second-order Fresnel lens. Present optic: VLB-44 (LED).

Characteristic: White flash every 15 seconds.

Fog signal: One blast every 30 seconds.

Thomas Laighton became keeper in 1839. His daughter, Celia, later gained widespread fame as Celia Thaxter, poet and author. In her book, *Among the Isles of Shoals*, Celia described the family's arrival at White Island: "It was at sunset in autumn that we were set ashore on that loneliest, lovely rock, where the lighthouse looked down on us like some tall, black-capped giant, and filled me with awe and wonder."

A new 58-foot brick lighthouse tower was built in 1859. The tower was fitted with a second-order Fresnel lens. In 1993, White Island became the property of the State of New Hampshire. Over the years, the lighthouse tower developed major cracks in its brick exterior. Seventh-grade students in North Hampton, New Hampshire, along with a science teacher, Sue Reyn-

olds, started an organization called the Lighthouse Kids, dedicated to the preservation of the lighthouse.

In 2005, money raised by the Lighthouse Kids was combined with a federal grant and state funds to allow a restoration of the tower. More than 1,000 bricks were replaced, and the brick courses were strengthened with the addition of stainless steel ties. Visit www.lighthousekids.com for more on the Lighthouse Kids.

In 2008, the rotating VRB-25 optic that had been in use at White Island for several years was replaced by a VLB-44 light emitting diode (LED) unit.

You can see the lighthouse very distantly from some points on the mainland, but it's best seen by boat. You can see it from sightseeing cruises offered by Portsmouth Harbor Cruises (603-436-8084, www.portsmouthharbor.com) and the Isles of Shoals Steamship Company (603-431-5500, www.islesofshoals.com) in Portsmouth. The Friends of Portsmouth Harbor Lighthouse hold lighthouse cruises periodically; check www.portsmouthharborlighthouse.org for the schedule. Island Cruises (603-964-6446, www.uncleoscar.com), leaving from Rye Harbor, also provides Isles of Shoals tours.

Fascinating Fact

The characteristic of the original lighthouse was unusually patriotic for a time, with red, white, and blue flashes. The blue flash was quickly discontinued because of its poor visibility.

PORTSMOUTH HARBOR LIGHT
(Fort Point Light)

The first lighthouse here was lighted by early July 1771. The shingled tower at Fort William and Mary on Great Island, a mile from the mouth of the Piscataqua River, was about 50 feet tall.

Early 1900s view

Accessibility:

Geographic coordinates: 43° 04' 18" N 70° 42' 30" W

Nearest town: New Castle. Located on the northeast point of Great Island, on the Piscataqua River.

Established: 1771. Present lighthouse built: 1878. Automated: 1960.

Height of tower: 48 feet. Height of focal plane: 52 feet

Optic: Fourth-order Fresnel lens.

Characteristic: Fixed green.

Fog signal: One blast every 10 seconds.

Present optic: VLB-44 (LED).

In 1793, President George Washington ordered that the light be maintained at all times, with a keeper living on site. A new 80-foot-tall octagonal wooden tower was constructed in 1804, about 100 yards east of the 1771 tower. A new 48-foot cast-iron tower was erected in 1878 on the same foundation as the 1804 tower. In fact, the new lighthouse was assembled inside the old one, which was eventually removed.

The keeper who served the longest was Joshua Card, who retired at the age of eighty-six in 1909 after thirty-five years at the station. When people would ask Card what the "K" on his uniform stood for, he'd tell them, "Captain."

Keeper Joshua Card

Elson Small became keeper in 1946. He and his wife, Connie, left the lighthouse in 1948 when the Coast Guard moved in and made the site their station for Portsmouth Harbor. Years later, Connie Small wrote the book, *The Lighthouse Keeper's Wife*. Connie, who lived to the age of 103, gave hundreds of lectures on lighthouse life.

A chapter of the American Lighthouse Foundation, the Friends of Portsmouth Harbor Lighthouses, was founded in 2001 to care for the lighthouse. The group holds periodic open houses in summer as well as cruises and other events. See www.portsmouthharbor lighthouse.org for more information.

The grounds of adjacent Fort Constitution are open to the public during the day, but visitors are not allowed into the area near the lighthouse except during open houses. To reach the lighthouse from I-95, take exit 5 (Portsmouth Circle). Follow the signs for the Route 1 Bypass South. At the sixth traffic light (two miles from the traffic circle), turn left onto Elwyn Road (the sign says To Route 1A). Follow for 1.4 miles to a small traffic circle. Take the exit for Route 1A north and follow for .4 mile to the intersection with Route 1B. Turn right onto Route 1B. About

2.2 miles from the turn onto Route 1B, you'll see signs for the Coast Guard Station Portsmouth Harbor and Fort Constitution. Follow these signs to the right and proceed to the free parking area for Fort Constitution. You can see the lighthouse from the fort. (From downtown Portsmouth, follow Marcy Street along the waterfront past Prescott Park and follow the signs for Route 1B, New Castle. The Coast Guard station and lighthouse are about 2.5 miles from Prescott Park.)

The lighthouse can also be seen from sightseeing cruises leaving Portsmouth offered by Portsmouth Harbor Cruises (603-436-8084, www.portsmouth harbor.com) and the Isles of Shoals Steamship Company (603-431-5500, www.islesofshoals.com), as well from

Fascinating Fact

The first lighthouse established here in 1771 was the first lighthouse in the American colonies north of Boston.

cruises leaving Kittery Point (207-439-3655, www.capandpatty.com). Friends of Portsmouth Harbor Lighthouses offers periodic lighthouse cruises; check www.portsmouthharborlighthouse.org for the schedule. New England Lighthouse Tours offers van trips to this lighthouse and others, based in Portsmouth, NH; see www.newenglandlight housetours.com or call 603-431-9155.

LAKE SUNAPEE LIGHTHOUSES

Herrick Cove Light.

Ten-mile-long, three-mile-wide Lake Sunapee (about a half-hour's drive northwest of Concord, and a 90-minute drive from Portsmouth) has drawn summer vacationers for well over a century. Vacationers in the late 1800s arrived at the lake by train and then boarded steamships to get to their destinations around the lake. A number of large resort hotels and private estates lined the lake's shores.

In 1891, the steamer *Edmond Burke* struck an underwater ledge. This led to the construction of a lighthouse for $400 on Loon Island in 1893. The builders were the Woodsum Brothers, owners of the steamships that serviced the lake. Two other small wooden lighthouses were also built in the 1890s. All of them are now owned by the state of New Hampshire's Marine Patrol Bureau and maintained by the Lake Sunapee Protection Association (603-763-2210, www.lakesunapee.org).

Lightning struck Loon Island Lighthouse in 1960, and it burned down. It was promptly rebuilt. Burkehaven Lighthouse, destroyed by ice in 1935, was rebuilt by the Lake Sunapee Protective Association in 1983. In 2003, Herrick Cove Lighthouse was lifted by helicopter for a thorough renovation.

Fascinating Fact

In October 2003, Herrick Cove Lighthouse was lifted by helicopter off its base for a thorough renovation.

All three of the lighthouses can be seen from narrated trips offered by Lake Sunapee Cruises aboard the *Mt. Sunapee II* (603-938-6465, www.sunapeecruises. com). To reach the dock from I-89 in New Hampshire, take exit 12 from the south or exit 12A from the north, and follow Route 11 to Sunapee. Follow the signs for Sunapee Harbor (left onto Main Street at a flashing traffic light). For more on visiting the Lake Sunapee region, visit www.lakesunapeenh.org.

Burkehaven Light

Loon Island Light

Maine

There's no doubt that lighthouses rank as one of the most ubiquitous icons of the Pine Tree State, right up there with lobsters, maple syrup, and moose. Several of the state's light stations are as breathtaking as any you'll find in the world.

The state's coastline is long and ragged, with some 3,500 miles of shore (5,000 if you include islands) twisting along sandy beaches, rocky peninsulas, lobster-boat-filled harbors, and sparkling bays. The Maine coast is probably best appreciated by cruising along it, and the opportunities for public sightseeing cruises are plentiful.

As commerce developed in Portland after the American Revolution, Portland Head was the site selected in 1791 for the state's first lighthouse, Portland Head Light. Ultimately, five additional light stations were established in the Casco Bay region, making it a prime destination for lighthouse peepers.

One of the most beautiful and lighthouse-rich parts of Maine is the midcoast region and Penobscot Bay. Rockland is home to the nation's largest collection of lighthouse lenses at the Maine Lighthouse Museum. Some of the area's lighthouses can be reached by car, but many of them can only be viewed from a boat or from the air.

Too many tourists never make it father north than Acadia National Park and Bar Harbor. Some natives will tell you that the "real" Maine coast doesn't start until you get past that area. Lighthouse buffs with time for the drive will want to make it all the way to the nation's easternmost lighthouse at West Quoddy Head.

Maine's coastal communities range from relatively unspoiled fishing villages like Port Clyde and Stonington to noisier tourist havens like Boothbay Harbor and Camden. The more touristy towns might be better visited in the spring or fall rather than in the heart of the summer. Fog can crop up at any time but is less likely in the fall—another reason why that's one of the best times of the year to visit the Maine coast.

Southern Maine to the
Midcoast Lighthouses

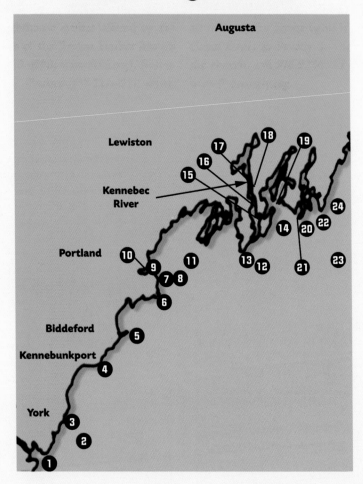

Augusta

Lewiston

Kennebec
River

Portland

Biddeford

Kennebunkport

York

Midcoast and Northern
Maine Lighthouses

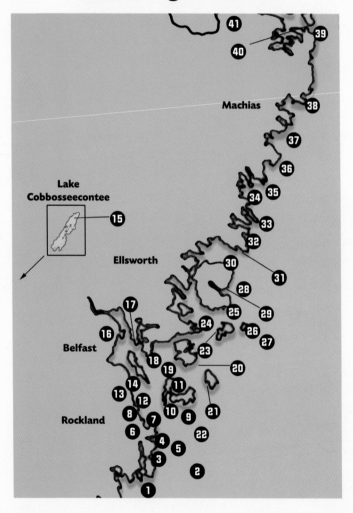

LIGHTHOUSE	PAGE

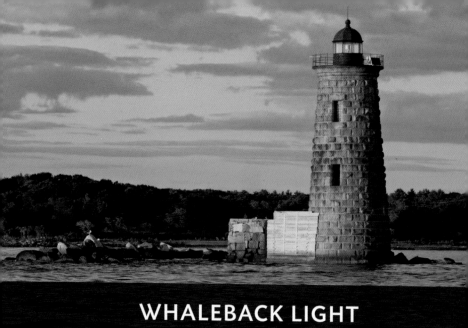

WHALEBACK LIGHT

Accessibility: 🏕 ⛵

Geographic coordinates:
43° 03' 31" N 70° 41' 48" W

Nearest town: Kittery. Located on a ledge at the entrance to the Piscataqua River.

Established: 1830. Present lighthouse built: 1872. Automated: 1963.

Height of tower: 50 feet. Height of focal plane: 59 feet

Earlier optic: Fourth-order Fresnel lens.

Present optic: VLB-44 (LED)

Characteristic: Two white flashes every 10 seconds.

Fog signal: Two blasts every 30 seconds.

The first lighthouse on Whaleback Ledge leaked badly in storms and heavy seas. Some wooden sheathing was added around the tower in 1837. This apparently helped the problem of the tower leaking, but keeper Samuel E. Hascall reported that during one great storm on July 7, 1837, the shaking of the tower was so violent that "some of the small stones of the tower were shaken out and fell upon the floors of the rooms, and articles of furniture were displaced by the motion of the tower."

In 1871, keeper Ferdinand Barr, a Civil War veteran, drowned in heavy seas while away from the lighthouse tending his lobster traps. He was about thirty years old and left his wife and three children.

A new tower was erected in 1872 for $75,000. The lighthouse was constructed of granite blocks dovetailed together in similar fashion to Minot's Ledge Light in Massachusetts. In 1878, a new iron tower was constructed next to the lighthouse to serve as a signal house for a new Daboll fog trumpet. The iron tower, which was a little more than half the height of the lighthouse, no longer stands.

In 2007, under the provisions of the National Historic Lighthouse Preservation Act, the lighthouse was made available to a suitable new steward. The American Lighthouse Foundation and its chapter, the Friends of Portsmouth Harbor Lighthouses, submitted a successful application. See www. lighthousefoundation.org and www. whalebacklighthouse.org for more information.

Whaleback Light can be seen from Fort Constitution, Fort Stark, and Odiorne Point on the New Hampshire coast. The closest mainland view is from the

Fascinating Fact

Surprisingly, although it's on the Maine side of the border, this lighthouse is south of Portsmouth Harbor Lighthouse in New Hampshire.

Maine side, at Fort Foster in Kittery. From Route 1 in Kittery, head east on Route 103 for 3.4 miles. Bear right onto Chauncey Creek Road. In about a half mile, turn right on Gerrish Island Lane and cross a bridge, then bear right onto Pocahontas Road and follow to the park entrance. From Memorial Day to Labor Day, there's a fee to drive into park. The gate to the park is closed in the off-season, but you can park outside the gate and walk in. For more information, call 207-439-3800.

The lighthouse can also be seen from cruises leaving Portsmouth offered by Portsmouth Harbor Cruises (603-436-8084, www.portsmouthharbor. com) and the Isles of Shoals Steamship Company (603-431-5500, www.islesof shoals.com), as well from cruises leaving Kittery Point (207-439-3655, www. capandpatty.com).

BOON ISLAND LIGHT

Accessibility: 🚻 ⛵

Geographic coordinates:
43° 07' 18" N   70° 28' 36" W

Nearest town: York. Located on a small island (approximately 400 square yards) about six miles southeast of Cape Neddick.

Established: 1811. Present lighthouse built: 1855. Automated: 1978.

Height of tower: 133 feet. Height of focal plane: 137 feet

Earlier optic: Second-order Fresnel lens. Present optic: VRB-25.

Characteristic: White flash every 5 seconds.

Fog signal: One blast every 10 seconds.

Before a lighthouse was established on this remote pile of granite off the southern Maine coast, shipwrecks on the island were not uncommon. The most famous was the wreck of the British ship *Nottingham Galley* on December 11, 1710. The survivors struggled to stay alive for over three weeks, finally resorting to cannibalism. After the *Nottingham Galley* disaster, local fishermen began leaving barrels of provisions on Boon Island in case of future wrecks.

An unlighted wooden 50-foot tower was erected on the island in 1799; a stone day beacon succeeded it in 1805. The island's first lighthouse was completed in late 1811. The first keeper, after witnessing the vulnerability of the low island to storms, left after only a few weeks. The lighthouse was destroyed by a storm in 1831 and was soon rebuilt, with a light exhibited 32 feet above the sea. The present granite lighthouse was constructed between 1852 and 1854, along with a new dwelling. The tower's second-order Fresnel lens went into operation on January 1, 1855.

Captain William C. Williams, a native of Kittery, served as keeper from 1885 to 1911. In an 1888 storm, Williams and the others on the island had to take refuge at the top of the tower for three days. One Thanksgiving, Williams and his assistants were unable to go ashore to buy a turkey. Providence intervened when a dozen black ducks smashed into the tower, providing the keepers with their Thanksgiving dinner.

The destructive blizzard of early February 1978 flooded the keeper's house and scattered boulders around like they were pebbles. The Coast Guard keepers were forced to take refuge in the tower; on the following day

SIDE TRIP: *Kittery Historical & Naval Museum*

This small museum next to Kittery Town Hall displays items and artifacts that reflect Kittery's rich past. Of special interest to lighthouse fans is the enormous second-order Fresnel lens that once served inside Boon Island Lighthouse. There are also ship models, old maps, scrimshaw, navigation instruments, a sea chest, a diving suit, and much more. The museum is open from June to Columbus Day, Tuesday through Saturday.

Kittery Historical & Naval Museum, Rogers Road Extension
P.O. Box 453
Kittery, ME 03904
Phone: 207-439-3080

Nineteenth-century view

they were removed by helicopter. The light was automated a short time later, and the remains of the keeper's house were destroyed.

In May 2000, the lighthouse was licensed by the Coast Guard to the American Lighthouse Foundation. On April 1, 2003, the "Republic of Boon Island" declared its (fictional) independence in an effort to raise funds for preservation by selling citizenships and political offices. For more information, visit the American Lighthouse Foundation web site at www.lighthousefounda tion.org or call 207-594-4174.

The slender tower can be seen very distantly from locations on the coast of southern Maine, including Sohier Park in York. Better views are available from occasional lighthouse cruises leaving Portsmouth offered by the Isles of Shoals Steamship Company (603-431-5500, www.islesofshoals.com). Friends of Portsmouth Harbor Lighthouse also holds lighthouse cruises periodically; check www.portsmouthharborlight house.org for the schedule.

Fascinating Fact

This is the tallest lighthouse tower in New England.

CAPE NEDDICK LIGHT
(Nubble Light)

The placement of a lighthouse on the island known as the Nubble, about two miles north of York Harbor, had been urged by local mariners since 1807. Congress finally appropriated $15,000 in 1874. The cast-iron tower, lined with brick, was first illuminated on July 1, 1879.

Early 1900s view

Accessibility: 🚡 ⛵

Geographic coordinates: 43° 09' 54" N   70° 35' 30" W

Nearest town: York. Located on a small island off the eastern tip of Cape Neddick.

Established: 1879. Present lighthouse built: 1879. Automated: 1987.

Height of tower: 41 feet. Height of focal plane: 88 feet.

Optic: Fourth-order Fresnel lens.

Characteristic: 3 seconds red alternating with 3 seconds darkness.

Fog signal: One blast every 10 seconds.

The station originally had a fog bell operated by automatic striking machinery. For a time, the Nubble's 3,000-pound fog bell could be heard by the keepers at Boon Island, six miles away.

On March 20, 1927, Eva Kimball, daughter of Keeper Fairfield Moore, went into labor during a severe snowstorm. Keeper Moore rowed across the channel and picked up a local doctor. The two men returned to the Nubble just in time for the last seconds of the birth of Eva's daughter, Barbara. Barbara lived at the lighthouse until she was six. Her favorite memory was accompanying her grandfather to the top of the tower to light the lamp.

The usual way of getting to and from the Nubble was by boat. For a time, the keepers used a bucket suspended on a line across the channel to the mainland to transport supplies. Around 1967, Coast Guard keeper David Winchester started putting his two children in the bucket each morning to send them on their way to school. A photographer snapped a picture of seven-year-old Ricky Winchester in the bucket, and the photo appeared widely in newspapers. When the district commander saw the picture, arrangements were made for the children to board on the mainland during the week.

The station was leased to the town of York in 1989. Under the Maine Lights Program, the lighthouse and other buildings officially became the property of the town in 1998. A volunteer group, the Friends of Nubble Light, provides support: Friends of Nubble Light, 186 York Street, York, ME 03909. Phone: 207-363-3078.

The lighthouse and other buildings are illuminated with white lights in the Christmas season. The view of the Nubble Light from York's Sohier Park is one of the most photographed scenes on the New England coast. There's a welcome center with a gift shop and restrooms (open from early May to Columbus Day) at the park, along with ample free parking. From I-95, take exit 7 and bear right at the lights onto Route 1 South. Turn left at a traffic light onto Route 1A. Travel one mile to a monument and bear left. Continue 0.6 miles and turn right onto Long Sands Road. Follow Long Sands Road to a stop sign; this is the intersection with Long Beach Avenue. Take a left onto Long Beach Avenue. The ocean and Long Sands Beach will be on your right. After passing the beach, turn right onto Nubble Road. After about a mile you'll see the entrance to Sohier Park on your right.

The lighthouse can also be seen from daily cruises offered by Finestkind Scenic Cruises (207-646-5227, www.finestkindcruises.com), leaving from Perkins Cove in Ogunquit, just up the road from York. The Isles of Shoals Steamship Company (603-431-5500, www.islesofshoals.com) offers occasional lighthouse cruises leaving Portsmouth, NH, that include a view of the Nubble Light, as do the Friends of Portsmouth Harbor Lighthouse; check www.portsmouthharborlighthouse.org for the schedule. New England Lighthouse Tours, based in Portsmouth, NH, offers van trips to this lighthouse and others; see www.newenglandlighthousetours.com or call 603-431-9155.

SIDE TRIP:
Lighthouse Depot

Any lighthouse buff will want to make a stop at Lighthouse Depot, the world's largest lighthouse gift store. There are more lighthouse collectibles here than you can imagine—clothing, jewelry, art, Harbour Lights replicas, and much more. Those interested in reading more about lighthouse history will appreciate the extensive book selection. The store is on Route 1 in Wells and is easily accessible by taking exit 19 (Wells/Sanford) from I-95; take a left onto Route 109 East and then turn left onto Route 1 North. The store will be on your left in less than two miles.

Lighthouse Depot
U.S. Route 1 North (2178 Post Road)
Wells, ME 04090
Phone: 1-800-758-1444
Web site: www.lhdepot.com

Fascinating Fact

In 1842, the bark *Isidore* was wrecked north of the Nubble near Bald Head Cliff. The vessel, according to legend, still reappears as a ghost ship with a phantom crew.

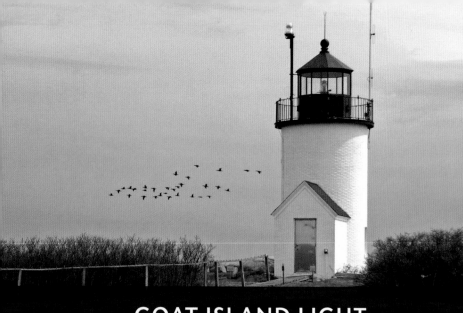

GOAT ISLAND LIGHT

Accessibility: 🏛

Geographic coordinates: 43° 21' 30" N 70° 25' 30" W

Nearest town: Kennebunkport. Located about a half-mile offshore from Cape Porpoise.

Established: 1833. Present lighthouse built: 1859. Automated: 1990.

Height of tower: 25 feet. Height of focal plane: 38 feet

Earlier optic: Fifth-order Fresnel lens. Present optic: VLB-44 (LED).

Characteristic: White flash every 6 seconds.

Fog signal: One blast every 15 seconds.

Goat Island Light was established in August 1833 to help guide mariners into the sheltered harbor at Cape Porpoise, a busy fishing center for many years. A 20-foot stone tower and dwelling were built, and John Lord of Kennebunk became the first keeper at a salary of $350 per year.

Early 1900s view

The extant brick tower and a new dwelling were built in 1859. Dangerous rocks in the vicinity continued to claim vessels, including forty-six between 1865 and 1920. There was not one death in all the wrecks, partly due to the keepers at Goat Island picking up survivors near the island.

Coast Guard keeper Joseph Bakken, who lived on Goat Island with his wife and three children, had a memorable experience during a severe storm in 1947. The waves washed over the island, damaging the boat slip and ripping out a fence. In the commotion the family forgot about their dog and her newborn puppies. Later that night, Bakken went into the cellar and found several feet of water. Floating in the seawater was the box that contained the dog and her puppies. All were safe and sound, and the keeper brought them upstairs out of harm's way.

This was the last lighthouse in Maine to be automated (1990). Brad Culp, his wife, Lisa, and their two children, Christian and Dakota, were Maine's last traditional lighthouse family.

In 1998, the lighthouse became the property of the Kennebunkport Conservation Trust (www.thekenne bunkportconservationtrust. org). Work

Fascinating Fact

For a time during the presidency of George H. W. Bush, secret service agents lived at Goat Island, which offers a good vantage point on Bush's estate at Walker's Point. The island served as an air-sea command center complete with a radar beacon.

began in 2011 to rebuild the station's fog bell tower and the walkway between the house and tower as part of a $380,000 restoration project.

Visitors with private boats are welcome to land at the island. The lighthouse can be seen at a distance from the public wharf in Cape Porpoise. From Route 1, take Route 9 to Kennebunkport. Continue to Cape Porpoise. Where the road takes a 90-degree turn to the left, continue straight onto Pier Road. Continue about 0.6 miles to the end at the town wharf. At low tide, it's possible to walk part of the way to the island for a closer look.

WOOD ISLAND LIGHT

Accessibility: 🚻 ⛵ 🏠

Geographic coordinates:
43° 27' 25" N   70° 19' 45" W

Nearest town: Biddeford.
Located on a 35-acre island
about a half mile northeast
of Biddeford Pool, about two
miles east of the mouth of
the Saco River.

Established: 1808.
Present lighthouse built:
1858. Automated: 1986.

Height of tower:
47 feet. Height of focal
plane: 71 feet.

Earlier optic: Fourth-order
Fresnel lens. Present optic:
VLB-44 (LED).

Characteristic: Alternating
white and green flash every
10 seconds.

Fog signal: Two blasts every
30 seconds.

The village of Biddeford Pool gets its name from a tidal inlet known simply as "The Pool," bounded by Fletcher's Neck to the south and Hills Beach to the north. Because Fletcher's Neck was considered a hazard to navigation, Congress appropriated $5,000 for a lighthouse on nearby Wood Island in March 1806.

Keeper Thomas Orcutt and his dog, Sailor

The original tower lasted until 1839, when a new 45-foot conical granite tower was built, along with new one-story granite dwelling. The extant stone tower was completed in 1858.

One of the best-known keepers in Wood Island's history was Thomas H. Orcutt, a veteran sea captain who was in charge from 1886 until his death in 1905. Orcutt had a pet that gained national fame. His dog, Sailor, became famous for ringing the station's fog bell with his mouth (or paws, according to one account). The dog was said to possess almost human intelligence. Sailor also served as a messenger, delighting in carrying letters and other small articles in his mouth. It was claimed that he understood all that was said to him.

In 2003, a chapter of the American Lighthouse Foundation was formed to care for the light station: Friends of Wood Island Lighthouse, P. O. Box 26, Biddeford Pool, ME 04006. Web site: www.woodislandlighthouse.org. In 2009–10, the lighthouse tower was restored. At this writing, the restoration of the keeper's house is slated to begin soon.

The lighthouse can be seen from a trail along the water at the East Point Audubon Sanctuary in Biddeford Pool.

Take Route 9/208 (Pool Road) south from Biddeford for five miles, turning left on 208 toward Biddeford Pool. After 0.6 miles, turn left at the T intersection, and then bear right through two forks to Lester B. Orcutt Boulevard, following it to the point. The gate entrance is on the left side. Parking is permitted along the street. It's about a 15-minute walk from the gate to the view of the island.

The volunteers of Friends of Wood Island Lighthouse offer tours of the light station during the summer, leaving from Vines Landing in Biddeford Pool. The boat takes 17 to 18 adults. The trip and tour take about 90 minutes. Call 207-286-3229 for reservations; see www.woodislandlighthouse. org/schedule.htm for the schedule and more infor mation.

Fascinating Fact

In 1972, the Coast Guard removed the lantern, and a rotating aerobeacon was installed. The public complained about the "headless" lighthouse, so the lantern was returned.

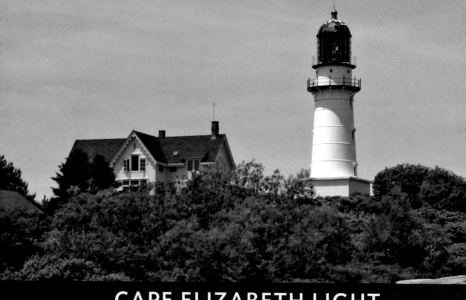

CAPE ELIZABETH LIGHT
(Two Lights)

Accessibility: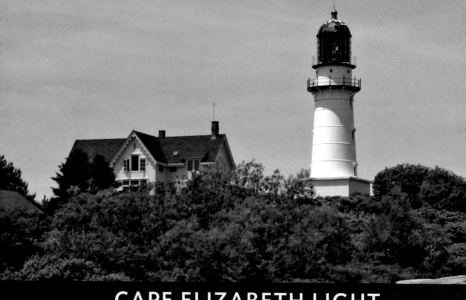

Geographic coordinates: 43° 33' 56" N 70° 12' 00" W

Nearest town: Cape Elizabeth. Located at the southern entrance to Casco Bay.

Established: 1828. Present lighthouse built: 1874. Automated: 1963.

Height of tower: 67 feet. Height of focal plane: 129 feet

Earlier optic: Second-order Fresnel lens. Present optic: VRB-25.

Characteristic: Four white flashes every 15 seconds.

Fog signal: Two blasts every 60 seconds.

To help mark the southern approach to Portland's harbor, a stone day beacon was erected in 1811 at Cape Elizabeth, about eight miles southeast of Portland. The stone marker was torn down in 1827 to make way for a pair of 65-foot rubble-stone lighthouses, built for $4,250. Elisha Jordan was appointed first keeper at a salary of $450 per year. The original towers were replaced in 1874 by 67-foot cast-iron towers 300 yards apart. Second-order Fresnel lenses were installed in both towers.

On January 28, 1885, a storm hit and increased in severity as the night progressed. Keeper Marcus Hanna sounded the fog whistle all night despite being ill with a cold and exhausted. Assistant keeper Hiram Staples relieved Hanna at 6:00 a.m. The keeper had to crawl through enormous snowdrifts back to the house. After Hanna was asleep, his wife looked out toward the ocean and saw a schooner aground near the fog signal building. The captain had already been swept away by the waves; only two crew members remained alive. The men had climbed to the rigging and were practically frozen alive in the bitter cold.

Keeper Marcus Hanna

Hanna and Staples hurried to the edge of the water near the schooner. Hanna said later, "I felt a terrible responsibility thrust upon me, and I resolved to attempt the rescue at any hazard." He tried a number of times to throw a line to the vessel but failed. Practically frozen, he waded waist-deep into the ocean and again threw a line to the schooner, this time hitting his target. The two crewmen were hauled safely to shore. After two days they had recovered enough to be taken to Portland by sled. Six months later, Hanna received a gold lifesaving medal for "heroism involving great peril to his life."

During World War I, military personnel patrolled the grounds around the station. One of the assistant keepers at the time was James Anderson. His daughter, Edwina Davis, later recalled that the soldiers swept off a pond so the lighthouse families could ice skate. Edwina and the other lighthouse children walked four miles each way to school every day.

After some military use in World War II, the west tower (deactivated in 1924) passed into private ownership. The 1878 Victorian principal keeper's house next to the east tower is now privately owned. The light in the east tower was automated in 1963, and the 1,800-pound second order Fresnel lens was removed in 1994. The lens is now on display at Cape Elizabeth Town Hall at 320 Ocean House Road.

In May 2000, Cape Elizabeth Light (the east tower) was licensed by the Coast Guard to the American Lighthouse Foundation (ALF). In the fall of

2008, ALF contracted Leslie Masonry to carry out repairs on the lighthouse's base. The grounds immediately around the lighthouse are not open to the public. For a good view, take Two Lights Road to the southeast from Route 77 in Cape Elizabeth (at a sign for Two Lights State Park). At a fork, bear left and follow to the end of Two Lights Road. There is free parking, often crowded in summer. You can also walk out onto the granite ledges near the parking area for a view of both the east and west towers. Adjacent Two Lights State Park encompasses 41 acres of rocky headlands and includes picnic sites; call 207-799-5871 for information.

Fascinating Fact

The deactivated west tower at Cape Elizabeth was owned for a time by actor Gary Merrill (Bette Davis's ex-husband).

The west tower

PORTLAND HEAD LIGHT

Portland was one of America's busiest ports, but Maine had no lighthouses before seventy-four merchants petitioned the government for a light to mark the entrance to Portland Harbor. A stone lighthouse was completed in January 1791. President Washington appointed Captain Joseph Greenleaf, a Revolutionary War veteran, to be the first keeper.

Keeper Joshua Strout

Accessibility:

Geographic coordinates:
43° 37' 24" N 70° 12' 30" W

Nearest town: Cape Elizabeth. Located at the southern approach to Portland Harbor, Casco Bay.

Established: 1791.
Present lighthouse built: 1791.
Automated: 1989.

Height of tower: 80 feet.
Height of focal plane: 101 feet.

Earlier optic: Fourth-order Fresnel lens (1855); Second-order Fresnel lens (1864); Fourth-order Fresnel lens (1883); Second-order Fresnel lens (1885); Present optic: DCB 224.

Characteristic: White flash every 4 seconds.

Fog signal: One blast every 15 seconds.

Captain Joshua Strout, a native of Cape Elizabeth and a former sea captain, became keeper in 1869 for $620 per year. Strout's wife, Mary, became assistant keeper at a salary of $480 per year. Joshua and Mary's son Joseph became keeper in 1904, and he remained until 1928, ending fifty-nine years of the Strout family at Portland Head.

In 1910, Joseph Strout was quoted in the *Lewiston Journal*: "We've all got the lighthouse fever in our blood. . . . Father was named for Captain Joshua Freeman. He kept the light, too, Captain Freeman did, in the days when they burned whale oil and had sixteen lamps. Old Cap'n Freeman used to sit in a big armchair with a coil of rope near him so if a shipwreck came sudden he would be prepared."

With the completion of Halfway Rock Light in Casco Bay in 1871, the Lighthouse Board felt that Portland Head Light had become less important. The tower was shortened by 20 feet in 1883, and the second-order lens was replaced by a weaker fourth-order lens. This met with many complaints. A year later, the tower was restored to its former height and a second-order lens was again installed. A new Victorian two-family keeper's house was built in 1891.

On Christmas Eve, 1886, the British bark *Annie C. Maguire* ran ashore on the rocks at Portland Head. The Strouts helped all aboard get safely to shore.

The lighthouse is in Fort Williams Park, and the grounds are open all year from sunrise to sunset. There's ample parking and plenty of room for picnicking or strolling. The Museum

at Portland Head Light opened in the former keeper's house in 1992. (Note: the lighthouse tower itself is not open to the public.) The museum is open daily from Memorial Day to the Friday following Columbus Day. From mid-April to Memorial Day and from Columbus Day to just before Christmas, the museum is open weekends only. Among the displays are a portion of the tower's old second-order lens and a fifth-order lens from Squirrel Point. There's also a gift shop in a former garage. For more information, contact the Museum at Portland Head Light, 1000 Shore Road, Cape Elizabeth, ME 04107. Phone 207-799-2661. Web site: www. portlandheadlight.com.

Maine's oldest lighthouse is easily accessible by land. From I-295 in Portland, take Route 77 South to South Portland. Turn left on Broadway, then right on Cottage Road. Cottage Road becomes Shore Road at the Cape Elizabeth town line. Follow to the entrance to Fort Williams Park and the lighthouse. You can also take Route 1 North to Oak Hill in Scarborough. Turn right onto Route 207, and then turn left onto Route 77 North to Cape Elizabeth. Turn right at a flashing traffic light onto Shore Road and follow to

Fascinating Fact

Poet Henry Wadsworth Longfellow, who was born in Portland, was a frequent visitor to Portland Head Light in his younger years. His poem, "The Lighthouse," was probably inspired by his many hours there.

Fort Williams Park.

You can get a view from the water from some of the cruises offered by the following companies: Lucky Catch Cruises (207-761-0941, www.lucky catch.com), Ophelia's Odyssey (207-590-3145, captainsearles.tripod.com), and Casco Bay Lines (207-774-7871, www.cascobaylines.com). Portland Discovery (207-774-6498, www.portland discovery.com) has a "Lighthouse Lovers Cruise" that includes Portland Head Light. Also, their "Land and Sea Tour" and "Portland Trolley Tour" both include a stop at Portland Head Light. New England Lighthouse Tours (603-431-9155, www.newenglandlight housetours.com), based in Portsmouth, NH, offers van trips to this lighthouse and others.

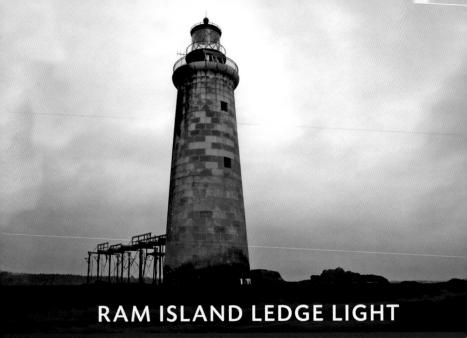

RAM ISLAND LEDGE LIGHT

Accessibility:

Geographic coordinates:
43° 37' 54" N 70° 11' 12" W

Nearest town: Cape Elizabeth. Located about one mile offshore on the southern approach to Portland Harbor, Casco Bay.

Established: 1905. Present lighthouse built: 1905. Automated: 1959.

Height of tower: 90 feet. Height of focal plane: 77 feet.

Earlier optic: Third-order Fresnel lens. Present optic: 300 mm.

Characteristic: Two white flashes every 6 seconds.

Fog signal: One blast every 10 seconds.

In 1902, Congress appropriated funds for the building of a lighthouse on Ram Island Ledge, about a mile offshore from Portland Head. The ledge was submerged much of the time, meaning that construction could only take place at low tide. The first stones were laid on Ram Island Ledge in July 1903. By the end of September, the tower reached a height of 32 feet. A crew of 25 men worked from April to July 1904 to complete the tower.

The first head keeper was William C. Tapley, who served until 1929. There were three keepers assigned to the station. Each man stayed for two weeks, with daily 12-hour shifts, followed by a week of shore leave. The keepers lived inside the tower. The lower part of the tower held a water cistern.

A scene from the construction of Ram Island Ledge Light

Joe Johansen was an assistant keeper from 1949 to 1950. Johansen told an interviewer for the Island Institute: "You could have been living in the 1800s because, other than the link with the radio, there were no conveniences at all. Nothing . . . You usually stood watch in the galley because that's where your only source of heat was: a kerosene stove, which we used for cooking and heat."

In 2009, the lighthouse became available to a new steward under the provisions of the National Historic Lighthouse Preservation Act. There were no applicants, so the lighthouse was put up for auction. It was sold to Dr. Jeffrey Florman of Windham, Maine, for $190,000. It can be seen distantly from the area around Portland Head Light. Closer views are available from cruises from Portland offered by the following companies: Lucky Catch Cruises (207-761-0941, www.luckycatch.com), Portland Discovery (207-774-6498, www.portlanddiscovery.com), Ophelia's Odyssey (207-590-3145, captainsearles.tripod.com), and Casco Bay Lines (207-774-7871, www.cascobaylines.com).

Fascinating Fact

Many fishing boats and schooners struck the ledges over the years, often while trying to make Portland Harbor in bad weather. On May 27, 1866, alone, there were four wrecks.

SPRING POINT LEDGE LIGHT

Accessibility: 🚗 🚶 🏠 ⚓

Geographic coordinates: 43° 39' 07" N 70° 13' 26" W

Nearest city: South Portland. Located on the west side of the main shipping channel from the south into Portland Harbor.

Established: 1897. Present lighthouse built: 1897.

Height of tower: 54 feet. Height of focal plane: 54 feet.

Earlier optic: Fifth-order Fresnel lens. Present optic: 300 mm.

Characteristic: White flash every 6 seconds, two red sectors.

Fog signal: One blast every 10 seconds.

Unlike many sparkplug-style lighthouses of its period, the tower here is built of brick rather than cast-iron. The lighthouse has a cistern in the basement, topped by four levels, including two floors of living quarters.

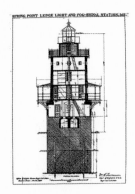

From the plans for the lighthouse

Keepers had to be creative in their means of exercise. Somebody figured that it took fifty-six jogs around the tower's main deck to make one mile. Once, a keeper was running laps and forgot to close a trap door. He slipped through the opening and only a ladder prevented him from falling 17 feet to a rock ledge and the waves below.

In 1951, a 900-foot breakwater was constructed with 50,000 tons of granite, joining the lighthouse to the mainland. In 1998, under the Maine Lights Program, the lighthouse was transferred to the Spring Point Ledge Light Trust. In 2004, a six-year effort by the trust culminated in the replacement of the badly deteriorated iron canopy over the structure's lower gallery.

There's free parking nearby, and the public may walk out on the breakwater to the lighthouse. From I-295 North, take exit 6A (Forest Avenue South). Turn right onto State Street. Follow State Street (Route 77) through Portland and over the Casco Bay Bridge to South Portland. The bridge feeds traffic directly onto Broadway. Go straight ahead off the bridge. Stay on Broadway until you reach the stop sign in front of the Spring Point Marina. Turn right on Pickett Street, then left on Fort Road.

Follow Fort Road through the Southern Maine Community College campus until it ends at the water. The lighthouse will be on your right.

The lighthouse is open weekend days, 11:00 a.m. to 3:00 p.m., from mid-June to early September. Climbing of narrow stairs and through hatches is required. Please note that children less

SIDE TRIP: *South Portland Historical Society Museum*

The South Portland Historical Society operates a small but fascinating museum, with a gift shop, adjacent to Bug Light Park. The museum's exhibits tell the story of the shipyards that thrived here during World War II. There are also displays on the local lighthouses and the sardine-canning industry.

To reach the museum, follow the directions for Spring Point Ledge Light. When you reach the stop sign in front of the Spring Point Marina, turn left. Turn right onto Madison Street and follow to Bug Light Park. The museum will be on your left, across from the park.

South Portland Historical Society Museum
55 Bug Light Park
South Portland, ME 04106
Phone: 207-767-7299

than 55 inches in height are not permitted inside the lighthouse. Call 207-699-2676 or visit www.springpointlight.org online to check for the latest schedule. You can get a good view from the water

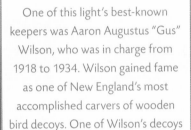

Fascinating Fact

One of this light's best-known keepers was Aaron Augustus "Gus" Wilson, who was in charge from 1918 to 1934. Wilson gained fame as one of New England's most accomplished carvers of wooden bird decoys. One of Wilson's decoys fetched $195,500 at a 2005 auction.

aboard some of the trips offered by Lucky Catch Cruises (207-761-0941, www.luckycatch.com), Portland Discovery (207-774-6498, www.portland discovery.com) and Casco Bay Lines (207-774-7871, www.cascobaylines. com). Also, the narrated 65-minute tour offered by Downeast Duck Adventures (207-774-DUCK, www.down eastducktours.com) includes the lighthouse. New England Lighthouse Tours (603-431-9155, www.newenglandlight housetours.com), based in Portsmouth, NH, offers van trips to this lighthouse and others.

PORTLAND BREAKWATER LIGHT
(Bug Light)

Construction of a 2,500-foot protective breakwater in Portland Harbor began in 1836 but was soon halted by lack of funds. The shortage of funds also delayed the building of a lighthouse, making the breakwater more of a navigational hindrance than help. Funds for a lighthouse were appropriated in 1854, and a small octagonal wooden tower was lighted for the first time by keeper W.A. Dyer on August 1, 1855. A keeper's house wasn't built until 1889.

Accessibility:

Geographic coordinates: 43° 39' 20" N 70° 14' 06" W

Nearest city: South Portland. Located at the entrance to Portland Harbor and the Fore River.

Established: 1855. Present lighthouse built: 1875. Deactivated: 1942; Relighted: 2002.

Height of tower: 26 feet.

Earlier optic: Sixth-order Fresnel lens. Present optic: 250 mm.

Characteristic: White flash every 4 seconds.

The breakwater was extended in the early 1870s, and a new lighthouse was erected at the end of the breakwater in 1875. The design of the cast-iron tower is unique: the cylinder is surrounded by six fluted columns.

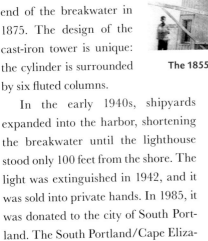

The 1855 tower

In the early 1940s, shipyards expanded into the harbor, shortening the breakwater until the lighthouse stood only 100 feet from the shore. The light was extinguished in 1942, and it was sold into private hands. In 1985, it was donated to the city of South Portland. The South Portland/Cape Elizabeth Rotary Club and the Spring Point Ledge Light Trust completed a restoration of the lighthouse, culminating in a relighting ceremony on August 14, 2002.

The lighthouse is now part of Bug Light Park, which also includes a Liberty Ship memorial. More than 250 Liberty Ships were built on the site during World War II.

Free parking is available near the lighthouse at Bug Light Park. To reach the park, follow the directions above for Spring Point Ledge Light. When you reach the stop sign in front of the Spring Point Marina, turn left. Turn right onto Madison Street and follow into Bug Light Park. Turn right as you approach a booth, into the parking area near the water. You can also view the lighthouse from some of the trips offered by Lucky Catch Cruises (207-761-0941, www.luckycatch.com), Portland Discovery (207-774-6498, www.portland discovery.com) and Casco Bay Lines (207-774-7871, www.cascobaylines. com). The narrated 65-minute tour offered by Downeast Duck Adventures (207-774-DUCK, www.downeastduck tours.com) includes the lighthouse. New England Lighthouse Tours (603-431-9155, www.newenglandlighthouse tours.com), based in Portsmouth, NH, offers van trips to this lighthouse and others.

Fascinating Fact

It's said that this lighthouse was modeled after the Greek Choragic Monument of Lysicrates, built in the fourth century B.C.

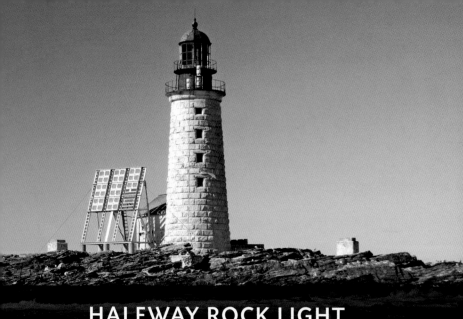

HALFWAY ROCK LIGHT

There are several treacherous ledges in the vicinity of Halfway Rock that claimed many vessels, including the brig *Samuel* in the spring of 1835. It wasn't until 1869 that $50,000 was appropriated for the building of a lighthouse. The granite tower was finished in the summer of 1871. The keepers originally lived in rooms inside the tower on the two-acre rocky islet. Reaching the mainland for supplies required an 11-mile row to Portland, often made difficult or impossible by rough seas or ice.

Accessibility: 🚹 ⛵

Geographic coordinates: 43° 39' 21" N 70° 02' 12" W

Nearest town: Harpswell. Located in Casco Bay, about 10 miles east of Portland Head.

Established: 1871. Present lighthouse built: 1871. Automated: 1975.

Height of tower: 76 feet. Height of focal plane: 77 feet.

Earlier optic: Third-order Fresnel lens. Present optic: VRB-25.

Characteristic: Red flash every 5 seconds.

Fog signal: Two blasts every 30 seconds.

George A. Toothaker, a keeper in the 1870s and 1880s, said years later, "Asleep or awake, the beacon haunts you. Often I would start, quick, sharp, out of profound sleep, a great, dark haunting shudder on me—the light has gone out. Even now it is my fear, and so nervous am I that all sounds startle me, even though it is years since I left the Rock."

In 1888, a new boathouse was built with an upper story containing keeper's quarters. This improved the living conditions, but the tower was always the safest place in a storm. In 1975, the last Coast Guard keepers were removed, and the light was automated. The third-order Fresnel lens went to the museum at the U.S. Coast Guard Academy in New London, Connecticut. In 2000, the American Lighthouse Foundation (207-594-4174, www.lighthouse foundation.org) was licensed by the Coast Guard to care for the tower.

Halfway Rock light can be seen distantly from Land's End at Bailey Island. From Route 1 in Brunswick, at Cooks Corner, head south on Route 24, passing through Orr's Island. After you cross the bridge to Bailey Island, continue down Route 24 for another 2.5 miles to the end. No regular cruises pass near the lighthouse, but you can get a distant view from the Bailey Island cruise offered by Casco Bay Lines (207-774-7871, www.cascobaylines. com). Sea Escape Cottages and Charters (207-833-5531, www.seaescape cottages.com) of Bailey Island can arrange a private charter to photograph this and other area lighthouses.

Early 1900s view

Fascinating Fact

Halfway Rock is so-named because it's halfway between Cape Elizabeth and Cape Small.

SEGUIN ISLAND LIGHT

For more than two centuries, a light on Seguin Island has been an important guide for mariners heading down the coast for Portland as well as those entering the Kennebec River toward Bath and other ports. The building of the original lighthouse was approved by President George Washington in 1794. The station was established a year later at a cost of about $6,400.

Accessibility: 🏛 ⛵ ⌂

Geographic coordinates:
43° 42' 30" N   69° 45' 30" W

Nearest towns: Phippsburg and Georgetown. Located about 1.5 miles south of the mouth of the Kennebec River.

Established: 1795. Present lighthouse built: 1857. Automated: 1985.

Height of tower: 53 feet. Height of focal plane: 186 feet.

Optic: First-order Fresnel lens.

Characteristic: Fixed white.

Fog signal: Two blasts every 20 seconds.

The first keeper was Count John Polereczky, a Hungarian Hussar who fought with French troops during the American Revolution. The original wooden tower had to be rebuilt in 1819, this time of stone. The 1819 lighthouse proved sturdier than the first, but a new 53-foot stone tower was built in 1857 after an appropriation of $35,000. Because of the heavy shipping in the area, a first-order Fresnel

The first-order Fresnel lens

lens, Maine's most powerful light, was installed in the lantern. It remains the only operational first-order Fresnel lens north of Rhode Island. The lens was restored in 2006.

Elson Small was keeper from 1926 to 1930. His wife, Connie, later wrote about Seguin in her book, *The Lighthouse Keeper's Wife*. Connie remembered spirited singalongs and wrestling matches between

the keepers and visiting carpentry crews. She especially loved being in the lantern at sunset, when it was time to "light up."

Frank Bracey, formerly on the Portland Lightship, was keeper at Seguin from 1926 to 1945. He claimed to have seen seagulls knocked from the air by the concussion of the station's powerful foghorn, which on at least one occasion was heard as far away as Bath, 14 miles distant.

A popular ghost story concerns a nineteenth-century keeper's wife who played the same tune over and over on her piano. The keeper was driven insane and destroyed the piano with an axe, then killed his wife and himself. Legend has it that the piano tune can still be heard drifting from the island on calm nights.

After its automation in 1985, the future of the station was uncertain. Concerned local citizens founded the Friends of Seguin Island in 1986. (Friends of Seguin Island Inc., Box 866, Bath, Maine 04530. 207-443-4808, www.seguinisland.org) In 1998, under the Maine Lights Program, the property was transferred to the group. Grants and donations paid for the restoration of the keeper's house. Since 1990,

caretakers have lived on the island in summer.

You can drive to Popham Beach for distant views. To reach the beach, take Route 209 South from Route 1 in Bath and follow the signs to Popham Beach State Park. For more information on the park, call (207) 389-1335.

The Friends of Seguin Island maintain an up-to-date list of boat operators who can take you to the island; check www.seguinisland.org for the current options. Atlantic Seal Cruises of Freeport offers a seasonal coastal cruise that includes a two-hour stop at Seguin; see www.atlanticsealcruises.com or call 207-865-6112.

You can get a view of the lighthouse from cruises offered by Cap'n Fish's Whale Watch and Scenic Boat Tours (207-633-6605, www.boothbayboattrips.com) in Boothbay Harbor and by the Maine Maritime Museum in Bath (207-443-1316, www.mainemaritimemuseum.org).

Fascinating Fact

This is the highest navigational light above the sea in Maine.

POND ISLAND LIGHT

Accessibility: 🏛 ⛵

Geographic coordinates: 43° 44' 24" N   69° 46' 12" W

Nearest towns: Phippsburg and Georgetown. Located on a 10-acre island just south of the mouth of the Kennebec River.

Established: 1821. Present lighthouse built: 1855. Automated: 1963.

Height of tower: 20 feet. Height of focal plane: 52 feet.

Earlier optic: Fifth-order Fresnel lens. Present optic: 250 mm.

Characteristic: 3 seconds white alternating with 3 seconds darkness.

Fog signal: Two blasts every 30 seconds.

In 1821, a quarter of a century after Seguin Light was erected in a commanding position near the mouth of the Kennebec River, the Pond Island Light Station was established on a rocky island off Popham Beach. The lighthouse was rebuilt in 1835; a stone tower, 13 feet tall to the lantern deck, was erected. In 1855, the present 20-foot brick tower was built and fitted with a fifth-order Fresnel lens.

In November 1849, the vessel *Hanover*, returning to Bath from Cadiz, anchored near Pond Island in a storm. As the storm raged, the captain tried to tack around the island and enter the western passage into the river. The ship ran into a bar off nearby Wood Island and soon sank with all twenty-four crewmen on board. Only a dog survived.

Fascinating Fact

Soldiers were quartered on Pond Island during the War of 1812 to prevent the British from entering the Kennebec River.

The light was automated in 1963, and all the buildings except the lighthouse tower were destroyed. The island is now managed as a bird refuge by the U.S. Fish and Wildlife Service. There are nesting roseate terns, common terns, and eiders. The lighthouse can be seen distantly from the Popham Beach area. Closer views are available from cruises offered by the Maine Maritime Museum (207-443-1316, www.maine maritimemuseum.org).in Bath, and by Cap'n Fish's Whale Watch and Scenic Boat Tours (207-633-6605, www.boothbayboattrips.com) in Boothbay Harbor. You can also check www.seguinisland.org for the latest offerings to Seguin Island.

Early 1900s view

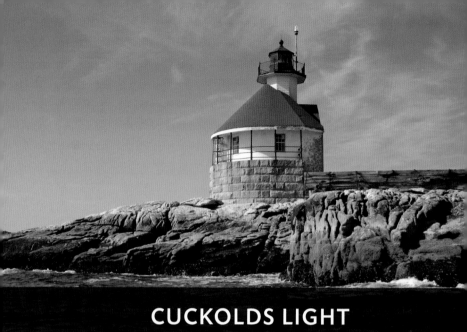

CUCKOLDS LIGHT

Accessibility: 🏛 ⛵

Geographic coordinates: 43° 46' 48" N 69° 39' 00" W

Nearest town: Southport. Located on a ledge off Cape Newagen, on the approach to Boothbay Harbor.

Established: 1892 (as fog signal station). Present lighthouse built: 1907. Automated: 1975.

Height of tower: 48 feet. Height of focal plane: 59 feet.

Earlier optic: Fourth-order Fresnel lens. Present optic: VRB-25.

Characteristic: Two white flashes every 6 seconds.

Fog signal: One blast every 15 seconds.

In 1890, a recommendation was made for a fog signal station on the ledges known as the Cuckolds, which were "much dreaded by mariners in thick weather." The station was established in 1892 for about $25,000, with a steam-driven Daboll fog trumpet.

Plans for the 1907 additions

{ 292 }

In January 1896, keepers Edward H. Pierce and Clarence Marr rescued the crew of the Canadian schooner *Aurora* by launching their dory in heavy seas and taking the three men to the fog signal station. The keepers were awarded silver watches by the Canadian government.

Local mariners believed a navigational light was called for, and the government agreed in 1907. The ledge was too small to build a separate lighthouse, so a small tower was built on the roof of the signal house. An attached two-story keeper's dwelling was also built.

Coast Guardsman Kelly Farrin lived with his wife at the Cuckolds in 1969–70. He later wrote, "They say lighthouses are romantic, but I do know that this one had quite a reputation concerning the divorce rate. I would say it takes a sturdy relationship to endure that much togetherness. There is no time apart, unless the wife goes ashore alone."

The keeper's dwelling was demolished in 1977. In May 2006, own-ership of the lighthouse was conveyed to a local nonprofit organization, the Cuckolds Fog Signal and Light Station Council (www.cuckoldslight.org). Reconstruction of the keeper's dwelling began in the summer of 2011. All of the building materials for the project were donated by Hancock Lumber.

Views are possible from the town landing at the southern tip of Southport Island. From Route 1 in North Edgecomb, take Route 27 South for about 12 miles through Boothbay Harbor to Southport. At its southern end, Route 27 takes a left turn before its junction with Route 238. Instead of turning north onto Route 238, bear right onto

Fascinating Fact

A keeper's wife was sewing near a second-story window in the keeper's quarters one August day when a "freak wave" poured through the window, damaging much of the furniture.

a paved road at a Town Landing sign. Continue a short distance to the small parking area. The lighthouse can be seen about a half mile offshore to the southeast.

Closer views are available from cruises offered by the Maine Maritime Museum (207-443-1316, www.maine maritimemuseum.org) in Bath, and by Cap'n Fish's Whale Watch and Scenic Boat Tours (207-633-6605, www.booth bayboattrips.com) and Goddess of the Sea Cruises (207-649-2628, www.goddess cruise.com) in Boothbay Harbor.

Aerial view circa 1980s

PERKINS ISLAND LIGHT

Several aids to navigation were established along the Kennebec River in 1898 to aid mariners headed for the shipbuilding center of Bath. A 23-foot octagonal wooden tower was erected on Perkins Island, near the mouth of the river. A six-room keeper's house was also built, along with a small barn. A boathouse, fog bell tower (1902), and brick oil house (1906) were added later.

Accessibility:

Geographic coordinates:
43° 47' 12" N 69° 47' 06" W

Nearest town: Georgetown. Located on a seven-acre island on the east side of the Kennebec River, about two miles from the river mouth.

Established: 1898. Present lighthouse built: 1898. Automated: 1959.

Height of tower:
23 feet. Height of focal plane: 41 feet.

Earlier optic: Fifth-order Fresnel lens. Present optic: 250 mm.

Characteristic: Red flash every 2.5 seconds with two white sectors.

On June 16, 1931, keeper Eugene Osgood left the light station to pick up his mail in Phippsburg. He happened to see a man struggling in the currents in a sluiceway. The man had been thrown from his rowboat as he tried to cross the sluiceway. Thinking quickly, Osgood launched his own boat and rescued the drowning man.

The station, except for the lighthouse tower, was transferred to the state of Maine in the 1960s. The keeper's house fell into a state of severe disrepair. In late 2000, a restoration of the bell tower took place. Local resident Joshua Bate was the project foreman, and volunteers from around the state helped with the restoration.

The lighthouse tower was licensed in May 2000 by the Coast Guard to the American Lighthouse Foundation (www.lighthousefoundation.org). A chapter, the Friends of Perkins Island Lighthouse (P.O. Box 376, Georgetown, Maine 04548) is working to restore the keeper's house.

The best views are from the water. Good opportunities are available from cruises offered by the Maine Maritime Museum (207-443-1316, www.mainemaritimemuseum.org) in Bath, and by Cap'n Fish's Whale Watch and Scenic Boat Tours (207-633-6605, www.boothbayboattrips.com) in Boothbay Harbor.

Fascinating Fact

The fog bell from Perkins Island is now on the grounds of Georgetown High School.

SQUIRREL POINT LIGHT

This is one of several aids to navigation authorized in 1895 and erected in 1898 on the Kennebec River, a bustling waterway at the time. The 25-foot wooden tower is very similar to the lighthouses built at nearby Doubling Point and Perkins Island. The keeper's house, garage, and barn were all built along with the tower in 1898. The boathouse and oil house were added a few years later. George Matthews, the first keeper, was in charge from 1897 to 1912.

Accessibility: 🚻 🚶 ⛵

Geographic coordinates: 43° 49' 00" N 69° 48' 06" W

Nearest town: Arrowsic. Located on Arrowsic Island, on the east side of the Kennebec River.

Established: 1898. Present lighthouse built: 1898. Automated: 1979.

Height of tower: 25 feet. Height of focal plane: 33 feet.

Earlier optic: Fifth-order Fresnel lens. Present optic: 250 mm.

Characteristic: 3 seconds red alternating with 3 seconds darkness.

Fog signal: One blast every 10 seconds.

Undated aerial view

Squirrel Point Light and its fog signal were for a time operated by the keeper at the Kennebec River (Doubling Point) Range Light Station. The light was automated in 1979. The original fifth-order lens can now be seen at the Museum at Portland Head Light.

The Coast Guard transferred ownership of the station to Squirrel Point Associates in 1998. The property later reverted to the U.S. government. In February 2008, the Chewonki Foundation (207-882-7323, www.chewonki. org) signed a 15-year license to manage the light station property. The foundation offers a broad array of environmental education, natural history, conservation, and wilderness programs. Donations toward restoration can be sent either to Citizens for Squirrel Point (www.squirrelpoint.org) c/o Susan Lubner, Treasurer, 51 Bedford St., Bath, ME 04530, or directly to the Chewonki Foundation.

The station is accessible via a fairly strenuous twenty- to thirty-minute walk through the woods at the end of Bald Head Road in Arrowsic. From Route 1 in Woolwich, take Route 127 South. After 4.2 miles, bear right onto Bald Head Road. Follow the road for 2.3 miles to its end. There is a well-defined path that leads to the light station. Keep to the left at a fork in the trail just after a footbridge.

Excellent views are also available from cruises offered by the Maine Maritime Museum (207-443-1316, www. mainemaritimemuseum.org) in Bath, and by Cap'n Fish's Whale Watch and Scenic Boat Tours (207-633-6605, www.boothbayboattrips.com) in Boothbay Harbor.

Fascinating Fact

Fort St. George, founded in 1607 on the Kennebec River near present-day Augusta, was Maine's first English settlement.

DOUBLING POINT LIGHT

oubling Point Light was established on the northwest end of Arrowsic Island near the busy shipbuilding harbor of Bath. A wood-frame keeper's house, a shed, and a bell tower were erected in 1898, along with an octagonal wooden lighthouse tower. In 1899, the lighthouse was moved offshore to a stone pier connected to the island by a footbridge. The fog bell was relocated to the lighthouse tower, and the bell tower was moved and converted into a garage.

Accessibility:

Geographic coordinates: 43° 52' 57" N   69° 48' 25" W

Nearest town: Arrowsic. Located on Arrowsic Island, on the east side of the Kennebec River.

Established: 1898. Present lighthouse built: 1898. Automated: 1988.

Height of tower: 23 feet. Height of focal plane: 23 feet.

Earlier optic: Fifth-order Fresnel lens. Present optic: 300 mm.

Characteristic: White flash every 4 seconds.

Only two keepers served here in the Lighthouse Service era: Merritt Pinkham (1898–1935) and Charles W. Allen (1931–35). The keeper's house was sold to a private owner in 1935.

Fascinating Fact

This lighthouse was lifted off its base in late 1999 so that the granite foundation could be restored. The granite blocks, each weighing about six tons, were reset. The foundation's core was filled with concrete, and steel tie rods were inserted to hold the blocks together.

In the mid-1970s, the Fresnel lens was removed; it's now at the Maine Lighthouse Museum in Rockland, Maine. The fog bell was removed in 1980. Under the Maine Lights Program, the lighthouse was transferred to the Friends of Doubling Point Light (c/o Betsy Skillings-Coleman, HCR 33 Box 61B, Arrowsic, ME 04530; www.doublingpoint.org) in 1998.

To reach this scenic little lighthouse from Route 1 in Woolwich, head south on Route 127 for about a mile and then turn right onto the road marked Whitmore's Landing to Doubling Point Rd. At a T intersection, turn left onto Doubling Point Road, go past a stone wall, and follow the road to its end. There is a small (free) parking area. You can walk out to the lighthouse. The keeper's house is privately owned, so be sure to respect the privacy of the residents.

Good photo opportunities are also available from cruises offered by the Maine Maritime Museum (207-443-1316, www.mainemaritimemuseum.org) in Bath, and by Cap'n Fish's Whale Watch and Scenic Boat Tours (207-633-6605, www.boothbayboattrips.com) in Boothbay Harbor.

DOUBLING POINT RANGE LIGHTS
(Kennebec River Range Lights)

This station was established on Arrowsic Island, on the Kennebec River, to mark an extreme double turn in the channel at Fiddler Reach. Mariners would line up the two lights to know they were on course. The octagonal wooden towers are 235 yards apart from each other. A two-story keeper's house and a shed were also built, with a raised wooden walkway above the marshy ground connecting the keeper's house to the two towers.

Accessibility:

Geographic coordinates: 43° 53' 00" N 69° 47' 42" W

Nearest town: Arrowsic. Located on Arrowsic Island, on the east side of the Kennebec River.

Established: 1898. Present lighthouses built: 1898. Automated: 1990.

Height of towers: Front range 21 feet; Rear range 13 feet

Height of focal plane: Front range 18 feet; Rear range 33 feet

Earlier optics: Fifth-order Fresnel lenses. Present optics: 250 mm.

Characteristic: Front range - Quick white flash. Rear range - 3 seconds white alternating with 3 seconds darkness.

Captain Harry L. Nye was keeper in the 1920s. On one occasion, he rescued four young men who were drifting past Doubling Point on an ice floe. Beginning in 1935, the keeper of the range lights had the added duty of tending Doubling Point Light around the bend, as well as the Fiddler's Reach fog bell. In 1979, the job of monitoring the range lights went to the keeper at Squirrel Point Light. Then, in 1982, the responsibility of looking after the lights and fog signals at Doubling Point, Squirrel Point, and the range lights was transferred to the range light station.

Under the Maine Lights Program, the property was transferred in 1998 to an organization called the Range Light Keepers (Iron Mine Road, Arrowsic, ME 04530, www.rlk.org). The group also has the responsibility of looking after the old fog bell tower at Fiddler's Reach near the range lights.

SIDE TRIP: *Maine Maritime Museum*

With galleries and exhibits spread across 25 acres of scenic waterfront, this museum brings Maine's rich seafaring history to life. The exhibits include artifacts, paintings, photographs, ship models, and dioramas. Walking tours are available, and boat cruises leave from the museum property. On the grounds is a life-size sculpture of the largest wooden sailing vessel ever built, the *Wyoming*. The museum is open daily, year round (except Christmas, New Year's Day, and Thanksgiving).

Maine Maritime Museum
243 Washington Street
Bath, ME 04530
Phone: 207-443-1316
Web site: www.mainemaritime
museum.org

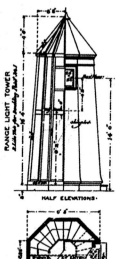

From the range lights plans

The grounds are open to the public; remember to respect the privacy of the residents of the keeper's house. To reach the station from Route 1 in Bath, head south on Route 127 for about a mile and then turn right onto the road marked Whitmore's Landing, to Doubling Point Rd. At a T intersection, turn left onto Doubling Point Road. After a very short distance, turn left onto a small dirt road. There's a small parking area near the station.

The best photographic views are from the water, from cruises offered by the Maine Maritime Museum (207-443-1316, www.mainemaritime museum.org) in Bath, and by Cap'n Fish's Whale Watch and Scenic Boat Tours (207-633-6605, www.boothbay-boattrips.com) in Boothbay Harbor.

Fascinating Fact

For several years in the 1980s, the Coast Guard keeper was Karen McLean, one of very few female lighthouse keepers under the Coast Guard.

HENDRICKS HEAD LIGHT

Accessibility: 🏛️ ⛵

Geographic coordinates:
43° 49' 22" N 69° 41' 23" W

Nearest town: Southport. Located on the east side of the entrance to the Sheepscot River.

Established: 1829. Present lighthouse built: 1875. Deactivated: 1933. Relighted: 1951.

Height of tower: 39 feet. Height of focal plane: 43 feet.

Earlier optic: Fifth-order Fresnel lens. Present optic: 250 mm.

Characteristic: Fixed white with a red sector.

The first lighthouse here was a granite keeper's dwelling with the tower on its roof. Jaruel Marr, who was born the same year the lighthouse was built, became keeper in 1866, after returning from the Civil War.

Keeper Jaruel Marr

A famous tale of this lighthouse concerns a vessel wrecked in a March gale sometime around 1870. The keeper and his wife could see those on board the wrecked ship hanging to the rigging, practically frozen to death. The rough seas made it impossible for the keeper to launch a dory. As evening arrived, the keeper saw a bundle floating toward the shore. He snatched the bundle from the waves with a boat hook and discovered that it was actually two featherbeds tied around a box. Opening the box, the keeper discovered a tiny baby girl.

The keeper and his wife adopted the girl, according to the story as it is usually told. Some local historians question whether the events ever took place, but according to some of the descendants of Jaruel Marr, the story is true. Some say the baby—named Seaborn—was adopted by a doctor and his wife, who were summer residents. The debate over the veracity of the story may never be settled, but it is one of New England's most enduring lighthouse stories.

The present square brick tower replaced the first lighthouse in 1875. Jaruel's son, Wolcott Marr, succeeded his father as keeper in 1895. In 1914, he rescued the crew of a wrecked schooner with the help of his sons.

Fascinating Fact

Keeper Wolcott Marr had an unusual distinction: he was born, married, and died in the same room at this light station.

The 1829 lighthouse

The light was discontinued in 1933, and the light station property was sold to a private owner. After electricity came to the house in 1951, the Coast Guard decided to reactivate the light, as boating traffic in the area had increased. In 1991, Benjamin and Luanne Russell of Alabama bought the property, and they subsequently restored all of the structures. Ben Russell has a web site for the lighthouse at www.benrussell.com/HH-home.htm.

Hendricks Head Light can be seen from a small beach. To reach the beach, take Route 27 south through Boothbay Harbor to West Southport. About 2 miles south of the intersection of Route 27 and Route 238, bear right around a triangular intersection with a statue and flagpole, past the Southport General Store. Where the road dips downhill onto Dogfish Head Road, bear left onto Beach Road and continue for a half-mile to the public beach. The view of the lighthouse tower from here is partly blocked by the keeper's house.

The lighthouse can also be seen distantly from across the river at the village of Five Islands. From Route 1 in Bath, head south on Route 127 and follow to the end, and walk out on the wharf for the view. (While here, you can get a meal or snack from the Five Islands Lobster Company.) In addition, you can get good views from cruises offered by the Maine Maritime Museum (207-443-1316, www.mainemaritime museum.org) in Bath, and by Cap'n Fish's Whale Watch and Scenic Boat Tours (207-633-6605, www.boothbay boattrips.com) in Boothbay Harbor.

RAM ISLAND LIGHT

The history of aids to navigation on Ram Island began in the mid-1800s when a fisherman began hanging a lantern at night for the benefit of local mariners. The fisherman left the area after a number of years, and the lantern was kept by a second keeper, then a third and a fourth. For some years after, there was no light. Locals talked of ghosts that warned mariners away from the dangerous rocks.

**Keeper
Samuel J. Cavanor**

〔 **307** 〕

Accessibility: 🏛 ⛵

Geographic coordinates: 43° 48' 14" N 69° 35' 58" W

Nearest town: Boothbay Harbor. Located about a half-mile offshore, south of Ocean Point, in Fisherman's Passage.

Established: 1883. Present lighthouse built: 1883. Automated: 1965.

Height of tower: 35 feet. Height of focal plane: 36 feet.

Earlier optic: Fourth-order Fresnel lens. Present optic: 250 mm.

Characteristic: 3 seconds red alternating with 3 seconds darkness.

Fog signal: One blast every 30 seconds.

Congress appropriated $25,000 for a lighthouse in 1883. The brick tower, with a granite base, was erected some yards offshore, and a wooden walkway connected it to the island. The first keeper was Samuel John Cavanor, a native of Halifax, Nova Scotia, who stayed at the light until he died in 1913. Cavanor had a wooden leg. He had been on the crew of a lighthouse tender, and a buoy raised by a derrick swung and crushed his leg.

In 1977, the Coast Guard repaired the lighthouse for $44,000 and removed the walkway, which had fallen into disrepair. During this renovation, 14,000 bricks were replaced in the tower, and the masonry base was repointed. The boathouse was destroyed in the great blizzard of February 6–7, 1978.

The property was transferred to the Grand Banks Schooner Museum Trust in 1998. The Ram Island Preservation Society, part of the trust, has restored the house and reconstructed the walkway from the shore to the lighthouse tower. For more information, contact the Ram Island Preservation Society, P.O. Box 123, Boothbay, Maine 04537. Phone: 207-633-4727.

You can see the lighthouse distantly from Ocean Point in East Boothbay.

From Route 27 in Boothbay Harbor, take Route 96 to the east and then south to Ocean Point. There's a two-mile loop road that will take you back to Route 96. You can pull to the side of the road for views of the lighthouse. You can get closer views from cruises offered by the Maine Maritime Museum (207-443-1316, www.mainemaritimemuseum.org) in Bath, and by Cap'n Fish's Whale Watch and Scenic Boat Tours (207-633-6605, www.boothbayboattrips.com), Balmy Days Cruises (207-633-2284, www.balmydayscruises.com), and Goddess of the Sea Cruises (207-649-2628, www.goddesscruise.com) in Boothbay Harbor.

Fascinating Fact

Legend has it that on one unusually dark night, before a lighthouse was established here, a sailor was approaching the ledges around Ram Island when he saw a woman in white waving a lighted torch over her head. The sailor veered off just in time to avoid being dashed on the rocks.

BURNT ISLAND LIGHT

Boothbay Harbor was a busy fishing port in the early 1800s. Burnt Island Light, one of the earliest lighthouses in the area, was established in 1821. The 30-foot stone tower was accompanied by a wooden keeper's house. In 1857, the original house was replaced by the wood-frame cottage that still stands. A covered walkway between the tower and house was also added that year.

Accessibility: 🚻 ⛵ 🏠

Geographic coordinates: 43° 49' 31" N 69° 38' 27" W

Nearest town: Boothbay Harbor. Located at the west side of the entrance to Boothbay Harbor.

Established: 1821. Present lighthouse built: 1821. Automated: 1989.

Height of tower: 30 feet. Height of focal plane: 61 feet.

Earlier optic: Fourth-order Fresnel lens. Present optic: 300 mm.

Characteristic: Red flash every 6 seconds.

Fog signal: One blast every 10 seconds.

For much of its history, this was a much sought-after family station. The island is close to the mainland, and the trip for supplies was usually not difficult. Keeper Joseph Muise lived with his wife and children on the island from 1936 to 1951. The Muises' children boarded on the mainland during the school year and spent summers on the island.

In 1998, as part of the Maine Lights Program, ownership of the station was transferred to the Maine Department of Marine Resources. Since then, the buildings at the light station have been gradually restored to the circa-1950 period.

Public tours are offered in summer. In recent years, former Coast Guard keeper James Buotte has been donning a Lighthouse Service uniform to portray his predecessor, keeper Joseph Muise, for the visiting tours. You can call 207-

Late nineteenth-century view

Fascinating Fact

In 1962, this became the last lighthouse in New England to be converted from kerosene to electric operation. It was also one of the last lights in Maine to be automated (in 1989).

633-2284 or visit www.maine.gov/dmr/burntisland/tour.htm for more information on the tours.

The lighthouse can also be seen distantly (about a mile offshore) from the road to Spruce Point from Boothbay Harbor, especially from Grandview Avenue. You can get much better views from cruises offered by Long Reach Cruises (1-888-538-6786, www.long reachcruises.com) and the Maine Maritime Museum (207) 443-1316, www. mainemaritimemuseum.org) in Bath, and by Cap'n Fish's Whale Watch and Scenic Nature Cruises (207-633-6605, www.capnfishmotel.com/boattrips. htm), Balmy Days Cruises (207-633-2284, www.balmydayscruises.com), and Goddess of the Sea Cruises (207-649-2628, www.goddesscruise.com) in Boothbay Harbor.

PEMAQUID POINT LIGHT

Congress appropriated $4,000 for the building of a lighthouse at Pemaquid Point in 1826. Isaac Dunham of Bath, later a keeper at Minot's Ledge Light, was the first keeper at $350 per year. The extant 38-foot stone tower was built in 1835. Pemaquid Point was usually not difficult to reach by land, but there was no landing place for vessels. Lighthouse tenders had to anchor on the rocks to bring supplies, making the lighthouse one of the least favorite of tender crews.

Accessibility:

Geographic coordinates:
43° 50' 12" N   69° 30' 21" W

Nearest town: Bristol. Located at the west side of the entrance to Muscongus Bay.

Established: 1827. Present lighthouse built: 1835. Automated: 1934.

Height of tower: 38 feet. Height of focal plane: 79 feet.

Optic: Fourth-order Fresnel lens.

Characteristic: White flash every 6 seconds.

On September 16, 1903, when Clarence Marr was keeper, the fishing schooner *George F. Edmunds* was driven by a strong gust into the rocks near Pemaquid Point and was dashed to pieces. The captain and thirteen crewmembers died in the wreck; only two were saved.

After the light was automated, the surrounding property became the town of Bristol's Lighthouse Park, and the keeper's house was converted into the Fishermen's Museum (Pemaquid Point Road, New Harbor, Maine 04554. Phone: 207-677-2494. Web site: www.pemaquidlighthouse.com). The museum opened in 1972 and has been operated since then by volunteers from the local area. The museum houses exhibits on the history of the local fishing and lobstering industries, as well as pictures of all the lighthouses on the Maine coast and a fourth-order Fresnel lens from Baker Island. The museum is open seven days a week in the summer for a small parking fee. A second floor apartment in the keeper's house is available for rent by the week; call Newcastle Square Vacation Rentals at 207-563-6500 for details.

In 2000, the lighthouse tower was licensed by the Coast Guard to the American Lighthouse Foundation (207-594-4174, www.lighthousefoundation.org). Volunteers of the Friends of Pemaquid Point Lighthouse (P.O. Box 353, Bristol, ME 04539-0353), a chapter of the American Lighthouse Foundation, open the tower in season (Memorial Day to Columbus Day) to the public every afternoon from 10:30 a.m. to 5:00 p.m. There is no charge to climb the tower, but donations are welcomed.

In February 2007, a $50,000 grant from Lowe's and the National Trust for Historic Preservation helped the American Lighthouse Foundation complete a $105,400 restoration of the tower. The work took place during the summer of 2007, leaving the lighthouse in its best condition in many years. More recently, restoration has also been completed on the interior of the tower.

Pemaquid Point is one of the most visited attractions of the Maine coast. To reach the lighthouse from the south

Fascinating Fact

This lighthouse is featured on the Maine state quarter, unveiled at a ceremony on June 9, 2003.

on Route 1, take the Damariscotta exit. Continue through Damariscotta's business district, and then turn right onto Route 129/130. Continue on Route 130 for 15 miles until you reach the parking area. From the north on Route 1, turn left onto Route 32 in Waldoboro and continue for 18 miles. Route 32 ends at Route 130; go left on Route 130 and travel three miles until you reach the parking area. You can also visit the Seagull Shop next door for a meal and some gift shopping.

MONHEGAN ISLAND LIGHT

Accessibility: 🚣 🧍 🏠

Geographic coordinates:
43° 45' 54" N   69° 18' 54" W

Nearest town: Monhegan. Located 12 miles offshore, on the southern approach to Muscongus Bay.

Established: 1824. Present lighthouse built: 1850. Automated: 1959.

Height of tower:
47 feet. Height of focal plane: 178 feet.

Earlier optic: Second-order Fresnel lens. Present optic: VRB-25.

Characteristic: White flash every 15 seconds.

Monhegan Island, about 700 acres, is a picturesque summer haven for artists and vacationers. For many voyagers coming across the Atlantic, Monhegan was the first sight of land. By the early 1800s, trade in the area was increasing. In 1822, Congress authorized the building of a lighthouse on one of Monhegan's highest points for $3,000. The 30-foot conical stone tower went into operation two years later. The extant 48-foot granite tower replaced the original lighthouse in 1850.

In 1861, keeper Joseph F. Humphrey left to fight in the Civil War, along with his two sons. His wife, Betty Morrow Humphrey, was left with her other eight children to tend the light. Joseph Humphrey died in 1861, and Betty became the official keeper. Betty Morrow Humphrey remained keeper at Monhegan until 1880.

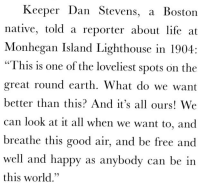

**Ernie DeRaps,
Coast Guard keeper
1956–57**

Keeper Dan Stevens, a Boston native, told a reporter about life at Monhegan Island Lighthouse in 1904: "This is one of the loveliest spots on the great round earth. What do we want better than this? And it's all ours! We can look at it all when we want to, and breathe this good air, and be free and well and happy as anybody can be in this world."

In 1962, the lighthouse grounds and buildings, except the lighthouse itself, were sold to the Monhegan Associates. A museum was opened in 1968 in the 1874 keeper's house, focusing on the island's rich history and wildlife. The Monhegan Museum (207-596-7003, Web site: www.monheganmuseum. org) is open daily in summer. Under the Maine Lights Program, the light-house became the property of the Monhegan Historical and Cultural Museum Association in 1998. The association has reconstructed an 1857 assistant keeper's house to serve as a museum for their art collection, and the lighthouse tower was restored by the J. B. Leslie Company in 2009.

Monhegan Island can be reached by ferry from Port Clyde (Monhegan Boat Line, 207-372-8848, www.monheganboat.com), New Harbor (Hardy Boat Cruises, 1-800-2-PUF-FIN, www.hardyboat.com), and Boothbay Harbor (Balmy Days Cruises, 207-633-2284, www.balmydayscruises. com). Reaching the lighthouse requires a moderate uphill walk.

Fascinating Fact

Some believe the Vikings visited this area around 1,000 A.D. and left carvings on the rocks of nearby Manana Island.

FRANKLIN ISLAND LIGHT

Accessibility: ⛵

Geographic coordinates:
43° 53' 32" N 69° 22' 29" W

Nearest town: Friendship. Located at the entrance to Muscongus Bay, about five miles south of Friendship.

Established: 1807. Present lighthouse built: 1855. Automated: 1930s.

Height of tower: 45 feet. Height of focal plane: 57 feet.

Earlier optic: Fourth-order Fresnel lens. Present optic: 250 mm.

Characteristic: White flash every 6 seconds.

Trade was booming in the early 1800s in the vicinity of Friendship and the St. George River, and many vessels were wrecked on the treacherous rocks near Franklin Island. The station was authorized by Congress and President Thomas Jefferson in 1803, but bad weather and lack of building supplies delayed completion until 1807. The extant 45-foot brick lighthouse on the island's northwest corner was erected in 1855. The tower was originally connected to the keeper's house.

Coleman George Woodward grew up on Franklin Island and several other Maine lighthouse stations, where his father, George E. Woodward, was keeper. He later recalled his time on Franklin Island in the 1920s: "On Franklin Island you didn't send messages back and forth. There was no telephone. If you needed assistance, you were to fly the American flag upside down from the top of the tower. . . . Each keeper had twenty-eight vacation days; I would do their job while they were on vacation. I just loved the island life."

All the buildings except the lighthouse tower and an 1895 oil house have been destroyed. The lighthouse is now cared for by a group called Franklin Light Preservation (P.O. Box 481, New Harbor, ME 04554) under an agreement with the Coast Guard. The island is part of the Maine Coastal Islands National Wildlife Refuge. Unfortunately, no regular public cruises pass close to here, so you'll have to charter a cruise or flight to get a good view. You might get a very distant view from the fall coastal cruise offered by Hardy Boat Cruises in New Harbor (1-800-2-PUFFIN, www.hardyboat.com).

Fascinating Fact

This is Maine's third oldest light station.

Early 1900s view

MARSHALL POINT

Accessibility:

Geographic coordinates:
43° 55' 03" N   69° 15' 41" W

Nearest town: Port Clyde (a village of the town of St. George). Located at the east side of the entrance to Muscongus Bay.

Established: 1832. Present lighthouse built 1857. Automated 1971.

Height of tower: 31 feet. Height of focal plane: 30 feet.

Previous optic: Fifth-order Fresnel lens. Present optic: 300 mm.

Characteristic: Fixed white.

Fog signal: One blast every 10 seconds.

The first lighthouse erected at Marshall Point to help mariners entering Port Clyde's harbor or passing to the west into Muscongus Bay was a 20-foot-high rubble-stone tower. The first keeper, John Watts, lived in a stone dwelling attached to the lighthouse tower. The extant brick and granite lighthouse was built at a cost of $5,000 in 1857. The original dwelling was replaced in 1895 after it was destroyed by a fire caused by lightning.

Charles Clement Skinner, a Civil War veteran, was keeper from 1874 to 1919. Skinner lived at the station with his wife and six children. Skinner's daughter, Eula, was born in the first keeper's house in 1891. She lived until 1993, spending her last years in a cottage near the light station. Eula's sister, Marion, was born in the new keeper's house in 1895 and lived until 1992. Both sisters attended the opening of the restored keeper's house in 1990.

The light was automated in 1971, and for several years the Coast Guard maintained a LORAN (long range navigation) station in the keeper's house. In 1980, the station was closed and the house was boarded up.

In 1986, the St. George Historical Society undertook the restoration of the house. The restoration was completed in 1990, and the first floor of the house now contains the Marshall Point Lighthouse Museum. The exhibits highlight area history as well as life at Marshall Point. The Marshall Point Lighthouse Museum (www.marshallpoint.org) is open weekends during

May, 1:00 to 5:00 p.m.; Memorial Day to Columbus Day, Sunday through Friday, 1:00 to 5:00 p.m., and Saturdays, 10:00 a.m. to 5:00 p.m. There's also a gift shop specializing in items made by local craftsmen and local artwork. The lighthouse tower itself is not open to the public.

Directions: Coming from the south on Route 1: After passing through the business district of Thomaston, turn right on Route 131 at the foot of the hill. Coming from the north on Route 1: After passing through Rockland and a large cement plant on your left, turn left onto Route 131 at the foot of the hill.

From the intersection of Routes 1 and 131, it is 15.2 miles to Marshall

Point. At mile 9.3, you'll see a Welcome II Tenants Harbor sign on your right. At mile 10.1, Route 131 bears left at the top of the hill. At mile 14.5, turn left off Route 131 at the blue Marshall Point Lighthouse sign. Turn right on Marshall Point Road and follow to the parking lot near the lighthouse.

You can also get a view from the water by taking one of the seasonal lighthouse cruises offered by the Monhegan Boat Line (207-372-8848, www.monheganboat.com) in Port Clyde.

Fascinating Fact

This lighthouse might be familiar to you from its brief appearance in the movie *Forrest Gump,* or from the children's book *Nellie the Lighthouse Dog.*

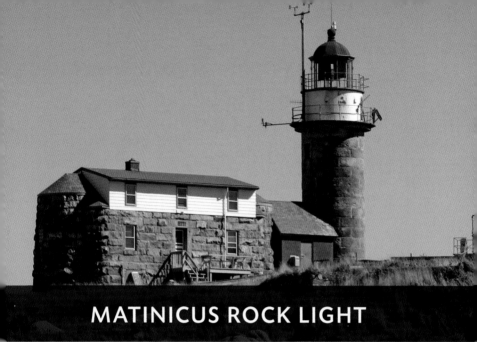

MATINICUS ROCK LIGHT

Matinicus Rock is a windswept 32-acre granite island about 25 miles from Rockland, the nearest port. Because of its prominent location on the approach to busy Penobscot Bay, President John Quincy Adams authorized the establishment of a light station in 1827. The first lighthouse building was a stone dwelling with a wooden tower at each end. In 1846, a new granite dwelling was built. Two years later, new granite lighthouse towers were erected 60 yards apart.

Accessibility: ⛵

Geographic coordinates: 43° 47' 00" N 68° 51' 18" W

Nearest town: Criehaven. Located about 18 miles offshore, in Penobscot Bay.

Established: 1827. Present lighthouse built 1857. Automated 1983.

Height of tower: 48 feet. Height of focal plane: 90 feet.

Previous optic: Third-order Fresnel lens. Present optic: VRB-25.

Characteristic: White flash every 10 seconds.

Fog signal: One blast every 15 seconds.

Second assistant keeper Austin Beal, first assistant keeper Arthur J. Beal, and keeper Frank O. Hilt circa 1920s

Samuel Burgess came to the isolated station as keeper in 1853 with his invalid wife and five children. The oldest girl, fourteen-year-old Abbie, soon learned how to light the whale oil lamps and perform other duties around the island. In January 1856, keeper Burgess left in his sailboat to pick up supplies in Rockland, leaving Abbie alone with her mother and younger sisters.

By the afternoon, a storm began to approach Penobscot Bay. Soon the waves grew large as the wind increased, and the gale continued to worsen. Abbie later wrote, "For four weeks, owing to rough weather, no landing could be effected on the Rock. During this time we were without the assistance of any male member of our family. Though at times greatly exhausted with my labors, not once did the lights fail. Under God, I was able to perform all my accustomed duties as well as my father's." Samuel Burgess finally made it back to the island.

Keeper Burgess lost his job in 1861 for political reasons. John Grant became the next keeper. The new keeper's son, Isaac, was the assistant keeper. Abbie Burgess and Isaac Grant were married within a year. Abbie was appointed assistant keeper at $440 per year. Abbie and Isaac had four children at Matinicus Rock before Isaac Grant's appointment to Whitehead Light in 1875.

A new pair of granite lighthouse towers, 180 feet apart, was built in 1857. The north light was discontinued on August 15, 1923. The third-order Fresnel lens from the north light is now on display at the Maine Lighthouse Museum in Rockland.

Fascinating Fact

A small metal lighthouse stands on the grave of Abbie Burgess, the heroine of Matinicus Rock, at a tiny cemetery in Spruce Head.

Under the Maine Lights Program, the station became the property of the U.S. Fish and Wildlife Service in 1998. The National Audubon Society researches and protects the island's seabird population. Matinicus Rock is home to a nesting colony of puffins, as well as terns and other seabirds.

There are no regularly scheduled cruises that go near Matinicus Rock. There is ferry service from Rockland to Matinicus Island (207-596-2202), and from there you can arrange a charter to Matinicus Rock with Matinicus Excursions (207-691-9030, www.matinicus excursions.com).

TENANTS HARBOR LIGHT
(Southern Island Light)

Accessibility: 🏛️ ⛵

Geographic coordinates: 43° 57' 40" N 69° 11' 05" W

Nearest town: Tenants Harbor (a village of St. George). Located on 22-acre Southern Island in western Penobscot Bay.

Established: 1858. Present lighthouse built 1858. Deactivated: 1933.

Height of tower: 27 feet.

Previous optic: Fourth-order Fresnel lens. Present optic: none.

Tenants Harbor Light was first illuminated on January 1, 1858. The 27-foot brick tower is connected to the keeper's house by a passageway. A storage shed was added in 1895, and an oil house was constructed in 1906.

Leonard Bosworth Dudley was keeper in the 1920s. His daughter, June, helped by cleaning the glass in the lighthouse, and she also learned to tend the light. When she was nineteen, June met a local lobsterman named Everett Watts, and the two were soon married.

After it was deactivated in 1933, the property was bought by a Rockland resident. It passed through several hands before it was bought in 1978 by artist Andrew Wyeth and his wife, Betsy James Wyeth. The Wyeths spent a number of summers on Southern Island. Since 1990, Betsy and Andrew's son, artist Jamie Wyeth and his wife, Phyllis Mills Wyeth, have lived on the island.

Andrew Wyeth, a history buff, designed a studio inside the base of the old 30-foot-tall bell tower. Jamie Wyeth once said, "I think I could spend two lifetimes here and not run out of subjects."

Southern Island can be seen distantly from the public landing in the picturesque village of Tenants Harbor, but the lighthouse is best seen by boat. You can get a good view from the seasonal lighthouse cruises offered by the Monhegan Boat Line (207-372-8848, www.moneganboat.com) in Port Clyde.

Fascinating Fact

This lighthouse has appeared in a number of paintings, including Andrew Wyeth's *Signal Flags* and Jamie Wyeth's *Iris at Sea*.

Early 1900s view

WHITEHEAD LIGHT

Accessibility: ⛵

Geographic coordinates:
43° 58' 43" N   69° 07' 27" W

Nearest town: St. George. Located at the western entrance to Muscle Ridge Channel, Penobscot Bay.

Established: 1804. Present lighthouse built 1852. Automated: 1982.

Height of tower: 41 feet. Height of focal plane: 75 feet.

Previous optic: Third-order Fresnel lens. Present optic: 300 mm.

Characteristic: Green light occulting every 4 seconds.

Fog signal: Two blasts every 30 seconds.

An octagonal wooden lighthouse, 30 feet tall, was established on 90-acre Whitehead Island by order of President Thomas Jefferson in 1807. The station had a scandal early in its history. It seems the first keeper, Ellis Dolph, had a side business selling oil intended for the light. Officials discovered that storekeepers in the nearby town of Thomaston had been buying whole barrels of oil from the keeper, who was immediately dismissed.

In 1837, new equipment was installed that created the first tide-driven fog bell. The "perpetual fog bell" was run by a complicated combination of timbers, chains, and weights. By 1842, the system was no longer in operation due to storm damage. The keeper had tied a line to the bell's clapper and run the line into his bedroom, where he sometimes amused himself by sounding the bell from his bed.

The extant granite lighthouse was built in 1852. Isaac Grant became keeper in 1875. Grant's wife was Abbie Burgess Grant, who had gained fame as the heroine of Matinicus Rock. Abbie was the assistant keeper under her husband.

Arthur Beal became keeper in 1929, after ten years as an assistant keeper at Matinicus Rock. Beal would go on to serve for twenty-one years at Whitehead. Under the Coast Guard, Whitehead Light became a males-only station instead of a three-family station. The 1899 Dutch Colonial principal keeper's house was razed, but the assistant keeper's duplex house near the tower still stands. The old third-order Fresnel lens is now at the Maine Lighthouse Museum in Rockland.

Under the Maine Lights Program, ownership was transferred from the Coast Guard to Pine Island Camp (207-465-3031, www.pineisland.org), an historic boys camp situated on Pine Island in Great Pond of the Belgrade Lakes in Maine. Visit www.whiteheadlight station.org for information on public educational programs and other activities on the island.

Cruises offered by the Monhegan Boat Line (207-372-8848, www.mon heganboat.com) in Port Clyde offer an excellent photographic opportunity.

Fascinating Fact

This is one of the foggiest spots on the coast, averaging eighty days of fog a year.

Nineteenth-century view

TWO BUSH ISLAND LIGHT

Accessibility: ⛵

Geographic coordinates: 43° 57' 51" N 69° 04' 26" W

Nearest town: St. George. Located in Two Bush Channel, Penobscot Bay.

Established: 1897. Present lighthouse built: 1897. Automated: 1964.

Height of tower: 42 feet. Height of focal plane: 65 feet.

Previous optic: Fifth-order Fresnel lens. Present optic: VRB-25.

Characteristic: White flash every 5 seconds with a red sector.

Fog signal: One blast every 15 seconds.

Two Bush Island was named for two lone pines, now gone, that served as day beacons before the building of the 42-foot square brick lighthouse and accompanying dwelling.

Undated aerial view

Leland Mann of nearby Spruce Head came to the station as an assistant keeper in 1919, and he became keeper in 1927. His son, Darrell, who was twelve when the family arrived on the island, helped with the lighthouse duties. On one occasion, he jumped out of a window of the keeper's house and ran to the top of the lighthouse to put out a fire that had started from the oil vapor.

The Manns successfully raised chickens on the island. In 1933, their hens laid 403 eggs. Apparently there was a competition with the keeper's family at Baker Island Light. Darrell Mann told a reporter, "If the Baker's Island hens read this, they will double up speed."

Around 1900, a fishing schooner was in danger of being smashed on the island in a snowstorm. The two men aboard took to a dory as a leak developed in the schooner. The men were desperately trying to find a place to land when they heard the frantic barking of Smut, keeper Alteverd Norton's dog. Norton, alerted by the dog, ran to the shore and saw the men in the dory. Their boat was overturned by a wave. The assistant keeper managed to get a line to the men and haul them ashore. Smut eagerly licked the faces of the fish-ermen, who later offered to buy the dog at any price. Norton refused to sell.

In 1970, the Coast Guard allowed the Green Berets to destroy the keeper's house as a demolition exercise. The lighthouse became the property of the U.S. Fish and Wildlife Service in 1998. The seasonal lighthouse cruises offered by the Monhegan Boat Line (207-372-8848, www.monheganboat.com) in Port Clyde offer excellent views.

Fascinating Fact

In February 1923, after the temperature hit zero for eighteen days in a row, a lifesaving crew had to smash their dory through the ice to get provisions to keeper Leland Mann and his family.

ROCKLAND HARBOR SOUTHWEST LIGH

Accessibility: 🚗

Geographic coordinates: 44° 04' 59" N 69° 05' 46" W

Nearest town: Owl's Head. Located at the southwest corner of Rockland Harbor.

Established: 1987. Present lighthouse built: 1987.

Height of focal plane: 44 feet.

Optic: Fifth-order Fresnel lens.

Characteristic: Flashing yellow every 2.5 seconds.

Dr. Bruce Woolett's love of lighthouses began when he was a boy. Years later, the Maine dentist had a house built in Owl's Head, with his own lighthouse included. The Coast Guard recognized the light as an aid to navigation marking dangerous Seal Ledge. In 1989, a fifth-order Fresnel lens from the Doubling Point Range Lights was installed.

John J. Gazzola purchased the property from Dr. Woolett in May 1998. According to Mr. Gazzola, "Much of the location has been extensively renovated including the lighthouse: new exterior wood shingle siding, combination storm sash with shutters, new doors both entrance and light level to exterior platform, also landscaping, interior first floor reading room, second floor bedroom, two watch bunks within tower to light level, new electrical wiring, insulation, interior and exterior painting, and other changes." The light is maintained as a private aid to navigation.

Visitors are welcome to visit the grounds near the lighthouse but are not allowed inside without permission. To reach the lighthouse from Route 73 between Thomaston and Rockland, turn right onto North Shore Drive. Drive for 0.6 miles (past Ash Point Road on the right) and turn left at a sign marked Shearmans Lane Prvt. Bear right at a fork into the driveway. As you enter the property, there is a small parking area to your right. Be sure to respect the privacy of the residents, and do not drive on the lawn when entering or leaving the property.

Fascinating Fact

Dr. Bruce Woolett was inspired to build this lighthouse when, while staying at his adopted grandparents' home, the flash of Rockland Breakwater Light entered his room each night.

OWL'S HEAD LIGHT

Accessibility: 🚗 🚶 ⛵

Geographic coordinates:
44° 05' 33" N   69° 02' 39" W

Nearest town: Owl's Head. Located at the south side of the entrance to Rockland Harbor, western Penobscot Bay.

Established: 1825. Present lighthouse built: 1852. Automated: 1989.

Height of tower: 30 feet. Height of focal plane: 100 feet.

Optic: Fourth-order Fresnel lens.

Characteristic: Fixed white.

Fog signal: Two blasts every 20 seconds.

The growing lime trade in Rockland and Thomaston led to the establishment of a light station, with a 30-foot stone tower at Owl's Head. Isaac Sterns was the first keeper at $350 per year. The present brick tower was built in 1852.

Owls Head Light Station circa 1860s

Author Edward Rowe Snow interviewed Clara Maddocks, wife of keeper Joseph Maddocks, when she was 102 years old. Maddocks became keeper at Owl's Head in 1873, and there were at least eleven shipwrecks in the vicinity during his twenty-three years as keeper. Mrs. Maddocks remembered a particularly cold winter when the bay was so frozen that she observed a horse and sleigh cross from Rockland to Vinalhaven.

Keeper George Woodward

Augustus B. Hamor came to Owl's Head as keeper in 1930. Keeper Hamor had a Springer spaniel named Spot who gained wide fame. Spot learned to pull the rope that rang the fog bell with his teeth, a ritual he repeated for every approaching vessel. Spot's unusual abilities turned out to be good for more than entertainment. The Matinicus mail boat almost ran aground one snowy night, but Spot's loud barking warned the captain and enabled him to steer clear of the rocks.

The 1854 keeper's house remains a residence for Coast Guard personnel, while the surrounding grounds are now a state park. The grounds at Owl's Head Light State Park (207-941-4014) are open daily; there is a large parking area and a moderate walk (about 10 minutes) to the lighthouse.

In December 2007, the lighthouse tower was licensed to the American Lighthouse Foundation (ALF). The effort is directed by a committee of the Friends of the Rockland Breakwater Lighthouse, a chapter of

SIDE TRIP: *Owl's Head Transportation Museum*

This gem of a museum has one of the finest collections of pioneer-era aircraft and automobiles in the world, with more than one hundred historic aircraft, automobiles, bicycles, carriages, and engines on display. Among the highlights are a 1963 prototype Mustang car and a 1935 Stout Scarab, called the world's first minivan. The museum is on Route 73 in Owl's Head, two miles from Route 1. It's open all year.

Owl's Head Transportation Museum
Phone: 207-594-4418
Web site: www.ohtm.org

ALF. A major overhaul was completed in 2010, thanks to a $248,000 joint project between the Coast Guard and ALF. The lighthouse is open for tours in summer; the schedule in 2011 was three days per week. Visit www.rockland lighthouse.com for more information.

From Route 1 North in Thomaston, go through two sets of lights; you will see the Knox Mansion on your right at the second set of lights. About one mile after this, turn right onto Buttermilk Lane. Follow to the end (2.6 miles) and turn left onto Route 73. Continue for 1.3 miles and then turn right onto North Shore Road. Continue for about 2.5 miles; turn left at a triangular intersection onto Main Street. After 0.2 miles, turn left at Lighthouse Road and continue about a half-mile to the large free parking area.

The lighthouse can also be seen from harbor tours out of Rockland (207-596-5660, www.mvmonhegan. com). Many other cruises in the area may also provide a view; check with the Camden-Rockport-Lincolnville Chamber of Commerce (207-236-4404, www. camdenme.org) and the Penobscot Bay Regional Chamber of Commerce (207-596-0376, www.rocklandchamber.org).

Fascinating Fact

A famous story concerns a schooner wrecked near here in December 1850. An engaged couple was found on the vessel, and it was reported that they were frozen in a block of ice when they were taken to the keeper's house at Owl's Head. They were gradually revived, and they lived to be celebrated as the "Frozen Couple of Owl's Head."

ROCKLAND BREAKWATER LIGHT

Between 1881 and 1899, a granite breakwater almost a mile long was built to help protect Rockland Harbor. As the work progressed, a small moveable beacon was moved farther out each time the breakwater was extended. Charles Ames served as the light's attendant for some years at $25 per month. He also struck a metal triangle when a fog signal was called for. Finally, in 1902 a permanent lighthouse was built at the breakwater's end.

Accessibility:

Geographic coordinates: 44° 06' 15" N 69° 04' 39" W

Nearest city: Rockland. Located at the end of a breakwater at Jameson Point, on the north side of the entrance to Rockland Harbor.

Established: 1902. Present lighthouse built: 1902. Automated: 1965.

Height of tower: 25 feet. Height of focal plane: 39 feet.

Earlier optic: Fourth-order Fresnel lens. Present optic: VRB-25.

Characteristic: White flash every 5 seconds.

Fog signal: One blast every 15 seconds.

The lighthouse consisted of a wood-and-brick keeper's house along with an engine room, with an attached 25-foot brick tower. The interiors of the engine room and lighthouse tower were lined with ceramic-faced brick.

This was a stag station, meaning the keeper's families did not live at the lighthouse. The keepers usually traveled by boat to Rockland Harbor, two miles away, rather than making the long trek over the breakwater. The keepers augmented their menu by trapping lobsters. A Coast Guardsman stationed at the lighthouse in 1951, Warren "Tommy" Ayres, once caught a 27-pound lobster. "The claw was as big as my shoe," he later remembered.

The city of Rockland obtained ownership of the lighthouse in 1998 under the Maine Lights Program. The Friends of the Rockland Breakwater Lighthouse (P.O. Box 741, Rockland, Maine 04841. Phone: 207-785-4609.

Web site: www.rocklandlighthouse.com), a chapter of the American Lighthouse Foundation, was established, and the group has been gradually restoring the building inside and out.

Open houses are held from 9:00 a.m. to 5:00 p.m. every Saturday and Sunday (also special events and holidays) from the end of May to the middle of October, weather and volunteer availability permitting. Volunteer docents are available to answer any questions about the lighthouse and its history, and lighthouse-related items are also available for purchase.

Directions: Turn off Route 1 onto Waldo Avenue. If you're heading north, it's a right turn about three miles north of Route 1's intersection with Route 1A. After about .4 mile, turn right onto Samoset Road. Continue to the parking lot at the breakwater park. Off to the left, there's a path leading to the breakwater. The walk to the lighthouse across the 4,346-foot breakwater is a pleasant one on a nice day, but in rough weather, waves sometimes lap over the granite blocks. Be sure to wear comfortable shoes and dress warmly. There are no restrooms in the lighthouse. Children must be at least four feet tall to climb the tower.

Fascinating Fact

The breakwater in Rockland Harbor required 697,627 tons of granite to complete.

The best views for photographing the lighthouse are from the water. Harbor tours out of Rockland Harbor (207-596-5660, www.mvmonhegan.com) offer a good view. Many of the day sails and longer windjammer cruises in the area may also provide views; check with the Camden-Rockport-Lincolnville Chamber of Commerce (207-236-4404, www.camdenme.org) and the Penobscot Bay Regional Chamber of Commerce (207-596-0376, www.rockland chamber.org) for the latest offerings.

SIDE TRIP: *Maine Lighthouse Museum*

This wonderful new museum on the Rockland waterfront is home to the largest collection of lighthouse lenses in the United States, as well as a landmark collection of lighthouse artifacts and Coast Guard memorabilia. There are a wide variety of Fresnel lenses, including the second-order lens from Petit Manan Light and the rotating third-order lens from Matinicus Rock.

The facility has its origins in the lighthouse displays at Rockland's old Shore Village Museum. The collection was amassed over more than thirty years by the late "Mr. Lighthouse," retired Coast Guard Chief Warrant Officer Ken Black. Black was the recipient of many honors, including a lifetime achievement award from the Coast Guard.

The building is also home to the Penobscot Bay Regional Chamber of Commerce. Open daily in summer with limited hours in the off-season. Group tours are available.

Maine Lighthouse Museum
One Park Drive
Rockland, ME 04841
Phone: 207-594-3301
Web site: www.mainelighthouse
museum.com

HERON NECK LIGHT

Accessibility: ⛵

Geographic coordinates:
44° 01' 30" N 68° 51' 44" W

Nearest town: Vinalhaven. Located at the southern end of Green's Island, off the south coast of Vinalhaven, eastern entrance to Hurricane Sound.

Established: 1854. Present lighthouse built: 1854. Automated: 1982.

Height of tower: 30 feet. Height of focal plane: 92 feet.

Earlier optic: Fifth-order Fresnel lens. Present optic: 300 mm.

Characteristic: Fixed red with a white sector.

Fog signal: One blast every 30 seconds.

This light station was established on 400-acre Green's Island to help guide mariners heading for Vinalhaven's Carver's Harbor. The 30-foot brick tower was attached to the keeper's house, also constructed of brick.

Undated aerial view

An 1890 report revealed that five people had died in the keeper's house, apparently because of unhealthy conditions. Insufficient mortar had been used in the building's construction, leaving it damp and leaky. The keeper's house was rebuilt in 1895; the 1854 tower remained and was attached to the new house.

In April 1989, an electrical fire broke out in the empty keeper's house, and the building was badly damaged. In November 1993, the Coast Guard agreed to hand over the station to the Island Institute of Rockland (www.islandinstitute.org). The institute in turn leased the property to a private party who successfully restored the house.

There's a wilderness camp on the island; see www.greensisland.com for details. The periodic lighthouse cruises offered by the Isle au Haut Company in Stonington (207-367-5193, www.isleauhaut.com) pass close by.

Fascinating Fact

In the early 1900s, a dog named Nemo was taught by Keeper Levi Farnham to bark loudly when he heard the horns of approaching boats. When Nemo retired, he was replaced by a new "fog dog" named Rover.

Early 1900s view

BROWN'S HEAD LIGHT

Accessibility: ⛵ + 🚗

Geographic coordinates:
44° 06' 42" N   68° 54' 36" W

Nearest town: Vinalhaven.
Located at the northwest
corner of Vinalhaven Island,
Penobscot Bay.

Established: 1832.
Present lighthouse built:
1857. Automated: 1987.

Height of tower:
20 feet. Height of focal
plane: 39 feet.

Earlier optic: Fifth-order
Fresnel lens. Present optic:
Fourth-order Fresnel lens.

Characteristic: Fixed white
with two red sectors.

Fog signal: One blast every
10 seconds.

Vinalhaven is a large island (8 miles long) in the middle of Penobscot Bay. In the second half of the nineteenth century, Vinalhaven developed a thriving granite industry. It was the busy fishing industry and passenger-cargo shipping that led Congress and President Andrew Jackson to authorize the establishment of a light station in 1832 to help guide mariners through the western entrance to the Fox Islands Thorofare.

A 20-foot stone tower and accompanying keeper's house were built for $4,000. The original keeper's house was in disrepair by 1857. A new wood-frame dwelling was constructed, connected by a covered passageway to the cylindrical brick tower.

Benjamin Eldridge Burgess became keeper in 1867. He was still in charge thirty-seven years later, at the age of 80, when the *Boston Globe* published an article about him. The article called Burgess "a good man, a good servant of Uncle Sam, and a saver of countless lives."

This was one of the last lighthouses in Maine to be automated. Under the Maine Lights Program, the lighthouse buildings were transferred to the Town of Vinalhaven in 1998. The station is the residence of Vinalhaven's town manager.

Vinalhaven can be reached by the Maine State Ferry (207-596-2202, www.maine.gov/mdot/msfs). To reach the lighthouse from the ferry terminal, turn right and follow Main Street to High Street. Turn left onto High Street. Turn right onto North Haven Road. Continue north for about 6.1 miles to a group of mailboxes. Turn left onto unpaved Crockett River Road.

After 0.3 miles, turn right onto the second dirt road on the right. Continue another half-mile past a cemetery to a small parking area. The lighthouse grounds are open to the public. Visitors should, of course, respect the privacy of the residents.

The lighthouse can also be viewed from the "Lighthouses Boat Trip" offered by Old Quarry Ocean Adventures (207-367-8977, www.oldquarry.com) of Stonington. Lighthouse cruises offered by the Isle au Haut Company in Stonington (207-367-5193, www.isleauhaut.com) also pass by.

Brown's Head Light Station circa 1860s

Fascinating Fact

Vinalhaven is part of a group called the Fox Islands. They were named by explorer Martin Pring after the gray foxes that were common there.

GOOSE ROCKS LIGHT

Accessibility: ⛵

Geographic coordinates: 44° 08' 08" N 68° 49' 50" W

Nearest town: North Haven. Located at the eastern end of the Fox Islands Thorofare.

Established: 1890. Present lighthouse built: 1890. Automated: 1963.

Height of tower: 51 feet. Height of focal plane: 51 feet.

Earlier optic: Fourth-order Fresnel lens. Present optic: 250 mm.

Characteristic: Red flash every 6 seconds with a white sector.

Fog signal: One blast every 10 seconds.

Goose Rocks Light is a typical spark-plug-style cast-iron lighthouse of its era, built on a cylindrical cast-iron caisson filled with concrete. The tower has three stories inside, including living quarters.

Goose Rocks Light circa 1890s

Charles L. Knight became an assistant keeper in 1926. He later said, "I enjoyed being on this character of light station, for it gave me no worry about my family, as they were nicely located in a fine home on shore and well cared for. My eight-day visit ashore with them was looked forward to every month of the year with much pleasure."

Jim Woods was part of the Coast Guard crew at Goose Rocks Light, circa 1959–60. He wrote: "It was a three-man crew, with one on liberty at all times. The fog signal was a large brass bell with a mechanism that worked on the same idea as a wind-up watch. It had to be wound up every 4 to 6 hours during periods of fog. . . . Local lobstermen kept us in lobster to eat. All in all, it wasn't bad duty, as no one was after your job."

In 2006, under the provisions of the National Historic Lighthouse Preservation Act, the lighthouse was sold to Beacon Preservation (203-736-9300, ext. 398, www.beaconpreservation.org). The organization has at times made the lighthouse available for overnight stays.

The lighthouse can be seen distantly from Vinalhaven and North Haven, but it's best seen by boat. An excellent view is available from the "Lighthouses Boat Trip," offered by Old Quarry Ocean Adventures (207-367-8977, www.oldquarry.com) of Stonington. Periodic lighthouse cruises offered by the Isle au Haut Company in Stonington (207-367-5193, www.isleauhaut.com) also provide a view.

Fascinating Fact

For some time after the light was automated, local people—known as "lamplighters"—were employed to control the fog signal.

INDIAN ISLAND LIGHT

Accessibility: 🏛 ⛵

Geographic coordinates:
44° 09' 57" N   69° 03' 38" W

Nearest town: Rockport.
Located at the east side of
the entrance to Rockport
Harbor, Penobscot Bay.

Established: 1850.
Present lighthouse built:
1875. Deactivated: 1934.

Earlier optic: Fourth-order
Fresnel lens. Present optic:
none.

Rockport Harbor was a center for ship-building and the export of lime in the mid-1800s. Established in 1850, the first lighthouse consisted of a lantern mounted on the roof of the keeper's house. The light was discontinued in 1859, but it was reactivated and a new lighthouse tower was built in 1875 for $9,000. The station consists of a square brick tower attached to the original T-shaped keeper's house.

Early 1900s view

Foster Reed was the keeper from 1925 to 1933. His granddaughter Barbara frequently spent weekends and vacations on the island, according to an article by Diane Roesing O'Brien in *Lighthouse Digest*. "Barbara never remembers being lonely on the island," wrote Roesing. "There wasn't a tree on the island in her childhood, and she wandered the beach, looking for things or digging clams."

In 1934, the lighthouse was replaced by an automatic light on nearby Lowell Rock. The property has been privately owned since then. It can be seen distantly (more than a mile) from Rockport Marine Park. To reach the park from Route 1 North, turn right off Route 1 at a traffic light in Rockport (Route 90 will be on your left). Drive .25 miles and then turn left at a T intersection. The park is less than .25 miles away on the right.

The lighthouse is best viewed from the water. Cruises leaving Camden aboard the *Betselma* (207-236-4446) offer a good view. You can also charter a trip with Rockport Charters (207-691-1066, www.rockportcharters.com).

Fascinating Fact

Indian Island was so named because local Native Americans took refuge there during the French and Indian War.

CURTIS ISLAND LIGHT

Accessibility: 🏠 ⛵

Geographic coordinates: 44° 12' 06" N   69° 02' 54" W

Nearest town: Camden. Located at the entrance to Camden Harbor, Penobscot Bay.

Established: 1835. Present lighthouse built: 1896. Automated: 1972.

Height of tower: 25 feet. Height of focal plane: 52 feet.

Earlier optic: Fourth-order Fresnel lens. Present optic: 300 mm.

Characteristic: Green light occulting every 4 seconds.

Camden's well-protected harbor helped the town develop major lime kiln and shipbuilding industries in the nineteenth century. The first brick lighthouse on the small island was built in 1835, by order of President Andrew Jackson. H. K. M. Bowers was the first keeper.

Early 1900s view

The keeper's house was rebuilt in 1889. The extant 25-foot brick tower replaced the earlier lighthouse in 1896. Six Coast Guardsmen were stationed on the island during World War II. It was reported that the men were treated like sons by keeper Myrick Morrison.

In the mid-1960s, John R. French, a Coast Guard keeper, transported four of his children—aged 6 to 12—to shore for school each day in his outboard motorboat. Two younger children sometimes went along for the ride. This was a vast improvement over the days when French was assigned to remote Matinicus Rock and saw his family only about once a month.

The town of Camden acquired the island after the light was automated. A fog bell from the station is on display in

SIDE TRIP: *Mount Battie and Camden Hills State Park*

A highlight of 5,500-acre Camden Hills State Park is the scenic panorama from the summit of Mount Battie, with sweeping views of Penobscot Bay, including Curtis Island and its lighthouse. The park and the entrance to the Mount Battie Auto Road are just a few minutes north of Camden on Route 1. There are hiking trails, a campground, and picnic areas. The auto road is open from early May to early October.

Camden Hills State Park
280 Belfast Road
Camden, ME 04843
Phone: (207) 236-3109
Web site: www.maine.gov/doc/parks/

Fascinating Fact

Curtis Island was previously called Negro Island, after an African cook who lived on the island. The name of the island was changed in 1934 in memory of Cyrus H.K. Curtis, publisher of the Saturday Evening Post and other publications and a longtime summer resident and benefactor of Camden.

the public parking lot at Camden Harbor, and the old fourth-order Fresnel lens is on display in the Camden Public Library at 6 High Street. Under the Maine Lights Program, the lighthouse officially became the property of the town of Camden in 1998.

This picturesque light station is difficult to see from land, but you might be able to get a partially obstructed view on Bayview Street. The lighthouse is best seen from cruises leaving Camden, including the *Betselma* (207-236-4446), the schooner *Olad* (207-236-2323, www.maineschooners.com), the *Lively Lady Too* (207-236-6672, www.livelyladytoo.com), the schooner *Appledore II* (207-236-8353, www.appledore2.com), and the schooner *Surprise* (207-236-4687, www.camdenmainesailing.com). For other sailing opportunities, check with the Camden-Rockport-Lincolnville Chamber of Commerce (207-236-4404, www.camdenme.org).

GRINDLE POINT LIGHT

Islesboro is a 10-mile-long, narrow island in upper Penobscot Bay. The largest commercial shipping fleet in the bay was based at the island in the nineteenth century. A light station, with a 28-foot-tall tower was established in 1851 to help mariners entering Islesboro's Gilkey Harbor.

Accessibility:

Geographic coordinates:
44° 16' 56" N 68° 56' 34" W

Nearest town: Islesboro. Located on the west side of the entrance to Gilkey Harbor at the southwest end of Islesboro Island, Penobscot Bay.

Established: 1851. Present lighthouse built: 1874. Deactivated: 1934. Relighted: 1987.

Height of tower: 39 feet. Height of focal plane: 39 feet.

Earlier optic: Fifth-order Fresnel lens. Present optic: 250 mm.

Characteristic: Green flash every 4 seconds.

The extant lighthouse is a square brick tower attached by a covered walkway to the keeper's house. The tower originally had a fifth-order Fresnel lens. A boathouse was built in 1886, and an oil house was added in 1906.

SIDE TRIP: *Penobscot Marine Museum*

The exhibits at Maine's oldest maritime museum, located right along Route 1 in the old seafaring town of Searsport, focus on the history and industry of Penobscot Bay in the 1800s. The museum is also known for its collection of fine marine art, featuring one of the largest collections of Thomas and James Buttersworth paintings. The facility is spread through a series of historic buildings, including one that has been set up to resemble a typical sea captain's home. There's also an extensive museum store.

Searsport is also known to many as the antiques capital of Maine, with numerous shops and flea markets.

Penobscot Marine Museum
5 Church Street, P.O. Box 498
Searsport, ME 04974
Phone: 207-548-2529
Web site: www.penobscotmarine
museum.org.

Francis Grindle sold the land for the station to the government and later became keeper in 1853. Grindle had spent years at sea and achieved the title of master mariner.

Keeper James E. Hall, who had been an assistant keeper under William Grant at Matinicus Rock, was killed in a rock-blasting accident at Grindle Point in 1916.

In 1934, the light was deactivated and replaced by a nearby light on a skeleton tower. The lighthouse and grounds became the property of the

town of Islesboro. The keeper's house was converted into the Sailor's Memorial Museum, which opened in 1938. The people of Islesboro convinced the Coast Guard to reactivate the lighthouse in 1987. A solar-powered optic was installed with a flashing green light, and the skeleton tower was removed.

The Sailor's Memorial Museum is open in summer; for information, you can call the Islesboro town offices at 207-734-2253. The ferry (207-734-6935, www.maine.gov/mdot/msfs/) from Lincolnville Beach docks right next to the lighthouse, so there's no need to bring your car if lighthouse viewing is your main goal. The ferry terminal is on Route 1 in Lincolnville.

Fascinating Fact

Islesboro was once the haunt of wealthy people like J. P. Morgan. Today, actors John Travolta and Kirstie Alley are among those who live part-time here.

LADIES DELIGHT LIGHT

Accessibility: 🏛 ⛵

Geographic coordinates:
44° 18' 16" N   69° 53' 48" W

Nearest town: Manchester. Located on a small island in the northern part of Lake Cobbosseecontee.

Established: 1908. Present lighthouse built: 1908.

Height of tower: 25 feet.

Lake Cobbosseecontee is just west of the state capital of Augusta. Around 1900, the lake became a resort with many cottages and inns. The central part of a large, jagged reef in the lake forms a small island called Ladies Delight, located about a mile south of Island Park in Manchester. A lighthouse designed by Frank Morse, a Boston marine architect, was built on the island in 1908. The purpose of the light was to keep a passenger launch in the south end of the lake from going aground on the reef.

The light source was originally kerosene lanterns. A volunteer keeper would go out each evening to trim the wicks, clean the globes, and light the beacon. A system of grandfather clock weights was used to rotate a reflector. The lighthouse now receives its power via a cable from Manchester.

The Cobbosseecontee Yacht Club (P. O. Box 17, Manchester, ME 04351. Web site: www.cycmaine.org) maintains the lighthouse during the summer. A 2005 restoration included the installation of a new aluminum lantern. The lighthouse can be seen distantly from shore; contact the yacht club for information about getting a closer look by boat. Lakeside Motel and Cabins (207.395.6741, www.lakesidelodging.com) at the northern end of the lake has can oes available to guests; the adventurous might want to paddle to the lighthouse.

Fascinating Fact

Personnel of the Cobbosseecontee Yacht Club erected the lighthouse with the help of two oxen. The builders could transport only one ox at a time on their barge. After taking the first ox to the island, the workers returned to get the second one. In the meantime, the first ox grew lonely and started swimming back to the mainland as the workers returned to the island. They finally succeeded in getting both oxen on the island, and the lighthouse was built over the course of the summer.

MOONLIGHT ON LAKE COBBOSSCEC

FORT POINT LIGHT

Accessibility: 🚶

Geographic coordinates:
44° 28' 02" N 68° 48' 42" W

Nearest town: Stockton Springs. Located on Cape Jellison, on the west side of the mouth of the Penobscot River.

Established: 1836. Present lighthouse built: 1857. Automated: 1988.

Height of tower:
31 feet. Height of focal plane: 88 feet.

Optic: Fourth-order Fresnel lens.

Characteristic: Fixed white.

Fog signal: One blast every 10 seconds.

This light was established in 1836 to aid vessels bound for Bangor, a leading lumber port. The town of Stockton Springs was also a lumber port and a shipping point for Maine's potato industry. The first lighthouse was a granite tower. The first keeper was William Clewly, who had sold his land to the government for the station.

Nineteenth-century view

The extant 31-foot square brick lighthouse was built in 1857. A new two-story keeper's house, attached to the tower, was built the same year. In 1890, a bell tower and a barn were added, and an oil house was built in 1897. All of these buildings are still standing, making Fort Point Light an unusually well-preserved light station. The pyramidal bell tower is one of the few left in New England and is listed on the National Register of Historic Places. The bell, replaced by a foghorn, hangs outside the tower. There are historic photos displayed inside the tower, and it's sometimes opened to the public in summer.

Larry Baum was the last Coast Guard keeper at the family station. Under the Maine Lights Program coordinated by the Island Institute of Rockland, the lighthouse became the property of the Maine Bureau of Parks and Land in 1998. The lighthouse grounds are now part of 154-acre Fort Point State Park.

Since 1988, the resident "keepers" for the Maine Bureau of Parks and Lands have been Terry and Jeralyn Cole. Terry was the keeper at Fort Point Light back when he was in the Coast Guard in the early 1970s

There are signs on Route 1 in

Fascinating Fact

The lighthouse gets its name from adjacent Fort Pownall, built by order of Massachusetts Governor Pownall (Maine at that time was part of Massachusetts) in 1759 to guard against the French.

Stockton Springs pointing the way to Fort Point State Park and the lighthouse. After turning off Route 1 (a right turn if you're heading north) onto Main Street, continue for 0.6 miles and then turn right onto Cape Jellison Road. Turn left after 0.9 miles and continue to the entrance to the park on the left. Follow to the parking area on the right, near the fort and lighthouse. For more information on the park, you can call 207-567-3356.

DICE HEAD LIGHT
(Dyce Head Light)

Accessibility: 🚗

Geographic coordinates: 44° 22' 57" N 68° 49' 07" W

Nearest town: Castine. Located at the east side of the entrance to the Penobscot River.

Established: 1828. Present lighthouse built: 1829. Deactivated: 1935.

Height of tower: 51 feet.

Earlier optic: Fourth-order Fresnel lens. Present optic: 250 mm.

Dice Head Light served to guide mariners headed into the Penobscot River toward Bangor, a leading lumber port. First lighted in June 1829 by keeper Jacob Shelburne, the conical stone tower is lined with brick. In 1858, the entire tower was surrounded with a six-sided wooden frame. The frame was removed in the late 1800s.

Dice Head Light Station circa 1860s

Shipping in the area fell off, and in 1935 the light was discontinued and replaced by a skeleton tower by the edge of the water. The keeper's house and surrounding property became the property of the town of Castine in 1937. In 1956, the lighthouse itself was turned over to the town.

Early 1900s view

The keeper's house is rented by the town to help pay for the upkeep of the property.

The tower lost some chunks of mortar over the years. Inspectors found interior disintegration in the lighthouse that could have eventually caused serious problems. A 1998 renovation involved a method called "slurry injection." Slurry—clay or cement mixed with a liquid—was injected through holes in the tower.

In September 2007, a wind storm or "microburst" toppled the skeletal tower. A short time later, it was announced that the Coast Guard would install a new optic in the lighthouse tower, making it an active aid to navigation again after 72 years in darkness. A 250-mm optic went into service on January 1,

Fascinating Fact

Castine is one of America's oldest communities. Beginning in the early 1600s, it was the site of trading posts, forts, missions, and permanent settlements of France, Holland, England, and colonial America.

2008, exhibiting a white flash every 6 seconds.

Directions: From Route 1 in Orland, take Route 175 South. In about eight miles, Route 175 goes to the left. Continue straight onto Route 166. In approximately one mile, bear right onto Route 166A. At the next junction with Route 166, take Route 166 and

continue into Castine. Take a right at a golf course onto Battle Avenue. Follow Battle Avenue past the Maine Maritime Academy for about a mile to the lighthouse on your right. There's free parking, and a path leads around the tower, affording good views. The grounds are open to the public daily until sunset; be sure to respect the privacy of the residents of the keeper's house.

SIDE TRIP: *Fort Knox State Historic Site*

Fort Knox, on the west bank of the Penobscot River, was built between 1844 and 1864. It's a National Historic Landmark and one of the most beautifully preserved forts in New England. Visitors can stroll the scenic grounds and learn about the rich history of the site. The fort also features two complete Rodman cannons. Guided tours are available daily during the summer season.

Fort Knox State Historic Site
711 Fort Knox Road
Prospect, ME 04981
Phone: 207-469-7719
Web site: fortknox.maineguide.com

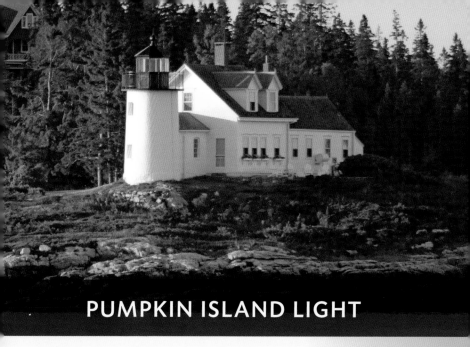

PUMPKIN ISLAND LIGHT

This light in eastern Penobscot Bay marks the south side of the western entrance to the body of water known as Eggemoggin Reach. In the nineteenth century, this waterway, which connects Penobscot Bay and Blue Hill Bay, was bustling with maritime traffic. The station consists of a 25-foot brick tower and a colonial cape keeper's house attached to the tower by a work shed. The first keeper, at $350 yearly, was J. C. Tibbetts, who stayed until 1861.

Accessibility: 🚶 ⛵

Geographic coordinates: 44° 18' 33" N   68° 44' 33" W

Nearest town: Deer Isle. Located off the northwestern tip of Little Deer Isle, at the western entrance to Eggemoggin Reach.

Established: 1855. Present lighthouse built: 1854. Deactivated: 1934.

Height of tower: 28 feet.

Earlier optic: Fifth-order Fresnel lens. Present optic: none.

In 1934, Pumpkin Island Light was discontinued and put up for auction by the government. George Harmon of Bar Harbor bought the station along with two other lights. Since then, the island has passed through several private owners.

From Route 1 in Orland, take Route 175 South. After about 22 miles, turn right onto Route 15 and continue for about 5 miles south across a bridge to Little Deer Isle. On Little Deer Isle, where Route 15 turns left, bear right through a triangular intersection onto Eggemoggin Road. Continue for 2.7 miles to the end of the road and park at a fishing pier, with a view of the lighthouse about 1,000 feet offshore.

The lighthouse can also be viewed from the "Lighthouses Boat Trip" offered by Old Quarry Ocean Adventures (207-367-8977, www. oldquarry.com) of Stonington. Some of the schooners out of Rockland, Rockport, and Camden occasionally pass nearby. Check with the Camden-Rockport-Lincolnville Chamber of Commerce (207-236-4404, www. camdenme.org) and the Penobscot Bay Regional Chamber of Commerce (207-596-0376, www. rocklandchamber.org) for the latest offerings. You can also arrange a trip with Sea Venture Custom Boat Tours (207-288-3355, www.svboat tours.com) in Bar Harbor to see this and other area lighthouses.

Fascinating Fact

Granite quarries at Deer Isle supplied material for many buildings, including Boston's Museum of Fine Arts, the U.S. Naval Academy, and the Manhattan Bridge.

Nineteenth-century view

EAGLE ISLAND LIGHT

Eagle Island Light was established on the east end of the 260-acre island to help guide vessels toward the Penobscot River. The first keeper was John Spear, who died at the station in 1848 and was replaced for a time by his widow. A two-story keeper's house was built at the same time as the stone lighthouse; a fog bell tower was added later.

Accessibility: ⛵

Geographic coordinates: 44° 13' 04" N   68° 46' 04" W

Nearest town: Deer Isle. Located in east Penobscot Bay.

Established: 1838. Present lighthouse built: 1838. Deactivated: 1959.

Height of tower: 30 feet. Height of focal plane: 106 feet.

Earlier optic: Fourth-order Fresnel lens. Present optic: 300 mm.

Characteristic: White flash every 4 seconds.

Eagle Island Light Station circa 1860s

Eagle Island could be a harsh place for lighthouse families in the winter. In the winter of 1917–18 there was solid ice from Eagle Island to Bangor. It wasn't until 1919 that the government furnished a boat for the keeper.

After automation, the Coast Guard put all the buildings, except the tower itself, up for bid with the condition that the buyer would remove the buildings. Nobody was willing to try this. In February 1964, a Coast Guard crew demolished the buildings, leaving the old lighthouse tower standing alone except for the bell tower.

Under the Maine Lights Program, the lighthouse was transferred in 1998 to a nonprofit group, the Eagle Light Caretakers (c/o Sam Howe, 2742 Normandy Drive NW, Atlanta, GA 30305).

The lighthouse is difficult to see from the mainland. It can be viewed from the "Lighthouses Boat Trip" offered by Old Quarry Ocean Adventures (207-367-8977, www.oldquarry. com) of Stonington. It can also be seen from Eagle Island mailboat cruise aboard the Sunset Bay Company's *Katherine* (207-348-9316, www.eagle islandrentals.com/transportation. html), with morning cruises departing from Sylvester's Cove in Deer Isle every day except Sunday, mid-June to mid-September. Reservations are required.

Fascinating Fact

This light station had no well for water until 1947 and no indoor plumbing until 1949. These basic conveniences were obtained partly through the help of Senator Margaret Chase Smith.

DEER ISLAND THOROFARE LIGHT
(Mark Island Light)

Deer Island Thorofare, between Deer Isle to the north and smaller islands to the south, was a busy waterway in the nineteenth century, with booming granite quarries in the area and a strong fishing industry. A light station on the west side of 6-acre Mark Island was established in 1857 to help mariners negotiate the narrow passage. Thomas Colby Small became the first keeper. The square brick tower was first lighted on New Year's Day in 1858.

Accessibility: ⛵

Geographic coordinates: 44° 08' 03" N   68° 46' 04" W

Nearest town: Stonington. Located on Mark Island in the Deer Island Thorofare, east Penobscot Bay.

Established: 1858. Present lighthouse built: 1858. Automated: 1960.

Height of tower: 25 feet. Height of focal plane: 52 feet.

Earlier optic: Fourth-order Fresnel lens. Present optic: 250 mm.

Characteristic: White flash every 6 seconds.

Fog signal: One blast every 15 seconds.

In February 1935, keeper Elmer Conary was stricken by an apparent heart attack. A tugboat reached the island with a local doctor, and Conary was carried aboard the tug. As the vessel reached Stonington Harbor, the ice was too thick to continue. The sick man was transported in a lifeboat through a narrow channel in the ice. Conary recuperated with his family on the mainland.

In 1959, an explosion and fire badly damaged the keeper's house. A short time later, the light was automated, the Coast Guard crew was removed, and all the buildings except the tower were destroyed.

In 1998, under the Maine Lights Program, ownership of the lighthouse was transferred to the Island Heritage Trust (P.O. Box 42, Deer Isle, ME 04627, 207-348-2455, www.island heritagetrust.org). The organization maintains the island as a wildlife refuge. Mark Island's birds include bald eagles and nesting eider ducks.

The lighthouse can be seen distantly from the mainland, but the best views are from the water. It can be seen from the "Lighthouses Boat Trip" offered by Old Quarry Ocean Adventures (207-367-8977, www.oldquarry.com) of Stonington. Seasonal lighthouse cruises offered by the Isle au Haut Company (207-367-6516, www.isleauhaut.com) of Stonington also provide a view.

Fascinating Fact

A Civil War veteran, Samuel E. Holden, became keeper in 1868. When he died in 1874, his widow, Melissa Colby Holden, became keeper. A local legend claims that the feisty Melissa once dumped a chamber pot on the heads of some unlucky intruders.

ISLE AU HAUT LIGHT

This brick tower on a granite base is very similar to the lighthouses built earlier at Ram Island and Marshall Point. The tower is slightly offshore and is reached via a wooden walkway. The original optic, a fourth-order Fresnel lens, is now at the Maine Lighthouse Museum in Rockland.

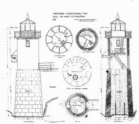

Original plans for Isle au Haut Light

Accessibility: ⛵ 🚤

Geographic coordinates: 44° 03' 54" N 68° 39' 06" W

Nearest town: Isle au Haut. Located at Robinson Point on the west coast of Isle au Haut, on the south side of the western entrance to Isle au Haut Thorofare.

Established: 1907. Present lighthouse built: 1907. Automated: 1934.

Height of tower: 40 feet. Height of focal plane: 48 feet.

Earlier optic: Fourth-order Fresnel lens. Present optic: 250 mm.

Characteristic: Red flash every 4 seconds with a white sector.

Early view of Isle au Haut Light Station

The light had only two keepers in its brief life as a staffed station. The property (except for the lighthouse) was sold to Charles E. Robinson, a resident of the island, after the light's 1934 automation.

In 1986, the property was purchased by Jeff and Judi Burke. The Burkes converted the keeper's house into a bed and breakfast called, appropriately enough, the Keeper's House Inn. Even the oil house was converted into a cozy guest room. The inn was the realization of a dream for the Burkes. The setting, with thick pine woods opening up to the sparkling ocean, is incomparable. Deer, osprey, eagles, and mink abound.

The keeper's house property was put on sale in the summer of 2007. At this writing, the inn is closed except for weekly rentals of a cottage on the property.

Under the Maine Lights Program, the lighthouse tower was turned over to the town of Isle au Haut in April 1998. A restoration of the lighthouse was finished in June 1999, thanks to the Isle au Haut Lighthouse Committee.

Isle au Haut is reached by taking the mailboat/passenger ferry (207-367-6516, www.isleauhaut.com) from Stonington. The lighthouse is a hike of a little less than a mile from the town landing. Maps of Isle au Haut can be obtained in Stonington or at the Acadia National Park visitor center in Bar Harbor. (Much of Isle au Haut is part of Acadia National Park.) The lighthouse can also be seen from the "Lighthouses Boat Trip" offered by Old Quarry Ocean Adventures (207-367-8977, www.oldquarry.com) of Stonington. Seasonal lighthouse cruises offered by the Isle au Haut Company in Stonington also provide a view.

Fascinating Fact

Charles E. Robinson, who bought the keeper's house after the light was automated, was the great-grandfather of writer Linda Greenlaw (*The Lobster Chronicles*).

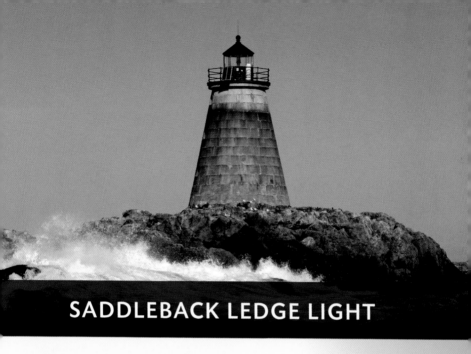

SADDLEBACK LEDGE LIGHT

Designed by noted architect and engineer Alexander Parris, this granite lighthouse was an expensive one for its day at $15,000. An attached wooden building was added later. The lower floor of the building was a boathouse, and two rooms for keepers were located on the second floor. Incredibly, for many years before the attached building was added, the upper part of the tower was home to the keepers and their families.

Accessibility: ⛵

Geographic coordinates:
44° 00' 54" N   68° 43' 36" W

Nearest town: Vinalhaven. Located about three miles southeast of the southeast corner of Vinalhaven Island, Isle au Haut Bay.

Established: 1839. Present lighthouse built: 1839. Automated: 1954.

Height of tower: 42 feet. Height of focal plane: 52 feet.

Earlier optic: Fourth-order Fresnel lens. Present optic: 300 mm.

Characteristic: White flash every 6 seconds.

Fog signal: One blast every 10 seconds.

The first keeper was Watson Y. Hopkins. He painted a dismal picture of the living conditions at the lighthouse in an 1843 report: "My family consists of nine persons. There is a living room and two chambers in the tower, besides a cellar. The iron railing,

Painting of keeper Watson Y. Hopkins

which was secured to the rock around the tower, has been all swept away; also, the privy, which was carried away the first storm after its erection. The windows all leak in storms."

Saddleback Ledge has no soil, so the keepers brought soil from the mainland each spring and planted a few vegetables and flowers. The soil would inevitably be swept away by winter storms.

By the 1920s, Saddleback Ledge had become a stag station attended by male keepers only. The light was automated in 1954, and the keepers were removed. The keeper's dwelling was blown up as a Green Beret assault exercise around 1960.

This remote lighthouse can be seen from the "Lighthouses Boat Trip" offered by Old Quarry Ocean Adventures (207-367-8977, www.oldquarry.com) of Stonington. Lighthouse cruises offered by the Isle au Haut Company in Stonington (207-367-5193, www.isleauhaut.com) also provide a view, weather permitting.

A hoist was used to get people, like the woman shown here, on and off Saddleback Ledge

Fascinating Fact

In 1836, three years before the light was established, the ship *Royal Tar*, carrying circus performers and animals, caught fire and sank near Saddleback Ledge.

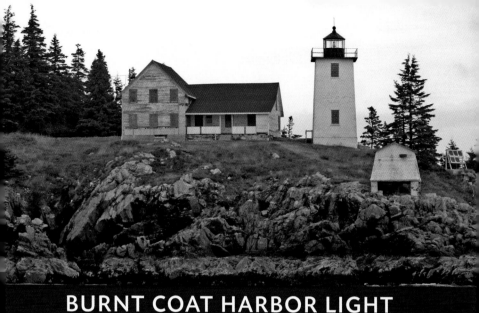

BURNT COAT HARBOR LIGHT
(Hockamock Head Light)

Swan's Island, about 7,000 acres, developed strong granite and fishing industries in the nineteenth century. Burnt Coat Harbor, on the island's south side, was a valuable sheltered spot. To mark the entrance to the harbor, a light station was established on the promontory called Hockamock Head.

Accessibility: ⛵ + 🚑

Geographic coordinates: 44° 08' 03" N   68° 26' 50" W

Nearest town: Swan's Island. Located at Hockamock Head at the entrance to Burnt Coat Harbor, south side of Swan's Island, Blue Hill Bay.

Established: 1872. Present lighthouse built: 1872. Automated: 1975.

Height of tower: 32 feet. Height of focal plane: 75 feet.

Earlier optic: Fourth-order Fresnel lens. Present optic: 250 mm.

Characteristic: White light occulting every 4 seconds.

Late 1800s view

Vessels frequently tried to make it into Burnt Coat Harbor in storms. In the early 1900s, a coal schooner on its way to Bar Harbor tried to make shelter but ran into a ledge and broke apart. The crew managed to escape, but the ship's cargo provided fuel for many Swan's Island residents that year.

The Coast Guard automated the light in 1975. The station became the property of the town of Swan's Island in 1994, and a committee was formed to oversee the management of the property. With nobody living at the station and no regular maintenance, the property quickly deteriorated.

In recent years, a number of grants have enabled the town to initiate the restoration of the dwelling. The town will continue fundraising toward the complete restoration of the station. You can learn more by visiting the town's website at www.swansisland.org. The Friends of the Swan's Island Lighthouse, a nonprofit corporation, assists the town in preserving the light station. See www.swansisland.org/lighthouse.htm for more information.

The six-mile ferry crossing to Swan's Island from Bass Harbor takes about 40 minutes. For information, call 207-244-3254 or visit www.maine.gov/mdot/msfs/ online. The grounds around the lighthouse are open to the public. From the ferry, drive about a half-mile to a T intersection, turn right, and continue straight along the main road through the village of Swan's Island. Continue straight to the parking area for the lighthouse. The drive from the ferry is about 4.5 miles.

You can arrange a trip with Sea Venture Custom Boat Tours (207-288-3355, www.svboattours.com) in Bar Harbor to see this and other area lighthouses.

Fascinating Fact

The first permanent white settler on Swan's Island was David Smith of New Hampshire in 1791. Smith had twenty-four children by two marriages, and his feats of strength earned him the nickname "King David." Many island natives can trace their ancestry to David Smith.

BLUE HILL BAY LIGHT

Green Island—about three-quarters of an acre at high tide and about three times that size at low tide—is one of a group of four islands called the Fly, or Flye, Islands after an early owner. In the mid-nineteenth century, the town of Ellsworth on Blue Hill Bay was said to be the second busiest lumber port in the world, making a lighthouse in the vicinity a necessity. The brick lighthouse was connected by a passageway to a colonial cape keeper's house.

Accessibility:

Geographic coordinates:
44° 14' 56" N 68° 29' 55" W

Nearest town: Brooklin. Located on Green Island in Blue Hill Bay.

Established: 1857. Present lighthouse built: 1857. Automated: 1933.

Earlier optic: Fourth-order Fresnel lens. Present optic: none.

Keepers augmented their food supplies by fishing and hunting in the area. On a summer camping trip in the 1920s, keeper Roscoe Chandler and his family caught almost 300 pounds of cod, hake, and cusk nearby. Duck and lobster were also staples.

Fascinating Fact

Lacking a telephone, the families at Green Island devised unique modes of communication. In the 1920s, when the keeper was needed on shore, a woman across on the mainland would hang a black suit outside her house as a signal.

The lighthouse was discontinued in 1933. It was replaced by a light on a skeleton tower. An automatic light, now solar powered, remains in use. The island was sold into private ownership. In 1976, it was purchased by Wilbur and Edith Trapp of New Jersey. The Trapps had the house and other buildings beautifully restored (even the outhouse is still standing). In 1995, the lighthouse was again sold.

The best views of the lighthouse are from the water; unfortunately, no regularly scheduled public cruises pass nearby. You can also arrange a custom trip with Sea Venture Custom Boat Tours (207-288-3355, www.svboattours.com) in Bar Harbor to see this and other area lighthouses. It is possible to walk to the island at low tide from Flye Point in Brooklin, but this isn't recommended; it's a strenuous walk, and some of the route may be underwater even at low tide.

Late 1800s view

BASS HARBOR HEAD LIGHT

This light served to warn mariners of the Bass Harbor Bar at the eastern entrance to Bass Harbor and also to mark the southeast entrance to Blue Hill Bay. The brick lighthouse is attached to the keeper's house by a covered walkway. A bell house from 1876 and a 1902 oil house also still stand. A boathouse was added in 1894.

Accessibility: car, boat

Geographic coordinates: 44° 13' 19" N 68° 20' 14" W

Nearest town: Bass Harbor (part of the town of Tremont). Located at the southern tip of Mount Desert Island, on the east side of the southern entrance to Blue Hill Bay.

Established: 1858. Present lighthouse built: 1858. Automated: 1974.

Height of tower: 32 feet. Height of focal plane: 56 feet.

Optic: Fourth-order Fresnel lens.

Characteristic: Red light occulting every 4 seconds.

Late 1800s view

The first keeper was John Thurston. Robert Thayer Sterling, in his classic 1935 book *Maine Lighthouses and the Men Who Keeper Them*, reported that keeper Joseph Grey "does not forget to salute all passing craft."

To reach the light station, follow Route 3 across the causeway onto Mount Desert Island. At a traffic light, bear right onto Route 102 South. Follow Route 102 for about 13 miles through Somesville and Southwest Harbor. Follow Route 102 and Route 102A south through Bass Harbor. Where Route 102A turns left, continue straight onto Lighthouse Road and follow to the free parking area. The grounds are open 9:00 a.m. to sunset. The station is now the residence for a Coast Guard family, and visitors are asked to respect the privacy of the residents.

A path and stairs lead down to the granite boulders neighboring the light station. To get a good view of the lighthouse, it is necessary to climb a distance over the rocks; extreme caution should be taken. A second path, leading to the right from the parking area, takes visitors to the area immediately around the lighthouse tower. The tower and house are not open to the public.

Island Cruises of Bass Harbor (207-244-5785, www.bassharborcruises.com) offers a cruise that affords the chance to see this lighthouse, one of the most scenic on the New England coast, from the water. You can also arrange a trip with Sea Venture Custom Boat Tours (207-288-3355, www.svboat-tours.com) in Bar Harbor to see this and other area lighthouses.

Fascinating Fact

A fourth-order Fresnel lens manufactured by the Henry-Lepaute Company in Paris has been in operation here since 1902.

GREAT DUCK ISLAND LIGHT

Great Duck Island Light was established to help mariners headed for Blue Hill Bay and the Mount Desert area. The light went into service on December 31, 1890, and the first keeper was William F. Stanley. Three keeper's dwellings were built side by side near the brick lighthouse, along with a shed and a fog signal building with a 1,200-pound bell. Only one of the keeper's houses survives.

Accessibility: ⛵

Geographic coordinates: 44° 08' 30" N 68° 14' 42" W

Nearest town: Frenchboro. Located on a 265-acre island about five miles south of Mount Desert Island, on the approach to Blue Hill Bay.

Established: 1890. Present lighthouse built: 1890. Automated: 1986.

Height of tower: 42 feet. Height of focal plane: 67 feet.

Previous optic: Fifth-order Fresnel lens (1890); fourth-order Fresnel lens (1902). Present optic: VRB-25.

Characteristic: Red flash every 5 seconds.

Fog signal: One blast every 15 seconds.

Undated aerial view

Keeper Nathan Adam "Ad" Reed, in charge from 1902 to 1912, and his wife, Emma, may hold the record for most children in a lighthouse family. Their seventeen children and the children of the other keepers, along with the children of the island's fishermen, attended a little white schoolhouse on the island. The state of Maine provided a teacher. One of the Reeds' older daughters, Rena, eventually got a teaching certificate in Castine and was able to teach her younger siblings in the

island's tiny schoolroom.

One of the last Coast Guard keepers was Larry Baum, who once commented, "The mental strain can be bad. We had guys who jumped into a peapod and tried to row to the mainland." Most of the island was purchased by the Maine Chapter of the Nature Conservancy in 1984. The Nature Conservancy estimates that Great Duck Island supports 20 percent of Maine's nesting seabirds. In 1998, the light station became the property of Bar Harbor's College of the Atlantic under the Maine Lights Program. The keeper's house is now occupied by students from the College of the Atlantic much of the year.

The College of the Atlantic's ongoing research projects on the island include the monitoring of the large nesting gull population, as well as detailed

Fascinating Fact

At one time, local people kept as many as 500 sheep on Great Duck Island, which got its name from an abundance of waterfowl.

study of the rare Leach's storm petrel. For more information, contact the College of the Atlantic, 105 Eden Street, Bar Harbor, ME 04609. Phone: 207-288-5015. Web site: www.coa.edu/html/greatduckisland.htm.

The island is not accessible to the public. You can also arrange a trip with Sea Venture Custom Boat Tours (207-288-3355, www.svboattours.com) in Bar Harbor to see this and other area lighthouses.

Banding a gull on Great Duck Island

MOUNT DESERT ROCK LIGHT

Accessibility: ⛵

Geographic coordinates:
43° 58' 06" N   68° 07' 42" W

Nearest town: Frenchboro.
Located on a small island
about 20 miles south of
Mount Desert Island.

Established: 1830.
Present lighthouse built:
1847. Automated: 1977.

Height of tower:
58 feet. Height of focal
plane: 75 feet.

Previous optic: Third-order
Fresnel lens. Present optic:
VRB-25.

Characteristic: White flash
every 15 seconds.

Fog signal: Two blasts every
30 seconds.

Far-flung Mount Desert Rock is home to one the most isolated light stations in the United States. The island's first lighthouse went into operation in 1830 to mark the entrances to Frenchman and Blue Hill bays. Esais Preble was the first keeper, and his son, William, was his assistant.

Nineteenth-century view

The first lighthouse was a short wooden tower at one end of a stone dwelling. The noted architect Alexander Parris designed the extant granite tower, which replaced the original one in 1847. The present keeper's dwelling was built in 1893.

In December 1902, the New York tugboat *Astral*, with a barge in tow, ran aground at the rock in a gale with eighteen men aboard. With the arrival of low tide, keeper Fred Robbins and an assistant managed to get close enough to the vessel to get a line aboard. All the crewmen except one were pulled to safety. The keeper's wife prepared gallons of steaming coffee for the survivors.

George York was keeper from 1928 to 1936. One year, after a storm, the supply boat couldn't get to the station, and the family nearly starved, living on biscuits and molasses.

After automation, the light station was leased to Bar Harbor's College of the Atlantic for use as a whale-watching station. The college's Allied Whale program compiles and maintains catalogs for the North Atlantic populations of finback and humpback whales. The station, along with Great Duck Island Light, became the property of the College of the Atlantic in 1998.

To learn more about the whale research effort at Mount Desert Rock, call Allied Whale at 207-288-5644 or visit www.coa.edu/mountdesert rockaw.htm. The lighthouse is best seen by charter cruise or from the air. Whale watches from Bar Harbor might occasionally pass near the island, but there's no guarantee, as the cruises go where the whales go.

Fascinating Fact

Waves mercilessly batter Mount Desert Rock; a 75-ton boulder was once moved 60 feet in a storm.

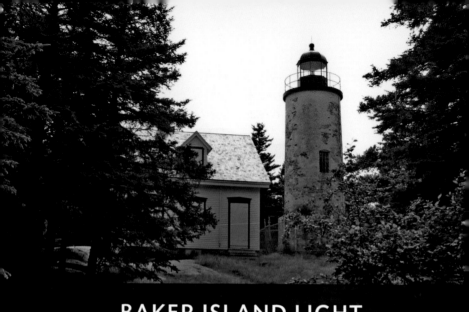

BAKER ISLAND LIGHT

Accessibility: 🛥 🚶

Geographic coordinates:
44° 14' 29" N   68° 11' 56" W

Nearest town: Islesford. Located in the Cranberry Islands, about 4 miles southeast of Mount Desert Island.

Established: 1828. Present lighthouse built: 1855. Automated: 1966. Deactivated: ca. 2002.

Height of tower: 43 feet. Height of focal plane: 105 feet.

Previous optic: Fourth-order Fresnel lens. Present optic: none.

Baker Island, about 123 acres, is one of five islands that make up the Cranberry Isles. Because of dangerous ledges and a sandbar nearby, and to help mark the western approach to Frenchman Bay, a lighthouse was established on Baker Island in 1828. The first lighthouse was a wooden tower built on the highest point on the island.

William and Hannah Gilley took possession of Baker Island in the early 1800s. When the lighthouse was built, William Gilley was appointed keeper at a salary of $350 per year. Gilley remained keeper until 1848 when he was dismissed for not being a member of the party that had come into power, the Whigs. Two of Gilley's sons harassed the succeeding keepers of the light until the government tried to evict the Gilley family from the island. The federal government eventually won the right to 19 acres for the light station and the necessary right-of-way, while the Gilley heirs retained the rest of the island.

The extant brick tower was built in 1855. In 1903, an extra layer of brick was added to the tower. The light station buildings are now owned by the Park Service as part of Acadia National Park. There has been some discussion of utilizing the former keeper's house as an island museum.

You can visit Baker Island on tours leaving from Bar Harbor, narrated by an Acadia National Park naturalist. The Bar Harbor Whale Watch Company also offers a "Lighthouse and Park Tour" that includes a view of Baker Island, but the tall trees make it very difficult to photograph the tower from

Fascinating Fact

A keeper's wife wrote in 1953: "Hope the fog goes away pretty soon so we'll know there are other people on this good earth besides ourselves."

the water. For information on both tours, contact the Bar Harbor Whale Watch Company (207-288-9800, www.barharborwhales.com). You can also arrange a trip with Sea Venture Custom Boat Tours (207-288-3355, www.svboattours.com) in Bar Harbor to see this and other area lighthouses.

BEAR ISLAND LIGHT

Accessibility: ⛵

Geographic coordinates:
44° 16' 59" N   68° 16' 10" W

Nearest town: Northeast Harbor. Located at the entrance to Somes Sound, about 1,200 feet offshore from Mount Desert Island.

Established: 1839. Present lighthouse built: 1889. Deactivated: 1981. Relighted: 1989.

Height of tower: 31 feet. Height of focal plane: 100 feet.

Previous optic: Fifth-order Fresnel lens.

President Martin Van Buren authorized the building of a lighthouse on the southeast point of Bear Island to help mariners entering Northeast Harbor and Somes Sound. The first lighthouse was a dwelling with a small tower on top. The first structure burned down in 1852.

Nineteenth-century view

The present 31-foot brick lighthouse was built in 1889 along with a new keeper's house and a barn. For a time, beginning in 1887, Bear Island had a buoy depot where navigational aids were maintained; the depot was later transferred to Southwest Harbor. There was also a coaling station so buoy tenders in the area could refuel.

One of the last Coast Guard keepers was Steve Loiver. He voiced his fears regarding automation: "I just hope that in the need to economize we don't destroy the things that give flavor and uniqueness to life."

In 1981, the light was discontinued and replaced by a lighted bell buoy. The property became part of Acadia National Park in 1987. Through most of the 1980s, the station fell into disrepair. In 1989, the Friends of Acadia refurbished the keeper's house, and the tower was relighted as a private aid to navigation. The National Park Service granted a long-term lease to an individual who is required to pay for the upkeep of the property.

The best views are from the water. The Bar Harbor Whale Watch Company (207-288-9800, www.barharbor whales.com) offers a "Lighthouse and Park Tour" that passes this lighthouse.

Sea Princess Cruises (207-276-5352, www.barharborcruises.com), leaving from Northeast Harbor, has narrated nature cruises that pass Bear Island. You can also arrange a trip with Sea Venture Custom Boat Tours (207-288-3355, www.svboattours.com) in Bar Harbor to see this and other area lighthouses.

Fascinating Fact

Nineteenth-century landscape artists, including Frederick Church and Albert Bierstadt, painted scenes of Bear Island's rugged beauty.

EGG ROCK LIGHT

Accessibility: 🏕️ ⛵

Geographic coordinates:
44° 21' 12" N   68° 08' 18" W

Nearest town: Winter Harbor. Located on a small island at the entrance to Frenchman Bay.

Established: 1875. Present lighthouse built: 1875. Automated: 1976.

Height of tower:
40 feet. Height of focal plane: 64 feet.

Previous optic: Fifth-order Fresnel lens. Present optic: VRB-25.

This light station consists of a brick tower on the center of a keeper's dwelling. The appearance of the building was altered in the late 1890s, when the original roof was replaced by the present roof with dormers.

Undated aerial view

A storm on March 2, 1900, was recorded as the worst storm in the area in twenty-four years. The gale sent waves over Egg Rock, but the heavy storm shutters prevented any damage to the dwelling. Another fierce storm in February 1908 broke through the shutters and flooded the house. Rocks weighing up to thirty tons were moved by the blizzard.

Keepers at Egg Rock generally rowed to Bar Harbor four miles away for supplies. The trip could be treacherous in bad weather and rough seas. In February 1935, assistant keeper Clinton "Buster" Dalzell drowned on his way to shore from the island.

After automation, the Coast Guard removed the lantern and installed rotating aerobeacons. After public complaints, the Coast Guard installed a new aluminum lantern and a new optic in 1986. Under the Maine Lights Program, the lighthouse was turned over to the U.S. Fish and Wildlife Service in 1998. It is managed as part of the Maine Coastal Islands National Wildlife Refuge. In the fall of 2009, a group of volunteers performed some renovation of the lighthouse. The crews were transported by Bar Harbor Whale Watch, which donated its services. The U.S. Fish and Wildlife Service provided materials for the work, which included staining and repairs.

The lighthouse can be seen distantly from high points on Mount Desert Island, but it's best seen by boat. A good view is available from the "Lighthouse and Park Tour" offered by the Bar Harbor Whale Watch Company (207-288-9800, www.barharborwhales.com). Trips aboard the four-masted schooner *Margaret Todd* (207-288-2984, www.downeastwindjammer.com), leaving from Bar Harbor, pass close by. You can also arrange a trip with Sea Venture Custom Boat Tours (207-288-3355, www.svboattours.com) in Bar Harbor to see this and other area lighthouses.

Fascinating Fact

Near the start of Bar Harbor's Shore Walk, close to the Bar Harbor Inn, two cannons are on display. The cannons were once on Egg Rock as part of a coastal defense battery.

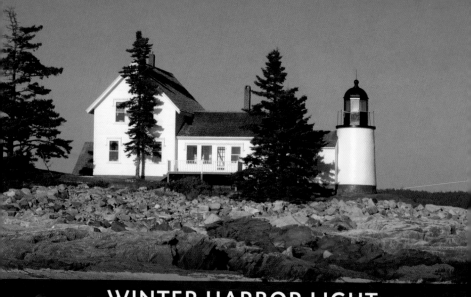

WINTER HARBOR LIGHT
(Mark Island Light)

Accessibility: 🏛 ⛵

Geographic coordinates:
44° 21' 40" N   68° 05' 13" W

Nearest town: Winter Harbor. Located on four-acre Mark Island at the entrance to Winter Harbor, off the west side of the Schoodic Peninsula.

Established: 1856. Present lighthouse built: 1856. Deactivated: 1933.

Previous optic: Fifth-order Fresnel lens. Present optic: none.

Winter Harbor was long a favorite safe harbor for mariners seeking shelter from storms. In 1856, a lighthouse was built for $4,000 on Mark Island to guide vessels into the harbor and to warn of dangerous ledges nearby. The first keeper was Frederick Gerrish.

In the light's seventy-eight years of active service, nine keepers and their families lived here. In 1933, the light was discontinued and replaced by a lighted buoy to the southeast. George Harmon of Bar Harbor bought the property.

Keeper Benjamin Maddox circa 1890

Three years later, the property was bought by writer Bernice Richmond and her husband, sociologist Reginald Robinson. Richmond wrote two books about the years she and her husband spent on Mark Island: *Winter Harbor* and *Our Island Lighthouse*. In the second book, she wrote, "I couldn't explain how I looked forward each morning to that first rush of salty air through my kitchen door, to the early tour I take over the vein-like paths to the gardens."

In the 1950s, René Prud-Hommeaux, an author of children's books, bought the island. It was later owned for a time by playwright Gerald Kean. Writer and retired banker William C. Holden III bought the property in 1995. While he lived on Mark Island, Holden renovated the property and wrote several novels. He sold the property in late 2004.

The lighthouse can be seen distantly from the loop road on Acadia National Park's Schoodic Peninsula, especially from off-road lookouts between 0.8 and 1.2 miles south of the park entrance. The best views are from the water. The "Lighthouse and Park Tour" offered by the Bar Harbor Whale Watch Company (207-288-9800, www.barharborwhales.com) provides an excellent view. You can arrange a trip with Sea Venture Custom Boat Tours (207-288-3355, www.svboattours.com) in Bar Harbor to see this and other area lighthouses.

Fascinating Fact

Winter Harbor gets its name from the fact that it rarely freezes over in the winter months. The harbor still has a substantial fleet of lobster boats.

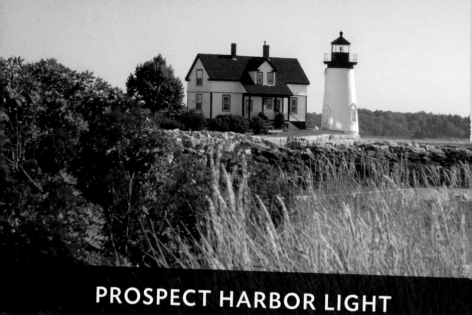

PROSPECT HARBOR LIGHT

Accessibility: 🚶 🚗

Geographic coordinates:
44° 24' 12" N   68° 00' 48" W

Nearest town: Prospect Harbor (a village of Gouldsboro). Located on the east side of the Schoodic Peninsula, east side of the entrance to Prospect Harbor.

Established: 1850. Present lighthouse built: 1891. Automated: 1951.

Height of tower: 38 feet. Height of focal plane: 42 feet.

Previous optic: Fifth-order Fresnel lens. Present optic: 250 mm.

Prospect Harbor developed a substantial fishing fleet in the nineteenth century. The first lighthouse to mark the east side of the harbor entrance was built in 1850. The original granite lighthouse attached to a dwelling was replaced in 1891 by the present 38-foot wooden lighthouse and a new farmhouse-style keeper's house.

Keeper Albion Faulkingham and family circa 1920s

Civil War veteran Ambrose Wasgatt became keeper in 1891. His two daughters later remembered playing croquet with guests at the light station, as well as annual open houses that included "boathouse dinners." Long tables would be set up inside the boathouse with large quantities of food for the visitors.

The light was automated in 1934, but a keeper remained at the station until 1953. The lighthouse is now on the grounds of a Navy installation (Detachment ALFA). The keeper's house, known as "Gull Cottage," is available for overnight stays for active and retired military families. Active Navy personnel receive reservation priorities. For information visit the Gull Cottage web page at www.militarycampgrounds.us/milcamps/64-maine/311-gull-cottage-at-prospect-harbor.

The tower was reshingled and repainted by the Coast Guard in April 2000. The lighthouse tower was licensed in May 2000 to the American Lighthouse Foundation (207-594-4174, www.lighthousefoundation.org). In August 2004, the foundation had the lantern removed by crane. Lead paint was removed, and the lantern was repainted. At the same time, the lantern

deck was rebuilt, and the windows were removed and replaced.

The grounds around the lighthouse are closed to the public, but you can drive to the entrance of the Navy installation for a good view. From Route 1, take Route 195 south for about five miles to Prospect Harbor. Turn left onto Main Street. After a very short distance, turn right onto Corea Road. Where the road bears left toward Corea, drive straight onto Lighthouse Point Road. Follow to the gate of the Navy installation. There are no real parking spaces; pull to the side of the road. Good views of the lighthouse are possible from the rocky beach, especially at low tide. The lighthouse can also be seen from across the harbor on Route 186 in Prospect Harbor.

Fascinating Fact

Some guests at the keeper's house have reported ghostly activity in the building. A statue of a sea captain seems to change positions by itself, and some guests claim to have seen or heard a ghost at night.

PETIT MANAN LIGHT

Accessibility: 🚶 ⛵

Geographic coordinates:
44° 22' 03" N 67° 51' 52" W

Nearest town: Steuben.
Located about two miles
southeast of Petit Manan
Point, on the southern
approach to West Bay, Dyer
Bay, Harrington Bay, and
Pleasant Bay.

Established: 1817.
Present lighthouse built:
1855. Automated: 1972.

Height of tower:
119 feet. Height of focal
plane: 123 feet.

Previous optic: Second-
order Fresnel lens. Present
optic: VRB-25.

Characteristic: White flash
every 10 seconds.

Fog signal: One blast every
30 seconds.

President James Monroe authorized the building of a lighthouse on Petit Manan Island to guide shipping traffic toward several bays and harbors in the vicinity and also to warn mariners of a dangerous bar between the island and Petit Manan Point on the mainland. The small original tower was replaced by the extant granite tower in 1855.

In 1869, a storm made the tower sway violently, causing the clockwork weights that turned the lens to come loose and fall. The falling weights destroyed some of the steps in the tower's cast-iron spiral stairway. In 1887, the tower was strengthened with the addition of iron tie rods driven from the top to huge bolts in the lower section.

Maizie Freeman Anderson grew up at Petit Manan, where her father, James H. Freeman, was keeper in the 1930s. She later recalled one particularly high tide when the entire island was under a foot of water and the chicken coops were floating in a cranberry bog.

The second-order Fresnel lens, almost 10 feet high, is now at the Maine Lighthouse Museum in Rockland. A fog bell from the station is at the elementary school in the town of Milbridge. After the light was automated, Petit Manan Island was turned over to the U.S. Fish and Wildlife Service and became part of the 3,335-acre Petit Manan National Wildlife Refuge. It's now part of the Maine Coastal Islands National Wildlife Refuge. The island supports a mixed-tern colony of common terns, arctic terns, and roseate terns. There's also a breeding colony of puffins as well as common eiders.

A renovation carried out in 1997-98 included repointing, lead paint removal, and the replacement of stair treads that were destroyed in 1869.

The tower can be seen very distantly from a trail at Petit Manan Point in the Maine Coastal Islands National Wildlife Refuge. Puffin-watch cruises out of Bar Harbor (207-288-9800, www.barharborwhales.com) go close to Petit Manan Island for an excellent view of its feathered residents as well as the lighthouse. Robertson Sea Tours Adventures (207-546-3883 or 207-483-6110, www.robertsonseatours.com) in Milbridge also offers a Petit Manan puffin cruise and a lighthouse cruise. Downeast Coastal Cruises (207-546-7720, www.downeastcoastalcruises.com), departing from Milbridge, offers a variety of options for charter cruises.

Fascinating Fact

This is considered one of the foggiest spots on the Maine coast, with an average of about seventy foggy days each year. A fog bell installed in 1855 was replaced by a steam-driven fog whistle in 1869.

NARRAGUAGUS LIGHT
(Pond Island Light)

Accessibility: ⛵

Geographic coordinates:
44° 27' 19" N   67° 50' 00" W

Nearest town: Milbridge.
Located on Pond Island in
Narraguagus Bay.

Established: 1853.
Present lighthouse built:
1853. Deactivated: 1934.

Height of tower: 31 feet.

Present optic: none.

In the nineteenth century, the little town of Milbridge was an important shipping point for lumber coming from the Narraguagus River. Established by order of President Franklin Pierce in 1853, on the east side of Pond Island, the Narraguagus Light Station originally consisted of a short tower and lantern on top of the keeper's dwelling.

In 1875, a new dwelling was built, and much of the original house was removed from around the tower. In 1894, the lighthouse was reinforced with a new layer of brick. The 31-foot granite tower was connected to the keeper's house by a workroom built in 1887.

Narraguagus Light circa 1860s

The station had a single keeper and his family until 1899, when assistant keepers were assigned. Access to the station was difficult, requiring a half-mile walk across the island. A boat slip was built near the lighthouse in 1900 but was for emergency access to the island only and was not used by the keepers.

The light was discontinued in 1934, and the property was sold at auction; it remains in private ownership. The lighthouse is best viewed by boat. Robertson Sea Tours Adventures (207-546-3883 or 207-483-6110, www. robertsonseatours.com) offers a scenic island cruise and a lighthouse cruise, both of which include this lighthouse. Downeast Coastal Cruises (207-546-

Fascinating Fact

An inn and clubhouse were built on Pond Island in 1878, and the three-story Pond Island House continues in operation today. A golf course was added to the island in 1920.

7720, www.downeastcoastalcruises. com), departing from Milbridge, offers a variety of options for charter cruises.

NASH ISLAND LIGHT

Accessibility: ⛵

Geographic coordinates:
44° 27' 50" N 67° 44' 45" W

Nearest town: Addison. Located at the southeastern entrance to Pleasant Bay.

Established: 1838. Present lighthouse built: 1874. Automated: 1947. Deactivated: 1981.

Height of tower: 36 feet. Height of focal plane: 51 feet.

Earlier optic: Fourth-order Fresnel lens. Present optic: none.

In 1837, Congress authorized the construction of a lighthouse at the mouth of the Pleasant River. The site chosen was Nash Island, the smaller of two islands known locally as Big Nash and Little Nashes Island. The first Nash Island Lighthouse, a round tower, was built for $5,000 in 1838. Major repairs were made to the original lighthouse, but the tower was rebuilt in 1874. The 51-foot square brick lighthouse still stands.

For a while, there were enough children living on the island for a small school to be put in operation with a teacher from the mainland. When they reached high-school age, the children boarded and attended school in Jonesport.

John Purington was keeper from 1916 to 1935. It was largely the inspiration of his daughter, Jenny Purington Cirone (1912–2004), that led to strong interest in the preservation of Nash Island Lighthouse. Jenny later owned half of Nash Island, as well as Big Nash Island. She started raising sheep as a girl and continued to keep sheep on her islands for the rest of her life.

The Friends of Nash Island Light (P.O. Box 250, Addison, ME 04606) became the owners of the lighthouse in 1998. Nash Island is now part of the Maine Coastal Islands National Wildlife Refuge. The lighthouse is best viewed from cruises offered by Robertson Sea Tours Adventures (207-546-3883 or 207-483- 6110, www.robertsonseatours.

com), Downeast Coastal Cruises (207-546-7720, www.downeastcoastal cruises. com), and Pleasant River Boat Tours (207-598-6993, www.pleasant riverboattours.com).

Fascinating Fact

Allen Carter Holt was keeper from 1910 to 1916. His children were assigned the task of counting gull nests on the local islands for the Audubon Society.

Jenny Purington as a teenager

MOOSE PEAK LIGHT

Accessibility: ⛵

Geographic coordinates:
44° 28' 26" N   67° 31' 34" W

Nearest town: Jonesport. Located at the eastern point of Mistake Island, entrance to Main Channel Way, about five miles from Jonesport.

Established: 1826. Present lighthouse built: 1851. Automated: 1972.

Height of tower: 57 feet. Height of focal plane: 72 feet.

Previous optic: Second-order Fresnel lens. Present optic: VRB-25.

Characteristic: White flash every 30 seconds.

Fog signal: Two blasts every 30 seconds.

This light station was established for $4,000 in October 1826. The present brick tower was built in 1851. For most of its history, the station had a keeper and one assistant, both of whom lived on the island with their families.

Moose Park Light Station circa 1860s

{ 396 }

Mistake Island is one of the foggiest locations on the Maine coast. In 1912, a signal house was erected with a powerful foghorn. The signal had to be sounded for 181 consecutive hours in 1916.

The dwelling was almost sold to a private party after automation, but the high cost of a sewage system caused the sale to fall through. In 1982, a military team blew up the keeper's house as a training exercise. The demolition didn't go exactly as planned; some of the timbers flew outward, breaking glass in the lighthouse lantern and damaging the helicopter pad.

The Coast Guard converted the lighthouse to solar power in 1999. Mis-

take Island is managed by the Nature Conservancy. A local group, Keepers of Moose Peak Light (PO Box 256, Jonesport, ME 04649) is working to preserve the lighthouse. It can be seen distantly from Great Wass Island; but it's best seen from the water or from the air. Downeast Coastal Cruises (207-546-7720, www.downeastcoastalcruises. com), departing from Milbridge, offers charter cruises that can include this lighthouse. Coastal Cruises & Dive Downeast (207-598-7473, www. cruisedowneast.com) of Jonesport offers cruises that include views of—and a possible visit to—this lighthouse.

Fascinating Fact

Between 1918 and 1934, the keepers here logged more hours of dense fog than any other Maine light station. The island averaged 1,607 hours per year, meaning it was foggy about 20 percent of the time.

LIBBY ISLAND LIGHT

Accessibility: ⛵

Geographic coordinates:
44° 34' 06" N   67° 22' 00" W

Nearest town: Machias-port. Located at the entrance to Machias Bay.

Established: 1823. Present lighthouse built: 1824. Automated: 1974.

Height of tower: 42 feet. Height of focal plane: 91 feet.

Previous optic: Fourth-order Fresnel lens. Present optic: VRB-25.

Characteristic: Two white flashes every 20 seconds.

Fog signal: One blast every 15 seconds.

Libby is actually two islands connected by a sandbar, with a total area of 120 acres. According to a report by the first keeper, Isaac Stearns, the extant tower was built in 1824. He wrote, "The [first] tower was built in the autumn of 1823, and in April following tumbled down. The present tower was immediately after erected."

A fog bell gave way to a Daboll fog trumpet housed in a building erected in 1884. Before the addition of the fog bell, Libby Island had a single keeper. The bell required an assistant keeper, so the Lighthouse Board eventually built two new houses for the keepers and their families.

Hervey Wass became keeper in 1919. His son, Philmore Wass, later wrote a book about his years on the island called *Lighthouse in My Life*. The delightful volume provides a detailed record of life on an offshore lighthouse station. During this period there were as many as twenty people living at Libby among the families of the keeper and two assistants. In his book, Phil Wass described his feelings of awe regarding the lighthouse inspector, Royal Luther. Inspector Luther would arrive unannounced on the tender *Hibiscus*, and the children would tag along as he met with Keeper Wass and toured the station. Young Phil's job was to polish the brass in the keeper's house.

Under the Maine Lights Program, the property was turned over to the U.S. Fish and Wildlife Service in 1998. It's managed as part of

Fascinating Fact

In 1918, the fog signal here was sounded for a total of 1,906 hours, the most of any Maine station.

the Maine Coastal Islands National Wildlife Refuge. The Coast Guard completed an overhaul of the tower in the summer of 2000, including the conversion of the light to solar power.

The lighthouse can be seen distantly from the mainland (including Jasper Beach in Machiasport) but is best viewed by boat. Downeast Coastal Cruises (207-546-7720, www.downeast coastalcruises.com), departing from Milbridge, offers charter cruises that can include this lighthouse. Coastal Cruises & Dive Downeast (207-598-7473, www.cruisedowneast.com) of Jonesport also offers cruises that can include a view of this lighthouse.

LITTLE RIVER LIGHT

Accessibility: 🔭 ⚓ ⊨

Geographic coordinates:
44° 39' 03" N   67° 11' 32" W

Nearest town: Cutler. Located on Little River Island at the entrance to Cutler Harbor.

Established: 1847. Present lighthouse built: 1876. Deactivated: 1975. Relighted: 2001.

Height of tower: 41 feet. Height of focal plane: 56 feet.

Previous optic: Fifth-order Fresnel lens. Present optic: VRB-25.

Characteristic: White flash every 6 seconds.

Fog signal: One blast every 10 seconds.

As trade, shipbuilding, and the fishing industry grew in Cutler Harbor, Little River Light was established in 1847 at the harbor's entrance. A stone dwelling was attached to the original stone lighthouse tower. In 1876, the extant cast-iron lighthouse was built. The old dwelling remained standing, but the top part of the old attached tower was removed. The extant dwelling was built in 1888.

Willie Corbett was keeper from 1921 to 1939. The Corbetts kept a cow, pigs, and chickens on the island. Keeper Corbett was an excellent fiddler and sometimes left the island on Saturday nights to play at dances at the lifesaving station at Cross Island down the coast.

The lighthouse was replaced by an automatic light on a nearby skeleton tower in 1975, and the property rapidly deteriorated. The station was licensed in early 2000 to the American Lighthouse Foundation (ALF). A chapter of ALF, Friends of Little River Lighthouse (207-259-3833, www.littleriverlight.org), was formed to care for the property.

During the summer of 2000, the wooden walkway from the boathouse to the lighthouse was completely rebuilt by the Coast Guard, with financial help from ALF. On October 2, 2001, after the lighthouse was restored, it was relighted as an aid to navigation. In 2002, ownership of the island was transferred to the American Lighthouse Foundation under the provisions of the National Historic Lighthouse Preservation Act.

The keeper's house has been restored, and overnight stays are available in summer. Call 207-259-3833 for more information and reservations. Boat transportation is provided, but you must bring your own food, towels and linens, and toiletries.

Little River Light can be viewed from Capt. Andrew Patterson's excellent nature cruises (207-259-4484, www.boldcoast.com) out of Cutler. A fairly distant view from the mainland is available from the hiking trail at Western Head, a two-mile loop that begins at the end of Destiny Bay Road in Cutler.

Fascinating Fact

Cutler Harbor is the last protected harbor on the Maine coast before Canada.

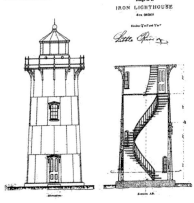

Plans for the 1876 tower

WEST QUODDY HEAD LIGHT

Accessibility:

Geographic coordinates:
44° 48' 55" N 66° 57' 04" W

Nearest town: Lubec.
Located at the eastern-
most point of the United
States, on the west side of
the southern entrance to
Quoddy Roads.

Established: 1808.
Present lighthouse built:
1858. Automated: 1988.

Height of tower:
49 feet. Height of focal
plane: 83 feet.

Optic: Third-order
Fresnel lens.

Characteristic: White flash
every 6 seconds.

Fog signal: Two blasts every
30 seconds.

In 1806, a group of concerned citizens chose West Quoddy Head as a suitable place for a lighthouse to help mariners entering Quoddy Roads, between the mainland and Campobello Island. The first rubblestone lighthouse on the site was built two years later by order of President Thomas Jefferson. The first keeper was Thomas Dexter, at a salary of $250 per year. The extant brick tower and accompanying dwelling were erected in 1858.

Nineteenth-century view

It's been claimed that fog is manu-factured in the Bay of Fundy. Keeper Arthur Marston, who was at West Quoddy in the 1920s, was once asked if the foghorn kept him awake. He answered, "Only when it stops!"

The keepers' children had to walk about two miles to school in Lubec. One day in the 1920s, Marston's chil-dren found some lumber that had washed ashore. One of the boys took the wood and built a cabin in the woods that long served as a meeting place for local children and was still standing into the 1990s.

In 1998, under the Maine Lights Program, the station became the prop-erty of the state of Maine. The light-house grounds are now part of Quoddy Head State Park. The grounds are open to the public, and trails through the park wind along the shore and past the lighthouse.

SIDE TRIP:
West Quoddy Gifts

The easternmost gift shop in the United States features clothing, spe-cialty foods, jewelry, toys, artwork, col-lectibles, books, and much more. There are many gifts depicting West Quoddy Head Lighthouse, including clothing with exclusive designs. The shop is easy to find on the road to West Quoddy Head State Park and the lighthouse.
West Quoddy Gifts
16 Loon Lane
Lubec, ME 04652
Phone: 1-866-218-3253
Web site: www.westquoddygifts.com

Fascinating Fact

At one time, West Quoddy Head had a fog cannon to warn mariners away from dangerous Sail Rocks. The station received one of the nation's first fog bells in 1820.

A local group, the West Quoddy Head Light Keepers Association (South Lubec Road, P.O. Box 378, Lubec, ME 04652. Phone: 207-733-2180. Web site: www.westquoddy.com), was formed to

enhance the experience of visitors with exhibits and displays. A seasonal visitor center is now open in the former keeper's house. The center is open daily from Memorial Day to mid-October. (The lighthouse tower is not open to the public.)

SIDE TRIP: *Campobello Island*

While you're in the Lubec area doing some lighthouse hunting, you'll probably want to make the short drive across the Roosevelt International Bridge to Campobello Island, New Brunswick. (Bring your passport.) Just over the bridge on the left, you'll see the pretty Mulholland Lighthouse. One of the island's main attractions is the Roosevelt Campobello International Park, the summer home of President Franklin D. Roosevelt. His thirty-four-room residence is preserved as a memorial and as a symbol of the close friendship between Canada and the United States.

At the eastern tip of Campobello is the Head Harbour Lighthouse, also known as East Quoddy Head Light. This was one of the earliest Canadian light stations and the second in the area after Maine's West Quoddy Head Light. A nonprofit group, the Friends of the Head Harbour Lightstation, is working to preserve this picturesque station.

To reach Head Harbour Lighthouse after crossing onto the island, continue for 2.5 miles. Bear right at a fork onto NM Route 774 North. Continue on this road for about seven miles until you reach a dirt road and a parking area for the lighthouse. The outcropping becomes an island at high tide. From about an hour before to an hour after low tide, access is possible via a series of stairs. Visitors should take care to note the tide situation in order to avoid being stranded at the station for hours.

Roosevelt Campobello International Park. Phone: 506-752-2922. Web site: www.fdr. net.

Friends of the Head Harbour Lightstation
P.O. Box 403, Route 774
Wilson's Beach, N.B. E5E 1Y2 Canada, or
P.O. Box 486
Lubec, ME, 04652
Web site: www.campobello.com/ lighthouse/

LUBEC CHANNEL LIGHT

Lubec Channel Light, built for $20,000 in 1889–90, is one of three surviving sparkplug-style cast-iron lighthouses in Maine. Its first keeper was Frederick W. Morong. The tower contained five levels, two of which were living quarters for the keepers. The lower deck was a combination living room and kitchen. The next deck was a bedroom.

Accessibility:

Geographic coordinates: 44° 50' 31" N 66° 58' 36" W

Nearest town: Lubec. Located in Johnson Bay, about a mile north of West Quoddy Head.

Established: 1890. Present lighthouse built: 1890. Automated: 1939.

Height of tower: 40 feet. Height of focal plane: 53 feet.

Earlier optic: Fifth-order Fresnel lens. Present optic: 155 mm.

Characteristic: White flash every 6 seconds.

Fog signal: One blast every 15 seconds.

Earl Ashby was the light's last keeper, leaving in 1939. An assistant keeper, Nathaniel Alley, was alone on duty in 1939 when he was overcome by gas from the coal stove. Alley was taken to Lubec for medical treatment, but he soon died. The light was automated a short time later.

In 1992, a $700,000 renovation included the stabilization of the foundation, which had developed a tilt over the years. The tower still has a 6-degree list but is considered stable.

In 2006, the lighthouse was made available to a suitable new steward under the guidelines of the National Historic Lighthouse Preservation Act. There were no applicants, so in July 2007 it was auctioned to Gary Zaremba, a restoration architect, for a high bid of $46,000.

Lubec Channel Light can easily be seen from many points on shore, including Quoddy Head Road in Lubec.

Lubec Channel Light circa early 1900s

Fascinating Fact

The light was to be discontinued in 1989, but local residents mounted a "Save the Sparkplug" campaign. Automobile sparkplugs were handed out to gain attention for the cause.

WHITLOCK'S MILL LIGHT

The city of Calais, midway between the equator and the North Pole, was an important lumber port in the nineteenth century. Beginning in 1892, a lantern displayed from a tree on the American side of the St. Croix River, near Calais, served local navigation. Complaints led to the construction of a brick lighthouse in 1910. The extant keeper's house was also built in 1910.

Accessibility: 🔒

Geographic coordinates: 45° 09' 46" N 67° 13' 39" W

Nearest city: Calais. Located on the south side of the St. Croix River.

Established: 1910. Present lighthouse built: 1910. Automated: 1969.

Height of tower: 25 feet. Height of focal plane: 32 feet.

Earlier optic: Fourth-order Fresnel lens. Present optic: 250 mm.

Characteristic: 3 seconds green alternating with 3 seconds of darkness.

SIDE TRIP: *Saint Croix Island International Historic Site*

At this beautiful site, you can learn about the events that took place during the settlement on Saint Croix Island, scene of one of the earliest European settlements in North America. Seventy-nine members of the French expedition passed the severe winter of 1604–05 on the island; thirty-five of them died and were buried in a small cemetery on the island. In spring 1605, the survivors went on to found the settlement of Port Royal, Nova Scotia.

From mid-June through August 31, an interpretive ranger is stationed at the mainland site, 8 miles south of Calais, Maine, on Route 1. When you look at Saint Croix Island from the mainland, you can see a boathouse that's left from the island's light station, established in 1857. The lighthouse burned down in 1976.

Saint Croix Island International Historic Site
c/o Acadia National Park
P.O. Box 177
Bar Harbor, ME 04609-0177
Phone: 207-288-3338
Web site: www.nps.gov/sacr/

Under the Maine Lights Program, the lighthouse was transferred to the St. Croix Historical Society (P.O. Box 242, Calais, ME 04619. Web site: www.stcroixhistorical.org) in 1998.

The keeper's house and other buildings are privately owned, meaning the grounds are not open to the public. The lighthouse can be viewed from the St. Croix River View Rest Area on Route 1 in Calais. The rest area is announced by a Rest Area 1,500 ft sign from the south. The view is largely obscured by trees in summer.

Fascinating Fact

The interior of the tower is lined with white ceramic-faced brick, a distinction shared with very few lighthouses.

Early 1900s view

Vermont

It often surprises people that New England's "west coast" has a number of lighthouses. There are four historic lighthouses on the Vermont side of Lake Champlain, plus two reconstructed ones at Burlington. There are also six on the New York side of the lake.

Lake Champlain, bordering New York, Vermont, and Quebec, was once a bustling waterway. The opening of the Champlain Canal in 1823 meant faster shipping to New York, and navigational aids were needed. There were many private aids to navigation placed by the shipping companies, but government officials eventually realized permanent aids were needed. More than ten lighthouses were built on the lake in the nineteenth century. Aside from crude early lanterns, Juniper Island Light in Burlington was the first lighthouse built on the lake.

Burlington was one of the most prosperous communities on the lake's eastern shore. The city grew into the third largest lumber port in the nation, and the two newly reconstructed lighthouses on the city's waterfront now serve as reminders of the illustrious past. They can be seen from the waterfront and from sightseeing cruises. Otherwise, only one of the Vermont lights—the old Colchester Reef Lighthouse, relocated to the Shelburne Museum—is visitor-friendly. The museum itself is a wonderful hodgepodge of New England architecture and ephemera that's not to be missed.

There were also three lighthouses built on Lake Memphremagog, which is partly in Quebec, Canada. None of these survive, but there has been talk of a possible reconstruction of Newport's Maxfield Point Lighthouse.

Vermont Lighthouses

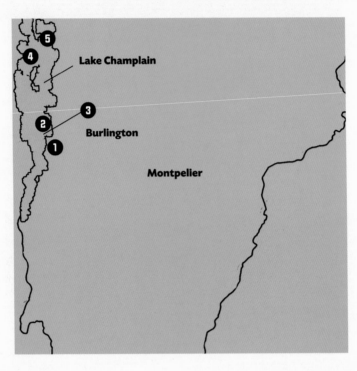

LIGHTHOUSE	PAGE

COLCHESTER REEF LIGHT

his lighthouse was originally located about a mile offshore from Colchester Point on Lake Champlain, a vital waterway bordering New York, Vermont, and Quebec. The light was established to mark a group of three dangerous shoals. Herman Melaney was the first of nine keepers, and he remained for eleven years. The lighthouse had four bedrooms on its second floor, and a kitchen and living room on the first floor.

Accessibility:

Geographic coordinates (original location): 44° 33' 32" N   73° 20' 00" W

Nearest town: Shelburne. Originally located off Colchester Point in Lake Champlain, now at the Shelburne Museum.

Established: 1871. Present lighthouse built: 1871. Deactivated: 1933.

Height of tower: 35 feet.

Optic: Sixth-order Fresnel lens.

Undated aerial view

August Lorenz was keeper from 1909 to 1931. Once, while Lorenz was keeper, a huge ice floe crashed right through the kitchen and opened an enormous hole in the house. The keeper's dory was torn away, but he managed to retrieve it from a floating cake of ice by snagging it with a long pole.

The lighthouse fell into disrepair after it was deactivated in 1933. In July 1952, Electra Havemeyer Webb, who founded the Shelburne Museum, purchased the lighthouse. A crew of five men dismantled the building and took it to Shelburne by barge, reassembling it in less than a month.

Today, the lighthouse is one of thirty-seven buildings on the grounds of the museum that has been called "New England's Smithsonian." Inside the lighthouse, which stands near the landlocked side-wheeler steamboat

Ticonderoga, there are exhibits on Lake Champlain history, steamboats, and lighthouse life.

After more than seventy years in darkness, the lighthouse was relit with a solar-powered light, largely through the efforts of the Coast Guard's Burlington base and lighthouse historian George Clifford. Clifford joked that now, with the lighthouse illuminated at night, partyers aboard the *Ticonderoga* will be able to navigate their way home safely.

The Shelburne Museum is located on Route 7, 7 miles south of Burlington. From I-89 in Vermont, take exit 13 and proceed south on Route 7. For more information: Shelburne Museum, P.O. Box 10, Shelburne, VT 05482. Phone: 802-985-3346. Web site: www.shelburne museum.org.

Fascinating Fact

The design for Colchester Reef Lighthouse was submitted by Albert R. Dow, a graduate engineer from the University of Vermont. His design was chosen over many entries in a national design competition.

BURLINGTON BREAKWATER LIGHTS

In the 1800s, Lake Champlain became a major shipping route after the establishment of canals connecting it to the Hudson River, the Great Lakes, and north to the St. Lawrence River. Burlington grew into the third-largest lumber port in the nation. In an effort to protect the city's harbor, a granite breakwater was constructed beginning in the 1830s.

Accessibility: 🏛 ⛵

Geographic coordinates (north light): 44° 28' 50" N 73° 13' 48" W

Nearest town: Burlington. Located in Burlington Harbor, Lake Champlain.

Established: 1857. Present lighthouses built: 2003.

Height of focal plane: North tower - 35 feet. South tower - 12 feet.

Characteristics: North tower - White flash every 2.5 seconds. South tower - White flash every 4 seconds.

Fog signal: One blast every 15 seconds.

In 1857, navigational lights were added to the north and south ends of the breakwater. The small lighthouses

The south breakwater light

were moved and rebuilt multiple times as the breakwater was expanded, and a middle light was added for a time, beginning in 1890. The lights were attended by keepers who lived nearby and reached the towers by boat, a dicey proposition in rough weather.

The wooden towers were plagued by ice, fire and wind; the North Light burned down in 1870, and in 1876, the South Light was knocked over in a storm. Automatic operation of the lights began in 1938, and eventually all the lights on the breakwater were replaced by modern steel skeleton towers.

The breakwater has been rehabilitated in recent years, and new replica lighthouses were built in 2003. The new wooden structures were built by Atlantic Mechanical Inc. of Wiscasset, Maine, under contract to the U.S. Coast Guard Civil Engineering Unit in Providence, Rhode Island. A number of other agencies helped with the project.

You can view the lighthouses from Burlington's Waterfront Park, at the foot of College Street. You can also get excellent views from sightseeing cruises aboard the *Spirit of Ethan Allen III* (802-862-8300, www.soea.com), leaving from the Burlington Boathouse, next to Waterfront Park.

Fascinating Fact

A keeper's residence was added to the breakwater in 1875 and remained for about a decade, but it was never used. It was eventually sold and moved to a neighborhood in Burlington, where it still remains as a private residence.

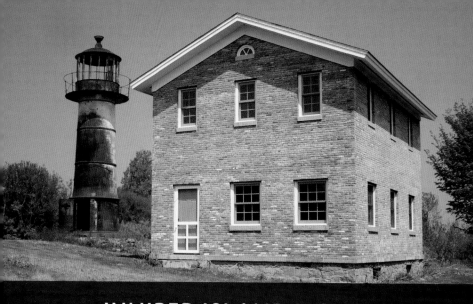

JUNIPER ISLAND LIGHT

side from crude early lanterns, Juniper Island Light was the first lighthouse built on Lake Champlain. The original 30-foot brick tower, built in 1826, was replaced by the extant cast-iron tower in 1846. A new stone dwelling was built in 1863. The station also had an automatic fog bell that sounded every 15 seconds.

Accessibility: ⛵

Geographic coordinates (north light): 44° 27' 04" N 73° 16' 36" W

Nearest town: Burlington. Located on the approach to Burlington Harbor, Lake Champlain.

Established: 1826. Present lighthouse built: 1846. Deactivated: 1954.

Height of tower: 30 feet. Height of focal plane: 93 feet.

Previous optic: Fourth-order Fresnel lens. Present optic: none.

senator, in 1956. A fire started by careless campers destroyed the keeper's house in 1962. Fayette's eleven children inherited the island after his death.

In the fall of 2001, work began on the reconstruction of the keeper's house. The bricks salvaged from the ruins of the old house were used to build the new one. Much of the work was done by volunteer labor, chiefly the Fayette family and their friends. Professionals were utilized for some aspects of the job, and the Coast Guard helped with the transportation of materials.

Juniper Island Light Station circa 1860s

For some time, Juniper Island also served as a depot for the Lighthouse Service on Lake Champlain. Coal, buoys, oil, and other supplies were stored on the island.

In 1954, the light was replaced by an automatic light on a steel skeleton tower. The island was sold at auction to Fred Fayette, a lawyer and state

The island is not open to the public. It's difficult to see the lighthouse from shore or from the water because of the tall trees that surround it. You can get a partial view from sightseeing cruises aboard the *Spirit of Ethan Allen III* (802-862-8300, www.soea.com), leaving from the Burlington Boathouse, next to Waterfront Park. If you take the cruise in the spring (they begin in mid-May), before the trees get too full, you have a better chance of seeing the lighthouse.

Fascinating Fact

This is the oldest standing cast-iron lighthouse in the United States.

ISLE LA MOTTE LIGHT

eginning around 1829 at Isle la Motte, a lantern was placed in an upper window of a stone house belonging to Ezra Pike Jr. to aid local navigation. The house still stands and is a private residence. In 1856, the federal government erected a stone pyramid with a lantern. Increased shipping traffic in the area made a more permanent lighthouse a necessity.

Accessibility: ⛵

Geographic coordinates (north light): 44° 54' 19" N 73° 20' 39" W

Nearest town: Isle la Motte. Located at the northern end of Isle la Motte, northern Lake Champlain.

Established: 1856. Present lighthouse built: 1880. Deactivated: 1933. Relighted: 2002.

Height of tower: 25 feet. Height of focal plane: 46 feet.

Previous optic: Sixth-order Fresnel lens. Present optic: 300 mm.

The extant cast-iron lighthouse was built in 1880 along with a new dwelling. Wilbur F. Hill was keeper of the old beacon starting in 1871, and he remained at the new lighthouse station until 1919, serving forty-eight years as keeper. During his years at Isle la Motte Light, Keeper Hill received awards for having the best-kept station in the district. He also maintained a 100-acre farm nearby. Hill retired from lighthouse keeping about six weeks before he died.

A skeleton tower with an automatic beacon replaced the lighthouse in 1933.

In 1949, the property was bought by the Clark family from their dentist, who had purchased it from the Coast Guard.

In 2001, the Coast Guard began looking at the possibility of reactivating some of Lake Champlain's lighthouses. They worked closely with Lockwood "Lucky" Clark and his family, owners of the station, to prepare for a relighting. On the evening of October 5, 2002, the lighthouse returned to service at dusk. As the light came on at 6:18 p.m., a cannon blazed and Lucky Clark vigorously rang the bell near the lighthouse.

The light station is a private residence and is closed to the public; you'll need a private boat or charter for a good view. The lighthouse, painted orange some years ago, has faded to a pinkish rose color, or as the locals call it, "Nantucket Red" or "salmon."

Fascinating Fact

Isle la Motte was the site of the first French settlement in Vermont. The Shrine of Ste. Anne stands today where the French under Captain Sieur de La Motte built Fort Ste. Anne in 1666.

WINDMILL POINT LIGHT

This light was established, according to some sources, as early as 1830. The first light at Windmill Point, reportedly the site of an early windmill, may have been a makeshift lantern on a post.

Nineteenth-century view

Accessibility: ⛵

Geographic coordinates (north light): 44° 58' 53" N 73° 20' 30" W

Nearest town: Alburg. Located in northern Lake Champlain, less than two miles from the border with Quebec.

Established: 1830. Present lighthouse built: 1858. Deactivated: 1931. Relighted: 2002.

Height of tower: 40 feet. Height of focal plane: 52 feet.

Previous optic: Sixth-order Fresnel lens. Present optic: 300 mm.

The present handsome 40-foot limestone tower was built in 1858 along with a keeper's house attached by a passageway to the tower. Similar towers were built around the same time on the New York side of the lake at Point aux Roches and Crown Point.

In 1931, the light was relocated to a nearby steel skeleton tower. The lighthouse and keeper's house passed into private hands. In 1963, a local man named Lockwood "Lucky" Clark was showing his bride-to-be around the area. As he was pointing out the lighthouse, the owner approached and asked if they were interested in buying it. Clark soon purchased the property, making two lighthouses in the family; his father had bought Isle la Motte Lighthouse in 1949.

On August 7, 2002, National Lighthouse Day, over three hundred onlookers cheered as the lighthouse was relighted, with the help of the Coast Guard. For the first time in almost seven decades, Lake Champlain had a working lighthouse.

Windmill Point Lighthouse is private property and is not open to the public. A private boat or charter is needed for a good view.

Lucky and Rob Clark receive an award from the Coast Guard at the relighting on August 7, 2002.

Fascinating Fact

Through the centuries, northern Lake Champlain has been the scene of many sightings of "Champ," a Loch Ness Monster–type creature.

Glossary

Fresnel lens: The 1822 invention of French physicist Augustin Jean Fresnel (pronounced "freh-NEL"). The Fresnel lens is composed of a succession of concentric rings, assembled in proper relationship, which magnify and concentrate the light and direct it in a horizontal beam.

Fresnel lenses were manufactured in as many as eleven sizes, known as orders. The order is determined by the distance of the light source to the lens. First-order Fresnel lenses (with an inside diameter of 6' 1") were the largest that were widely used; they were installed in many primary seacoast lights. Sixth-order lenses (with an inside diameter of 1') were the smallest used in the United States., but seventh- and eighth-order lenses were used in some other countries.

Fresnel lenses were in use in all American lighthouses by the early 1860s. Some of the lenses are still in operation, but most have been removed and replaced by modern optics. Some surviving Fresnel lenses are on display in museums, such as the Maine Lighthouse Museum in Rockland.

Height of focal plane: The distance from the surface of the water to the center of the optic.

Maine Lights Program: This program was conceived by the Island Institute of Rockland, Maine, and passed by Congress as part of the Coast Guard Authorization Act of 1996. Under the program, twenty-eight historic lighthouse properties were transferred to suitable new owners in 1998.

Modern optics

VRB-25: A powerful, reliable, and compact marine rotating beacon manufactured by Vega Industries of New Zealand. The heart of the VRB-25 is a high-performance acrylic Fresnel lens.

155 mm, 190 mm, 200 mm, 250 mm, and 300 mm optics are essentially one-piece acrylic Fresnel lenses. They are available in clear, red, green, and yellow versions. They are usually fitted with lamp changers—devices that permit a new lamp to go into service when the existing lamp burns out.

DCB-24, DCB-224, and DCB-36:
These large rotating optics, known as aerobeacons, were designed for use at airports. They were used in some lighthouses beginning in the 1940s. The aerobeacons consist of an aluminum drum (or two drums in the case of the DCB-224) fitted with a parabolic reflector and an automatic lamp changer. They have been replaced by the VRB-25 in many lighthouses.

National Historic Lighthouse Preservation Act of 2000: An amendment to the National Historic Preservation Act of 1966 (NLHPA), this act provides a mechanism for the disposal of federally owned historic lighthouse properties. The properties are transferred to new stewards at no cost. The legislation places nonprofit entities on equal footing with federal agencies and other public bodies in the application process.

The new steward must agree to comply with conditions set forth in NHLPA, and be financially able to maintain the property. The Department of the Interior is charged with choosing the most suitable applicant. In the event no new acceptable steward is found, the act authorizes the sale of the property at auction. For more on this process, see www.nps.gov/history/maritime/nhlpa/nhlpa.htm.

Range lights: Light pairs that indicate a specific position when they are in line. When a mariner sees the lights vertically in line, with the rear light above the front light, he is on the range line and in a safe channel.

Sparkplug-style lighthouse: This is a nickname for some caisson lighthouses, after their resemblance to automobile sparkplugs. Caisson lighthouses used a large cast-iron cylinder, sunk on the bottom and filled with rock and concrete to form a foundation. The superstructure is built on top of the caisson foundation. Some of these structures have also been likened to coffeepots.

Lighthouse-Viewing Flight Opportunities

Bird's Eye View/RI Aerials: Offering helicopter tours over the Rhode Island coastline, leaving from the Newport Airport in Middletown, Rhode Island. A 30-minute lighthouse tour is offered for a minimum of two passengers. The flight includes views of Castle Hill Light, Rose Island Light, Newport Harbor Light, the Ida Lewis Yacht Club (Lime Rock Light), and Beavertail Light. Arrangements can be made for custom flights to photograph other lighthouses. Phone 401-843-8687. Web site www.newportrihelicopter.com.

Helicopter Services of Boston: Flights leave from Beverly Airport, about 30 minutes north of Boston. A 30-minute lighthouse tour is offered, featuring Derby Wharf Light, Fort Pickering Light, Marblehead Light, Hospital Point Light, Baker's Island Light, Eastern Point Light, Ten Pound Island Light, the Thacher Island Twin Lights, and Straitsmouth Island Light. A 30-minute "Best of Boston" is available, and a 60-minute "New England's Best" tour combines the "Best of Boston" with the lighthouse tour. Custom flights are also available for up to four passengers. Phone 1-866-500-4354. Web site www.bostonhelicopter.com.

Adventure Sports: This company offers helicopter flights taking off from a number of locations around the U.S., including Boston and Newport, Rhode Island. You can customize a tour for optimum lighthouse viewing. Phone 1-800-497-3483. Web site www.thrill planet.com.

Ace Helicopter Tours: Departing from the Hampton Airfield in New Hampshire or the Lawrence Municipal Airport in Massachusetts. Offering 15- to 20-minute scenic tours or custom tours (up to three passengers) that can include area lighthouses such as Portsmouth Harbor Light, Whaleback Light, White Island Light, Cape Neddick Light, Boon Island Light, and others. Phone: 603-329-4963. Web site: www.acehelitours.com.

Southern Maine Aviation: Fly aboard a Cessna Skyhawk (up to three passengers) from the Sanford Airport in southern Maine. Custom tours can provide views of lighthouses from the New Hampshire seacoast to Portland, Maine. Phone 207-324-8919. Web site www.southernmaineaviation.com.

Penobscot Island Air: Flying Cessna 206/207 aircraft from the Knox County Regional Airport in Owls Head, Maine. You can take a pre-planned sightseeing trip, or they can design a custom tour to meet your needs. Penobscot Bay lighthouse tours are a specialty. Phone 207-596-7500 or 207-542-4944. Web site www.penobscotislandair.net.

Island Soaring: At the Bar Harbor/Hancock County Airport in Trenton, Maine, near Acadia National Park. Lighthouse flights pass these lights: Winter Harbor, Egg Rock, Baker Island, Bear Island, Bass Harbor Head, and Blue Hill Bay. The tour takes approximately 40 minutes. The pilots make at least 180-degree passes at slower airspeeds to make for the most viewing time per flight. Phone 207- 667-SOAR (7627).

Suggested Reading

Adamson, Hans Christian. *Keepers of the Lights*. New York: Greenberg, 1955.

Bachand, Robert G. *Northeast Lights: Lighthouses and Lightships, Rhode Island to Cape May, New Jersey*. Norwalk, CT: Sea Sports Publications, 1989.

Bachelder, Peter Dow. *Lighthouses of Casco Bay*. Portland, ME: Breakwater Press, 1975.

Caldwell, Bill. *Lighthouses of Maine*. Portland, ME: Gannett Books, 1986.

Clark, Admont G. *Lighthouses of Cape Cod, Martha's Vineyard and Nantucket - Their History and Lore*. East Orleans, MA: Parnassus Imprints, 1992.

Clifford, George. *Lake Champlain Lighthouses*. Plattsburgh, NY: Cumberland Head Tomorrow, 1999.

Clifford, Mary Louise and J. Candace Clifford. *Maine Lighthouses: Documentation of Their Past*. Alexandria, VA: Cypress Communications, 2004.

Clifford, Mary Louise and J. Candace Clifford. *Women Who Kept the Lights: An Illustrated History of Female Lighthouse Keepers*. Williamsburg, VA: Cypress Communications, 1993.

Davidson, Donald W. *America's Landfall: The Lighthouses of Cape Cod, Nantucket and Martha's Vineyard*. West Dennis, MA: The Peninsula Press, 1993.

D'Entremont, Jeremy. *The Lighthouses of Connecticut*. Beverly, MA: Commonwealth Editions, 2005.

D'Entremont, Jeremy. *The Lighthouses of Massachusetts*. Beverly, MA: Commonwealth Editions, 2007.

D'Entremont, Jeremy. *The Lighthouses of Rhode Island*. Beverly, MA: Commonwealth Editions, 2006.

De Wire, Elinor. *Guardians of the Lights: The Men and Women of the U.S. Lighthouse Service*. Sarasota, Florida: Pineapple Press, 1995.

Gleason, Sarah C. *Kindly Lights: A History of the Lighthouses of Southern New England*. Boston: Beacon Press, 1991.

Hamilton, Harlan. *Lights and Legends: A Historical Guide to Lighthouses of Long Island Sound, Fishers Island Sound and Block Island Sound*. Stamford, CT: Wescott Cove Publishing Company, 1987.

Harrison, Tim, and Ray Jones. *Lost Lighthouses*. Guilford, CT: Globe Pequot Press, 1999.

Holland, Francis Ross, Jr. *America's Light-houses: An Illustrated History.* New York: Dover Publications, 1972.

Jennings, Harold B. *A Lighthouse Family.* Orleans, MA: Lower Cape Publishing Company, 1989.

Jones, Dorothy H., & Ruth S. Sargent. *Abbie Burgess: Lighthouse Heroine.* New York: Funk & Wagnalls, 1969.

Rhein, Michael J. *The Anatomy of a Light-house.* Barnes and Noble Books, 2000.

Shelton-Roberts, Cheryl & Bruce Roberts. *Lighthouse Families.* Birmingham, AL: Crane Hill Publishers, 1997.

Skomal, Lenore. *The Keeper of Lime Rock.* Philadelphia, PA: Running Press Book Publishers, 2001.

Small, Constance. *The Lighthouse Keeper's Wife.* Orono, ME: University of Maine Press, 1986.

Snow, Edward Rowe. *The Lighthouses of New England.* Boston: Yankee Publishing, 1945. Annotated edition published in 2002 by Commonwealth Editions, Beverly, MA.

Sterling, Robert T. *Lighthouses of the Maine Coast and the Men Who Keep Them.* Brattleboro, VT: Stephen Daye Press, 1935.

Wass, Philmore B. *Lighthouse in my Life: Story of a Maine Light Keepers Family.* Down East Books, 1987.

Willoughby, Malcolm F. *Lighthouses of New England.* Boston: T.O. Metcalf Company, 1929.

Magazines

The Keeper's Log, published quarterly by the U.S. Lighthouse Society of San Francisco, CA. (www.uslhs.org)

Lighthouse Digest, published 11 times a year by FogHorn Publishing of Whiting, ME. (www.lhdigest.com)

Lighthouse Organizations

There are many organizations that care for specific lighthouses; information on them is included in this book in the appropriate sections. There are many other local, state, and regional lighthouse preservation organizations around the United States; we urge you to support the ones near you.

The following are organizations that support the preservation of lighthouses in general:

American Lighthouse Foundation
P.O. Box 565
Rockland, ME 04841
Phone: 207-594-4174
Web site: www.lighthousefoundation.org

American Lighthouse Coordinating Committee
Web site: www.alcc.ws

New England Lighthouse Lovers
Web site: www.nell.cc

Great Lakes Lighthouse Keepers Association
P. O. Box 219
Mackinaw City, MI 49701-0219
Phone: 231-436-5580
Web site: www.gllka.com

U.S. Lighthouse Society
244 Kearny Street 5th Floor
San Francisco CA 94108
Phone: 415-362-7255
Web site: www.uslhs.org

World Lighthouse Society
2nd Floor, 145-157
St. John Street
London EC1V 4PY
England
Web site: www.worldlighthouses.org

Lighthouse Index

State-by-State Index

Photo and Illustration Credits

All the recent color photos in this book were taken by Jeremy D'Entremont, with the exception of the photo of Ladies Delight Light on page 352, which was taken by Ross Tracy. The historical images are from the collection of Jeremy D'Entremont unless otherwise indicated. All lighthouse plans are courtesy of the U.S. Coast Guard.

Other image credits:

Pages 7, 14, 20, 26, 31, 104, 135, 153, 184, 216, 219, 229, 273, 284, 294, 298, 305, 328, 338, 341, 354, 356, 361, 376, 378, 384, 393, 396, 414, 418, 421: U.S. Coast Guard.

Page 4: Lois Valentine.

Page 10: Norwalk Seaport Association.

Page 19: Historical collections, Bridgeport Public Library.

Pages 30 (top), 109, 275: Lighthouse Digest.

Page 35: Margaret Bock.

Page 42: Barbara Gaspar.

Page 63: Bill and Carol Mack.

Page 69: Rodman Sykes.

Page 77: Crissie Stacey Derouchie.

Page 80: Marti Troy Rosalin.

Page 92: Rose Island Lighthouse Foundation.

Page 95: Joan Kenworthy.

Page 106 (both): Fred Mikkelsen.

Pages 127, 139, 143, 168, 171, 175, 187, 193, 212, 263, 279, 342, 368 (bottom), 369, 372: Collection of Edward Rowe Snow, courtesy of Dolly Bicknell.

Page 128: Jeremy Burnham.

Page 162: Bill Grieder.

Page 167 (top): Ruth E. Alt.

Page 191: Norman Poindexter.

Page 197: Paul Christian.

Page 270: Friends of Wood Island Lighthouse.

Page 304: Elisa Trepanier.

Page 307: Judy Armstrong.

Page 368 (top): Margo Burns.

Page 387: Merridee Marcus.

Page 388: Vicki Tuthill.

Page 395: Friends of Nash Island Light.

Page 422: PA3 Michael E. Hvozda, U.S. Coast Guard Public Affairs.

Author photo: John Whalen, Jr.

Icons & illustratons: ©iStockphoto.com/ Tom Nulens; compass ©iStockphoto. com/www.kyc.com.uy; ©2007 Jupiter Images

About the Author

Jeremy D'Entremont has been called New England's foremost lighthouse authority. He has been researching, writing, and photographing the lighthouses of New England since the mid-1980s. He launched his comprehensive web site "New England Lighthouses: A Virtual Guide" (www.lighthouse.cc) in 1997. He is a vice president and historian for the American Lighthouse Foundation, the founder of the Friends of Portsmouth Harbor Lighthouse, and vice president of the Friends of Flying Santa.

Jeremy's books include *The Lighthouses of Connecticut, The Lighthouses of Rhode Island, The Lighthouses of Massachusetts,* and the upcoming *The Lighthouses of Maine.* In addition, he has edited and annotated six new editions of books by the late maritime historian/storyteller Edward Rowe Snow, including *The Lighthouses of New England, The Islands of Boston Harbor,* and *Storms and Shipwrecks of New England.*

Jeremy has also written more than 300 magazine articles, in publications including *Lighthouse Digest and The Keeper's Log,* and he is the author of the "lighthouse" entry in *The World Book Encyclopedia.* His photos have been published in many magazines, including *Soundings, Offshore,* and *Captain's Guide.*

Jeremy has lectured to groups from Connecticut to Maine and has narrated lighthouse cruises and led tour groups all along the New England coast. He cites Edward Rowe Snow as an inspiration. Another important influence is Jeremy's own stepfather, William E. Meryman, who was descended from Maine sea captains and shipbuilders.

Jeremy lives in Portsmouth, New Hampshire, with his wife, Charlotte Raczkowski, and their tuxedo cat, Willy.

About Cider Mill Press Book Publishers

Good ideas ripen with time. From seed to harvest, Cider Mill Press strives to bring fine reading, information, and entertainment together between the covers of its creatively crafted books. Our Cider Mill bears fruit twice a year, publishing a new crop of titles each spring and fall.

Visit us on the Web at
www.cidermillpress.com
or write to us at
12 Port Farm Road
Kennebunkport, Maine 04046

DUXBURY PIER LIGHT-HOUSE.

Designed by J.C. DUANE, Lt.Col. of Engineers .... June, 1870.
Plan approved by Light-House Board .... July 23, 1870.
Tower completed .... June 30, 1871.

Scale ⅛ to 1.

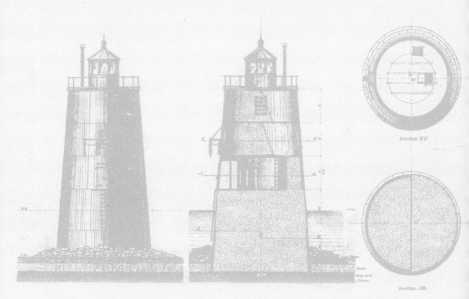

Section EF.

Section AB.